Intelligent Decision Aiding Systems Based on Multiple Criteria for Financial Engineering

Applied Optimization

Volume 38

Series Editors:

Panos M. Pardalos
University of Florida, U.S.A.

Donald Hearn
University of Florida, U.S.A.

The titles published in this series are listed at the end of this volume.

Intelligent Decision Aiding Systems Based on Multiple Criteria for Financial Engineering

by

Constantin Zopounidis and Michael Doumpos

Technical University of Crete,
Deptartment of Production Engineering and Management,
Chania, Greece

KLUWER ACADEMIC PUBLISHERS

DORDRECHT / BOSTON / LONDON

A C.I.P. Catalogue record for this book is available from the Library of Congress.

ISBN 0-7923-6273-X

Published by Kluwer Academic Publishers,
P.O. Box 17, 3300 AA Dordrecht, The Netherlands.

Sold and distributed in North, Central and South America
by Kluwer Academic Publishers,
101 Philip Drive, Norwell, MA 02061, U.S.A.

In all other countries, sold and distributed
by Kluwer Academic Publishers,
P.O. Box 322, 3300 AH Dordrecht, The Netherlands.

Printed on acid-free paper

Printed in the Netherlands.

This volume is dedicated to:

Helene Zopounidis and Kleanthi Koukouraki

Chris Doumpos and Catherine Doumpos

ACKNOWLEDGMENTS

We are grateful to Kiki Kosmidou, Ph.D. candidate at the Technical University of Crete, for her important notes on an earlier version of the book and her great help in the preparation of the final manuscript.

"Philosophy is the highest music"

Plato, Phaedo

TABLE OF CONTENTS

PROLOGUE xv

CHAPTER 1: FINANCIAL ENGINEERING 1

1. Mathematical modeling and financial management 1
2. Financial engineering 3
3. The relationship between financial engineering and financial risk management 5
4. Financial engineering methodologies 9
5. The multicriteria character of financial engineering 12
   - 5.1 The investment decision 14
   - 5.2 Portfolio management 16
6. Multicriteria decision aid 17
   - 6.1 Brief historical overview 18
   - 6.2 Decision aid activity 19
   - 6.3 MCDA approaches 21
     - 6.3.1 Methodological approach oriented classification 21
     - 6.3.2 Problem type oriented classification 29
   - 6.4 MCDA contributions to financial engineering 31

CHAPTER 2: DECISION SUPPORT SYSTEMS 37

1. Decision support systems: General framework and main features 37
2. DSSs' structure 39
   - 2.1 The user interface 40
   - 2.2 The database 42
   - 2.3 The model base 44
3. DSSs applications in financial engineering 47
4. Illustrations from credit granting and portfolio management 48
   - 4.1 Credit granting decisions: The FINCLAS system 48
     - 4.1.1 Problem domain 48
     - 4.1.2 General structure of the FINCLAS system 49
     - 4.1.3 The database 50

4.1.4 Financial model base 53
4.1.5 Preference disaggregation sorting methods 59
4.2 Portfolio management: The INVESTOR system 61
4.2.1 Problem domain 61
4.2.2 Structure of the INVESTOR system 63
4.2.3 The database 63
4.2.4 The model base 66
5. DSSs' contribution and limitations 71
Appendix: The UTADIS methods and its variants 74

CHAPTER 3: EXPERT SYSTEMS **83**

1. General framework 83
2. ESs' definition and basic characteristics 84
3. ESs' structure 86
3.1 The knowledge base 87
3.2 Knowledge acquisition and the knowledge engineer 92
3.3 The inference engine 94
3.4 The user interface 99
4. ESs applications in financial engineering 99
5. Illustration of ESs development and implementation: The ES part of the FINEVA system 101
5.1 Methodology of knowledge acquisition 102
5.2 Representation of knowledge 106
5.2.1 Production rules 108
5.2.2 Meta-rules 109
5.2.3 Incomplete information 110
5.3 An illustrative example 111
6. ESs benefits and limitations 118

CHAPTER 4: KNOWLEDGE-BASED DECISION SUPPORT SYSTEMS **121**

1. Connectives between Dsss and Ess technologies 121
2. Knowledge-based decision support systems 123
2.1 Integrating DSSs with ESs 123
2.2 Benefits of integrating DSSs and ESs in the KBDSS framework and new potentials 129

3. Alternative artificial intelligence techniques for intelligent decision support 133
3.1 Neural networks 134
3.2 Rough sets 137
3.3 Fuzzy sets 142
3.4 Case-based reasoning 143
3.5 Genetic algorithms 146
4. KBDSSs in financial engineering 148
4.1 Portfolio selection, management and trading 149
4.1.1 The ISPMS system 149
4.1.2 The PMIDSS system 151
4.1.3 The StockAdvisor system 152
4.2 Financial planning 154
4.2.1 The HYPER-SAVINGS system 154
4.2.2 The CASH MANAGER system 155
4.3 Credit granting 156
4.3.1 The LASS system 156
4.3.2 The MARBLE system 159
4.3.3 The KABAL system 160
4.4 Mergers and acquisitions 163
4.5 Bond rating 165

CHAPTER 5: INTELLIGENT MULTICRITERIA DSSs 167

1. Brief history on multicriteria decision support 167
2. MCDSSs functionality and main features 169
3. The contribution of artificial intelligence 173
3.1 The interaction between the user and the system 173
3.2 The operation of the methodological tools employed in the MCDSS 175
3.3 The special features of the problem domain 177
4. Applications of intelligent MCDSSs to financial engineering 178
4.1 Credit granting 178
4.1.1 The CGX system 178
4.1.2 The CREDEX system 182
4.2 Corporate performance and viability 185
4.2.1 The FINEVA system 185
4.3 Investment analysis 188
4.3.1 The INVEX system 188

CHAPTER 6: INTELLIGENT MCDSSs IN FINANCIAL ENGINEERING PRACTICE **193**

1. Is there any need for intelligent multicriteria decision support? 193
2. The road ahead 195

REFERENCES **197**

SUBJECT INDEX **213**

PROLOGUE

From the beginning of the 20th century, finance has consolidated its position as a science of major practical importance for corporate entities, firms, organizations and investors. Over this period finance has undergone significant changes keeping pace with the technological innovations that occurred after the second world war and the socio-economic changes that affected the global business environment. The changes in the field of finance resulted to a transformation of its nature from a descriptive science, involved with legislation issues, to an analytic science, involved with the identification of the relationship among financial decisions and the decision environment and ultimately to an engineering science, involved with the design of new financial products and the development of innovations with regard to financial instruments, processes and solutions.

Several financial researchers and practitioners consider this last phase of the above transformation as a new era in finance; Marshall and Dorigan (1996) used the term "new finance" to provide a general description of this new engineering phase of finance. This transformation has led to the introduction of the term "financial engineering" to describe the new approach of the study of financial decision making problems. Since the late 1980s financial engineering has consolidated its position among financial researchers and practitioners. An international association involved with financial engineering, the International Association of Financial Engineers, has already been founded since 1992. Nowadays, it counts nearly 2,000 members including practitioners and academic researchers.

The major characteristic of this new context is the extensive use of advanced decision analysis and modeling tools to manage the increasing complexity of the financial and business environment and the comprehensive consideration of all alternative solutions to financial decision making problems. These tools originate from a variety of different disciplines including statistical analysis, econometrics and operations research. Thus, the role of financial decision makers (financial engineers) within the financial engineering context becomes even more complex. They are not only involved in the application of the financial theory, but also in the knowledge of advanced methodological tools and quantitative analysis techniques in order to address effectively financial decision problems.

Within this new framework, information technology has become an integral part of the decision making process, not only in providing information processing tools, but most importantly in providing decision support tools. These tools enable real-time information management and processing similarly to traditional information management systems. They also enable financial decision makers to apply the modeling and decision analysis methodologies necessary within the financial engineering context. This is the decision support systems' framework, which has been developed from the early 1970s for more effective decision making.

Over the last two decades alternative forms of computerized systems have been developed to support and improve decision making and have already been applied in finance. The major feature of these alternative systems is the incorporation of artificial intelligence techniques in order to develop a new framework for addressing financial decisions. This new framework enables financial engineers to conduct qualitative analysis through systems that carry out both computation and inference procedures, to model highly non-linear systems as well as the uncertainty and the fuzziness that are evident in financial decision making. The term "intelligent systems" describes all systems that provide such capabilities. The expert systems' technology is probably the most influential part of the artificial intelligence approach to financial engineering, although over the last decades other artificial intelligence techniques have gained significant interest among financial researchers.

This brief initial discussion characterizes the topic and the goals of this book, whose aim is to provide a comprehensive discussion of the aforementioned approaches, their integration and synergetic results, and the expected benefits/contributions to the field of financial engineering. Furthermore, the present book goes one step further from the presentation of the aforementioned forms of computerized systems for financial engineering; it extends this framework through the introduction of a multiple criteria approach to the study of financial engineering problems. The multiple criteria approach constitutes a significant alternative to the traditional single-objective perspective from which financial decisions are often taken. It considers the existence of all factors (quantitative and qualitative) that are involved in the financial decision making process and enables the financial engineer to examine the existing tradeoffs among these factors according to his/her system of beliefs and preferences, in order to make realistic and rational decisions. The book is divided into six chapters.

Initially, chapter 1 introduces the concept of financial engineering, describes its relation to financial risk management and reports, from a critical point of view, the main methodological approaches employed in the financial engineering context. The limitations of the traditional optimization framework with regard to financial engineering are discussed and a new context is introduced based on the multicriteria decision aid approach.

In chapter 2 the methodological framework of decision support systems (DSSs) is presented. Emphasis is given on the basic characteristics and features of DSSs along with the illustration of their major structural components. Moreover, in the same chapter the benefits of the implementation of DSSs in financial institutions, companies and organizations as well as their limitations are discussed from the financial engineering point of view, and some applications of DSSs in financial decision making are also presented regarding credit risk assessment, portfolio selection and management.

Chapter 3 is devoted to the presentation of the expert systems' (ESs) technology. The chapter introduces the reader to the key concepts and the functionality of ESs through the detailed discussion of their architecture. Emphasis is given on topics related to knowledge engineering, as well as on the knowledge acquisition and representation processes. The advantages and disadvantages of ESs in facing real world decision problems, especially in the field of financial engineering, are discussed and some applications of the ESs technology in financial decision making are presented.

Chapter 4 focuses on the integration of DSSs and ESs within the framework of knowledge-based decision support systems (KBDSSs). The contribution of alternative artificial intelligence techniques, including neural networks, fuzzy sets, rough sets, case-based reasoning and genetic algorithms are also explored. The way that the integration of artificial intelligence techniques with the DSSs can be achieved is illustrated along with the expected benefits examined from the financial engineering point of view. The implementation of the KBDSSs' framework to the study of several financial engineering problems is also illustrated through the presentation of some representative financial engineering KBDSSs.

Chapter 5 extends the methodological framework of KBDSSs that was discussed in the previous chapter, through the investigation of the new capabilities provided by the combination of knowledge-based systems and artificial intelligence in general, with multicriteria decision aid (multicriteria intelligent decision aiding systems).

Finally, the concluding chapter of the book (chapter 6) discusses some issues regarding the implementation of intelligent DSSs based on multiple criteria to the financial engineering practice of financial institutions, corporate entities and organizations, along with some guidelines of future research that is required.

Chapter 1

FINANCIAL ENGINEERING

1. MATHEMATICAL MODELING AND FINANCIAL MANAGEMENT

During the last decades the globalization of financial markets, the intensifying competition among firms, financial institutions and organizations as well as the rapid economic, social and technological changes, have led to an increasing uncertainty and instability in the financial and business environments. This new context has given a new rise to the role of financial management for the operation of firms and organizations. Furthermore, along with the increasing significance of financial management, the complexity of financial decisions has also increased. The intensifying competitive environment and the continuous flow of a vast volume of information worldwide increases further this complexity.

In combination with the changing financial, business and social environment, the past decades have witnessed several theoretical and empirical advances in the understanding of financial decision making problems. These advances in the broad field of finance have led to a rapid increase in the variety and volume of new financial products and services that are available to financial decision makers for managing more efficiently the financial operation of corporate entities and organizations.

This new context within which financial decisions are taken necessitates the study of financial decision problems within an integrated realistic context that is based on well-structured quantitative and qualitative analyses to make rational decisions. Such analyses can not be performed only on the basis of empirical knowledge; it is also necessary to implement more sophisticated decision analysis techniques. Thus, the connectives between the financial theory and the mathematical modeling becomes apparent. Actually, the field of finance has been one of the most challenging fields for the application of applied mathematics and operations research. Techniques from the field of optimization, stochastic processes, simulation, forecasting, decision support systems, multicriteria decision aid, fuzzy logic, etc., are considered valuable tools for financial decision making.

This relationship between financial theory and operations research and applied mathematics in general, has been evident even from the beginning of the 20th century, despite the fact that by that time finance was mainly a descriptive science focusing on institutional and legal aspects (Merton, 1995); the application of mathematics has been limited to the determination of the net present value and the internal rate of return. The wide use of mathematics in finance began during the 1950s with the introduction of Markowitz's portfolio theory (1952, 1959) that was based on statistical measures (i.e. mean and variance) to estimate the expected return and the risk of the stocks, and on mathematical programming techniques to determine the most appropriate portfolio of stocks that meets the investor's expectations with respect to the risk-return framework.

Since the 1950s operations research has contributed to several financial decision making problems including portfolio selection and management, venture capital investments, bankruptcy prediction, financial planning, corporate mergers and acquisitions, country risk assessment, etc. These contributions are not limited to academic research, but they also involve the daily practice of many corporate entities and organizations. Actually, nowadays many firms, financial institutions and organizations use advanced operations research techniques to improve their financial decision making, to estimate and reduce the financial risks to which they are exposed to, and generally to advance their financial operation and decision making processes.

2. FINANCIAL ENGINEERING

The connection of mathematical modeling using tools from the field of operations research with the financial theory constitutes the underlying basis of a new field that emerged during the last decade, the *financial engineering*. According to Finnetry (1988) financial engineering refers to the design, development and implementation of innovative financial instruments and processes and the formulation of innovative solutions to financial decision making problems. The International Association of Financial Engineers, the first professional society for financial engineers founded in 1991, defines financial engineering in a similar broad context as "the development and creative application of financial technology to solve financial problems and to exploit financial opportunities". Other researchers define financial engineering in a more narrow context, such as "the art (with contributions from science) of creating desirable cash flow and/or market value patterns from existing instruments or new instruments to meet an investment or risk management need" (Gastineau, 1992), or consider financial engineering as a field that is exclusively related to financial risk management (Dahl et al., 1993a).

Despite the differences in the realization of financial engineering, the common concept among all definitions is financial innovation with regard to: (i) financial instruments, (ii) solutions and (iii) processes:

- The financial instruments involve a variety of products and investment vehicles that the finance industry provides to consumers, corporate entities and organizations. These instruments range from the traditional ones with a widespread application in daily practice, such as bank accounts, several forms of securities (e.g. bonds, mutual funds, stocks, treasury bills, etc.), financing products and insurance products, to the non-traditional instruments among which financial derivatives are the most significant ones (e.g. options, futures, swaps, etc.).

- The solutions refer to every financial problem that interests a corporate entity, an organization or an individual. Some examples of innovative solutions involve the development of innovative financial planning strategies, the construction of portfolios that meet the investors' preferences, the development of appropriate financing policies, the design of dynamic trading strategies as well as the development of credit risk evaluation models.

- Finally, the processes involve the steps that should be undertaken in order to structure and formulate the problem at hand and to implement the solutions that are developed. The ultimate goal of innovative financial processes such as electronic trading systems, or credit risk monitoring systems, is to reduce the time and cost of financial decisions.

For an analyst (practitioner or academic researcher) to be able to address these three aspects in an innovative way, that is a non-trivial one, the knowledge of financial theory is not enough. While the financial theory constitutes the underlying knowledge required to address financial engineering problems, some synthesis and analysis approaches are also necessary for innovation. This necessity has become apparent even from the late 1950s with the work of Markowitz (1959) on portfolio selection and later, during the 1970s, with the work of Black and Scholes on option pricing (Black and Scholes, 1973). These pioneering works have demonstrated that the descriptive character of financial theory was gradually progressing towards a more analytic one, that ultimately led to the engineering phase of finance by the late 1980s (Marshall and Dorigan, 1996). This transformation from the descriptive phase to the engineering one is evident in all sciences and finance could not be an exception.

The reasons that affected this transformation in the field of finance and the intensification of the relationship between financial theory and mathematical modeling can be summarized in the following aspects (Mulvey et al., 1997):

1. The globalization of the markets and the regulatory and structural changes that affect their operation along with the increasing volatility in the worldwide financial, economic and business environments. This has created new potentials as well as new risk factors.

2. The intensified competition in the global business environment that forces all corporate entities, organizations and investors to advance their financial operation, through the development of new instruments, products and processes, enabling them to be more competitive and ensuring an increased performance and viability.

3. The rapid technological advances of the last two decades on the theoretical and practical (implementation) aspects of decision making that enable the development and use of complex decision analysis models through computationally tractable procedures. Real-

time financial decision making is crucial within the context of the new financial environment formed over the last decades. Therefore, decision makers cannot proceed towards the use of sophisticated analysis and decision making tools, unless they meet the requirements that the financial environment poses on the time and the cost necessary to make a decision. The advances in decision analysis approaches have resulted towards the development of new methodologies to minimize the time required to obtain solutions to complex decision problems; the development of advanced optimization techniques is a typical example. At the same time the rapid developments of information technology and computer science provided the means to implement the advances made at the theoretical level through the development of user-friendly computerized systems providing real-time support to financial decision makers.

All of these three reasons have affected the promotion of financial engineering. Therefore, financial engineering is expected to increase its significance for the achievement of a more efficient financial operation of corporate entities, organizations and investors worldwide.

3. THE RELATIONSHIP BETWEEN FINANCIAL ENGINEERING AND FINANCIAL RISK MANAGEMENT

Risk is an integral part of every financial decision taken. Almost all financial decision making problems, including venture capital investment, bankruptcy prediction, portfolio selection and management, country risk evaluation, financial planning, investment analysis, etc., involve some form of financial risk analysis to identify how exogenous factors related to the general economic environment, or endogenous factors related to the financial operation of a corporate entity or organization can affect the outcome of a financial decision. The significance of the financial risk management process has been pointed out by several researchers who have focused on identifying the several forms of financial risks and on developing tools and methodologies to assess and manage these risks.

Generally, the financial risk management process involves the three stages presented in Figure 1.1 (Dahl et al., 1993a).

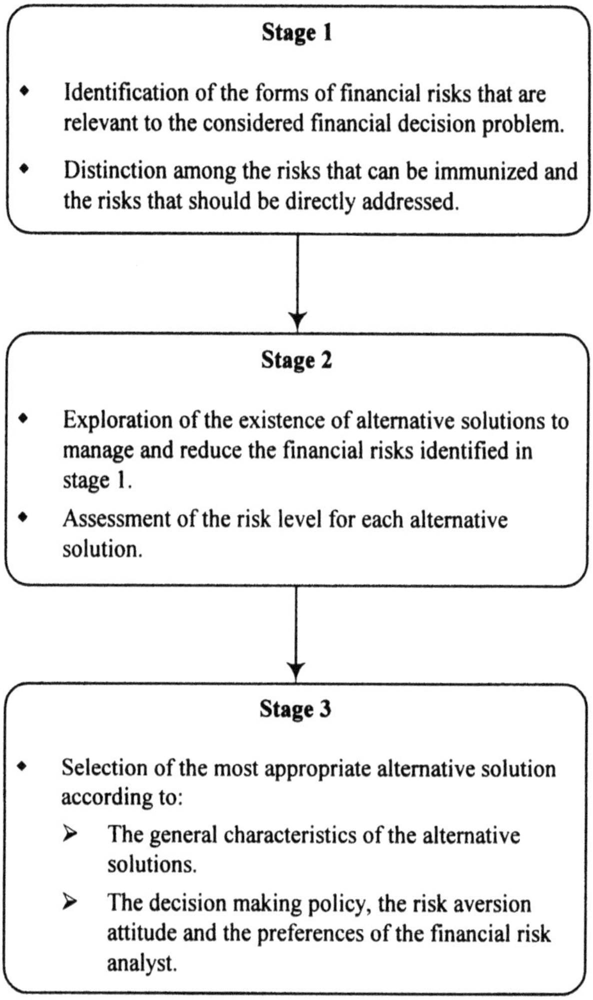

Figure 1.1. Stages of the financial risk management process

Since risk is evident in any financial decision problem, any innovation regarding the developed instruments, processes and/or solutions obtained in the field of finance should accommodate the risk factor. In that regard it is clear that there is a sort of relationship between financial engineering and financial risk management. However, practitioners and academic researchers in the fields of financial risk management an(engineering have considered the form of this relationship in tw ways.

1. Financial engineering is a risk management approach.
2. Financial engineering comprises several different aspects of financial management including financial risk management but it is not restricted to it.

A representative example of the former definition of the relationship among financial engineering and financial risk management is the approach presented by Dahl et al. (1993a, 1993b). The authors consider financial risk management as a broader field within which financial engineering falls in as an approach to develop financial risk management tools. In that regard, financial engineering provides a methodological framework based on sophisticated operations research techniques to manage financial risks on the three-stage context described above. More specifically the authors concentrate their discussion on the construction of portfolios of different forms of securities such as mortgage-backed securities, collateralized mortgage applications, asset/liability management and fixed-income securities that can be used as risk management instruments. They, therefore, focus on the third stage of the risk management process described in Figure 1.1. The main financial engineering tools proposed by the authors to manage financial risks, originate from the field of optimization, including linear, non-linear and integer programming, global optimization techniques, stochastic programming, network optimization, etc. (Dahl et al., 1993a;b). The restriction by the authors of the financial engineering concept on the construction of portfolios of securities justifies this risk management approach of financial engineering.

However, such a narrow definition of the relationship among financial engineering and financial risk management is rather limited. The process of financial innovation, a core concept within the financial engineering context, does not only comprise instruments, processes and solutions that involve securities. On the contrary, financial innovation involves all aspects of the financial operation of a corporate entity or organization. Not all of these aspects are related to risk analysis. Despite the fact that risk is a crucial concept within the context of financial management, the financial operation of a corporate entity or organization is not solely risk-driven. In that respect, the relationship between financial engineering and financial risk management can be defined within a broader context. This alternative approach was adopted by Mulvey et al. (1997), who considered that the role of financial engineering covers four major aspects of financial management (Figure 1.2).

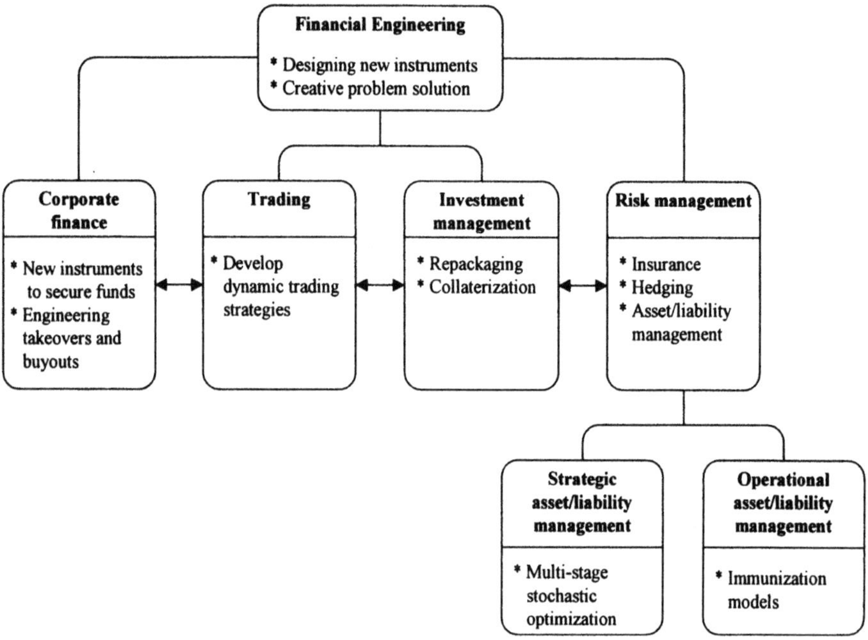

Figure 1.2. The multidimensional role of financial engineering according to Mulvey et al. (1997)

According to Mulvey et al. (1997) financial engineering contributes in four interrelated aspects of modern financial management: (1) corporate finance, (2) securities trading, (3) investment management and (4) financial risk management. With regard to corporate finance, financial engineering contributes in obtaining the funds necessary for the operation of a firm or organization as well as in structuring of mergers and acquisitions, which are of special interest within the reforming global business environment. With regard to securities trading, financial engineering provides the tools to develop appropriate trading strategies taking into account the dynamic nature of the markets. In investment management, financial engineering supports the design and development of new investment instruments, such as high yield mutual funds, or the transformation of high-risk investments into low risk investments using techniques such as repackaging and overcollaterization. Finally in financial risk management, financial engineering provides the required methodological framework to design appropriately financial risk management techniques including asset/liability management, hedging strategies and insurance policies. With regard to asset/liability management, Mulvey et al. (1997) distinguish between asset/liability management on the strategic level and asset/liability management on the operational level. At the strategic level the authors propose the use of multi-stage stochastic optimization techniques, while at the operational level they propose the use of immunization models. This is done to distinguish the risk caused by the sensitivity of an asset portfolio into interest rate changes from the risk caused by the influence that such changes have on the level of liabilities.

However, even in this broader concept of financial engineering, financial risk management is restricted to asset/liability management, while ignoring other aspects of financial management, where financial decision making requires the assessment of several forms of financial risks. For instance, one could mention the assessment of business failure risk, venture capital investments, credit risk evaluation, portfolio selection and management, country risk assessment, financial planning etc. (Zopounidis, 1998a).

4. FINANCIAL ENGINEERING METHODOLOGIES

Except for the theoretical aspects regarding the concept of financial engineering and its relation to financial risk management, researchers have proposed several methodological approaches to support the decision making process in problems encountered within the financial engineering context.

The fact that the financial theory addresses most financial decision making problems from an optimization perspective has led several researchers to employ operations research techniques to study these problems within the financial engineering context. The classical modeling of decision problems in operations research consists in formulating an optimization (maximization or minimization) problem under specific constraints. In fact, it is the best choice problem.

The operations research techniques were actually among the first to be used in the solution of some financial problems. Ekeland (1993) wonders "why finance, rather curiously, has remained so long away from the techniques of operations research (i.e. optimization techniques), except for those concerning portfolio selection models". According to the same author, the Capital Asset Pricing Model (CAPM) is a static optimization model based on the principle according which, the best portfolio (i.e. optimal portfolio) is the one that maximizes the expected return for a given level of risk in the period of time considered.

The interest of the financial community to integrate the financial theory with operations research is not surprising. According to Ashford et al. (1988) the operations research approach to address financial decision making problems differs from the approach employed within the context of the financial theory in three significant aspects.

1. The operations research approach is mainly oriented towards the managers of the firms and organizations rather than the external shareholders and the market. On the other hand, the analysis of financial decisions according to the financial theory is based on the valuation of the decisions taken by the market without considering the preferences and the judgment of the actual decision makers who are the ones mostly concerned with the decisions taken.
2. Operations researchers consider the market as imperfect. This approach justifies the imposing of specific constraints during the study of financial decisions. The financial theory assumes the existence of well-functioning capital markets, which implies that the market can be used as a credible factor in financial decision making.
3. The methodological approaches employed within the context of operations research are useful in addressing both short-term financial decisions, such as working capital management, as well as long-term financial decisions regarding, such as investment and financing decisions. On the contrary, financial theory is mainly concerned with long-term financial decisions.

Table 1.1 reports some contributions of several operations research techniques to financial engineering.

Table 1.1. Operations research techniques to financial engineering

Techniques	Contribution
Inventory control	Management of inventories Working capital management
Linear/integer/non-linear programming	Cash management Portfolio construction Asset/liability management Bankruptcy prediction Credit scoring
Stochastic programming	Asset/liability management
Graph theory/network optimization	Financial planning
Simulation	Investment appraisal
Markov processes	Management of accounts receivable

Except for the operations research approach, statistical analysis (both univariate and multivariate) as well as econometrics have also contributed to financial engineering, by providing the necessary means to perform hypothesis testing, experimental design, regression analysis, discriminant analysis, time series analysis and forecasting, data analysis, etc.

Despite the significant contributions of such approaches to financial engineering, one should also point out some major limitations. These limitations involve the restriction of the study of financial engineering problems to a quantitative analysis that is often based on the traditional probabilistic return-risk (mean-variance) framework. Such an approach often fails to comprise other factors that are relevant to the problem being studied and are commonly used in the daily practice of financial engineers. Considering also the fact that many of these factors are qualitative, it becomes apparent that an alternative analysis framework is required to facilitate the analysis of the multiple factors that are involved in financial engineering problems, both quantitative and qualitative ones, taking into account the preferences and the decision making policy of the actual decision makers (i.e., financial engineers). Multicriteria decision aid is one of the most promising methodological approaches suitable for addressing this issue and it has gradually gained an increasing interest among researchers to study financial engineering problems.

5. THE MULTICRITERIA CHARACTER OF FINANCIAL ENGINEERING

Traditional optimization, statistical and econometric analysis approaches used within the financial engineering context are often based on the assumption that the considered problem is well posed, well-formulated regarding the reality involved and they usually consider the existence of a single objective, evaluation criterion or point of view that underlies the conducted analysis (i.e., monocriteria paradigm). In such a case the solution of financial problems is easy to obtain. But in reality, the modeling of financial problems is based on a different kind of logic. In that case, their solution should take into consideration the following elements (i.e. multicriteria paradigm, cf. Roy, 1988):

- The existence of multiple criteria.
- The conflicting situation between the criteria.
- The complex, subjective and ill-structured nature of the evaluation process.
- The introduction of financial decision makers in the evaluation process.

Financial and operation researchers have recently started to adapt this innovative, comprehensive and realistic perspective, which overcomes the restrictive framework of optimization (Zopounidis, 1990; 1995). For example, in capital budgeting decision making, Bhaskar and McNamee (1983) pose the following questions:

(a) In assessing investment proposals, do the decision makers have a single objective or multiple objectives?

(b) If decision makers do have multiple objectives, which are those and what is the priority structure of the objectives?

In another similar study, Bhaskar (1979) notes that microeconomic theory has largely adopted a single objective function, which is the principle of utility maximization for the consumer unit and profit maximization for firms. Bhaskar (1979) presents three categories of criticism regarding the use of this single objective function principle for firms:

(a) there exist alternatives to the profit maximization approach which are based on equally simple hypotheses and can better explain reality;

(b) the profit maximization or any other equally simple hypothesis is too naive to explain the complex process of decision making;

(c) the real-world firms do not have suitable information to enable them to maximize their profits.

Furthermore, several other theories of the firm have been postulated and have proposed different objectives than that of the traditional microeconomic theory. One can cite the revenue maximizing model (cf. Baumol, 1959), the manager's utility model (cf. Williamson, 1964), the satisfying model (cf. Simon, 1957) and the behavioral models (cf. Cyert and March, 1963).

On the basis of the above remarks it is possible to distinguish three main reasons which have motivated a change of view in the modeling of the financial problems (Zopounidis, 1999a).

- Formulating the problem in terms of seeking the optimum, financial decision makers (i.e. financial analysts, portfolio managers, investors, etc.) get involved in a very narrow problematic, often irrelevant to the real decision problem.
- The different financial decisions are taken by humans (i.e. financial managers) and not by the models; the decision makers get more and more deeply involved in the decision making process. In order to solve problems, it becomes necessary to take into consideration their preferences, their experiences and their knowledge.
- For financial decision problems such as the choice of investment projects, the portfolio selection, the evaluation of business failure risk, etc., it is an illusion to speak about optimality since multiple criteria must be taken into consideration.

The subsequent two subsections illustrate the multicriteria character of two significant financial engineering problems, investment and portfolio management, and discuss the way that a multicriteria approach could improve the decision making process in these fields.

5.1 The investment decision

The choice of investment projects entails an important decision for every firm, public or private, large or small one. In fact, considering its duration, its amount and its irreversible character, an investment decision is regarded as a major and strategic one. Therefore, the process of an investment decision should be conveniently modeled. In general, the investment decision process consists of four main stages: perception, formulation, evaluation and choice. The financial theory intervenes only in the stages of evaluation and choice (cf. Colasse, 1993). With its empirical financial criteria (i.e. the payback method, the accounting rate of return) and sophisticated ones, based on discount techniques (i.e. the net present value, the internal rate of return, the index of profitability, the discounted payback method, etc.), the financial theory proposes either a ranking from the best to worst when there are more than one alternative investment projects or an acceptance or refusal if there is only one investment project.

Although the tools of the financial theory should be improved so that they could take into account time, inflation and risk (i.e. analytical methods, simulation methods, game theory, CAPM, etc.), there are still problems concerning the evaluation and selection of investment projects. Among the most important ones, one could mention the restriction of the investment concept in a time series of monetary flows (i.e. inflows, outflows), the choice of the discount rate, the conflicts between financial criteria (i.e. net present value versus internal rate of return), etc. According to the financial theory, the discount rate (sometimes called rate of return) plays the role of acceptance or rejection rate (a cut off rate) of an investment project in the case where the criterion of internal rate of return is used. Thus, one can see that the investment decision of a firm depends only on one variable, the discount rate. As far as the conflicts between criteria are concerned, the criteria that express the goal of the profitability of projects could lead to divergent rankings (for example, the net present value and the index of profitability or even the net present value and the internal rate of return). Consequently, the financial approach to the investment decision seems limited and unrealistic. It is limited because it involves only the stages of evaluation and choice and it is unrealistic because it is based only on financial criteria.

On the other hand, a multicriteria decision aid (MCDA) approach could contribute in a very original way to the investment decision process. Initially, it intervenes in the whole process of investment, from the stages of perception and formulation to the stages of evaluation and choice. Concerning the stages of perception and formulation, MCDA contributes to the identification of possible actions (i.e. investment opportunities) and to the definition of a set of potential actions (i.e. possible variants, each variant constituting an investment project in competition with others). This set of projects can be global, fragmented, stable or evolutionary. Then, it is necessary to choose a reference "problematique" which is well adapted to the investment decision problem (i.e. choice, sorting, ranking).

- Choice "problematique" P.α: enables us to choose the best investment project or develop a selection procedure for investment projects.
- Sorting "problematique" P.β: enables us to sort investment projects according to norms or build an assignment procedure for investment projects.
- Ranking "problematique" P.γ: enables us to rank the investment projects according to a decreasing preference order or build an ordering procedure for investment projects.

Concerning the stages of evaluation and choice, MCDA offers a much more realistic methodological framework than financial theory, by introducing in the study of investment projects both quantitative and qualitative criteria. Criteria such as the urgency of the project, the coherence of the objectives of the projects with those of the general policy of the firm (Evrard and Zisswiller, 1982), the social and environmental aspects should be taken into consideration in an investment decision. Therefore, MCDA contributes through the identification of the best investment projects according to the "problematique" chosen, the satisfactory resolution of the conflicts between the criteria, the determination of the relative importance of the criteria in the decision making process, and the revealing of the investors' preferences and system of values. It is very interesting to mention that many authors have already used MCDA methods in the evaluation of investment projects (list non exhaustive): ELECTRE II and ORESTE methods (Danila, 1980); multiattribute utility theory (Evrard and Zisswiller, 1982); multiobjective mathematical programming (Lin, 1978; Bhaskar, 1979; Khorramshahgol and Okoruwa, 1994); the Analytic Hierarchy Process (AHP) method (Kivijärvi and Tuominen, 1992); PROMETHEE method (Ribarovic and Mladineo, 1987; Zopounidis, 1993a).

Finally, in order to examine if the firms really apply multiple criteria in their investment decisions, we present the results of the empirical study of Bhaskar and McNamee (1983). The survey that the two authors conducted in large United Kingdom companies, has shown that most companies appear to have more than one objectives when an investment is being appraised (96%). The most common number of objectives that companies had was eight. Concerning the priority of the objectives, most companies (77%) had profitability as the primary objective. The next most important objective was company's growth. Other criteria less important but with a significant role in the investment decisions are the risk, the liquidity, the environment, the age of assets, the flexibility, the depth of skills, etc.

5.2 Portfolio management

In the field of portfolio management it is possible to cite the pioneering work of Harry Markowitz (1952), the founder of the classical approach of the portfolio management, who developed the mean-variance optimization model. According to Ekeland (1993), the problem of portfolio selection in the mean-variance model is a multicriteria one, because the investor will try simultaneously to maximize the return and minimize the risk; but determining the acceptable level of risk, one comes back to maximize the return, which is a classical monocriteria problem. After this bi-criteria, and even more the monocriteria portfolio selection consideration (i.e. market model, CAPM), the development of multi-factor models has started where there are more types of risk and not only market risk. The arbitrage pricing theory developed by Ross (1976) is a well-known example of such multi-factor models. Thus, the problem of portfolio selection becomes multidimensional. The necessity of having multidimensional methods (i.e. statistics and econometrics) for the selection of stocks has been presented by specialist researchers in finance (Jacquillat, 1972). The multidimensional nature of risk in portfolio management has also been demonstrated by specialist researchers in multicriteria analysis. One refers to the works of Zeleny (1977, 1982) and Colson and Zeleny (1979) regarding the "Prospect Ranking Vector (PRV)" method. Today an arsenal of multidimensional and multicriteria methods such as factor analysis, goal programming, AHP, ELECTRE, MINORA, ADELAIS, etc. have been already applied in the field of portfolio management (cf. Ho and Paulson, 1980; Lee and Chesser, 1980; Saaty et al., 1980; Martel et al., 1988; Colson and de Bruyn, 1989; Martel et al., 1991; Zopounidis, 1993b; Khoury et al.,

1993; Hui and Kwan, 1994; Zopounidis et al., 1995b; Hurson and Zopounidis, 1995, 1997).

The multicriteria nature of the problem of portfolio selection is well presented by Khoury et al. (1993). The authors study the problem of the international portfolio selection. According to them, the classical optimization model of portfolio selection used in a national context can have even more chance of being sub-optimal in a situation of international diversification. In fact, in an international context, the M-V model does not always constitute a suitable method because it does not incorporate all the criteria that the portfolio managers and the investors use in their stock investment decisions. For such decisions, the authors propose new criteria such as: the return of the last five years on a monthly basis, the standard deviation of the return calculated in the last five years, the total cost of transactions, the country risk (or political risk), the direct available coverage for foreign currencies and the exchange risk. The multicriteria methodology used (i.e. ELECTRE IS, ELECTRE III) has the advantage of offering the portfolio manager a large set of investment opportunities, and also gives him the flexibility of choosing the relative importance of the different criteria during the process of portfolio selection. Finally, the authors believe that the use of an optimization model under constraints changes the nature of the portfolio selection problem because a constraint does not play the same role as a criterion in all decision problems. To show this new direction of research in portfolio management, it is convenient to mention the special issue of the Canadian journal "L'Actualité Economique", which is dedicated on the contribution of multicriteria analysis in the study of financial markets (cf. Khoury and Martel, 1993).

6. MULTICRITERIA CRITERIA DECISION AID

Real world decision making problems are usually too complex and ill-structured to be considered through the examination of a single criterion, attribute or point of view that will lead to the "optimum" decision. In fact, such a unidimensional approach is merely an oversimplification of the actual nature of the problem at hand and it can lead to unrealistic decisions. A more appealing approach would be the simultaneous consideration of all pertinent factors that are related to the problem. However, through this approach some very essential issues/questions emerge: how can several and often conflicting factors be aggregated into a single evaluation model? Is this evaluation model a unique and optimal one? Researchers from a variety of disciplines have tried to address the former question using statistical approaches, artificial intelligence techniques and operations research methodologies. The success and usefulness of these attempts should be examined with regard to the second question. Obviously, a decision problem is not addressed, in the same way, by all decision makers. Each decision maker has his/her own preferences, experiences and decision making policy. This is a significant issue that it should be considered during the development of decision making models.

Addressing the aforementioned issues constitutes the focal point of interest for multicriteria decision aid (MCDA). MCDA constitutes an advanced field of operations research devoted to the development and implementation of decision support tools and methodologies to confront complex decision problems involving multiple criteria, goals or objectives of conflicting nature. The tools and methodologies provided by MCDA are not just some mathematical models aggregating criteria, points of view or attributes but furthermore they are decision support oriented. Actually, "support" is a key concept in MCDA, implying that the models are not developed through a straightforward sequential process where the decision maker's role is passive. Instead, an iterative process is employed to analyze the preferences of the decision maker and represent them as consistently as possible in an appropriate decision model. This iterative and interactive preference modeling procedure constitutes the underlying basis of the decision support orientation of MCDA, and it is one of the basic distinguishing features of the MCDA as opposed to statistical and optimization decision making approaches.

6.1 Brief historical overview

From the very beginning of mankind, decision making always involved multiple criteria that have been treated either implicitly or explicitly, although no specific mathematical framework existed for this purpose. Pareto (1896) was the first to study, in an axiomatic way, the aggregation of conflicting criteria into a single evaluation index. He was also the first to introduce the concept of efficiency, one of the key aspects of the modern MCDA theory.

Several decades later, Koopmans (1951) extended Pareto's work introducing the notion of the efficient vector, i.e., the non-dominated set of alternatives. During the same period (1940s – 1950s) von Neumann and Morgenstern (1944) introduced the expected utility theory, thus setting the foundations of another MCDA approach. In the 1960s the concepts and procedures described in these early works have been extended by Charnes and Cooper (1961) and Fishburn (1965).

By the end of 1960s significant research has started to be undertaken in this field by the European operations research community too. Roy (1968), the founder of the European stream of MCDA, developed a new theoretical approach based on the concept of outranking relations. In the next subsequent decades, 1970s – 1990s, MCDA has evolved rapidly, scientific MCDA associations were formed, and numerous advances have been developed in the international literature both on the theoretical aspects of MCDA, as well as on its practical implementation.

The field has been significantly benefited by the widespread use of personal computers that enabled the development of software packages employing MCDA methods. These software packages, known as multicriteria decision support systems, provided the means to implement the theoretical advances of MCDA in user-friendly systems that enable real-time decision making through interactive and iterative procedures that enhance the decision makers' perception of the problem and his/her judgment and decision making policy.

6.2 Decision aid activity

Roy (1985, 1996) proposes a methodology of systematic intervention of multicriteria analysis in the decision process. In brief, this methodology comprises four levels presented in Figure 1.3.

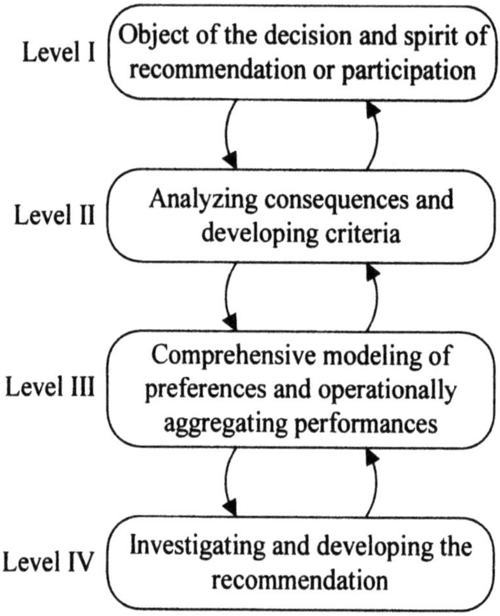

Figure 1.3. The intervention of multicriteria analysis in the decision process (Source: Roy, 1985)

It is important to emphasize that these four levels do not necessarily follow one another in the aforementioned order. The activity of decision aid does not necessarily constitute a sequential process; feedback due to the interaction between the decision maker and the analyst is possible. This general methodology has contributed to the development of several multicriteria methods, which have been applied successfully to real cases. Among these methods one could mention the ELECTRE methods developed by Bernard Roy and his collaborators, the PROMETHEE and GAIA methods (Mareschal and Mertens, 1990; Mareschal and Brans, 1993) the AHP method (Saaty, 1980), multiobjective/goal programming approaches (Lee and Chesser, 1980; Spronk, 1981) as well as preference disaggregation methods (the UTA method, the UTADIS method, etc.; cf. Jacquet-Lagrèze and Siskos, 1983; Zopounidis and Doumpos, 1997).

6.3 MCDA approaches

6.3.1 Methodological approach oriented classification

Among the MCDA methods and tools, several approaches and theoretical disciplines can be defined, although their distinction and the existing boundaries among them are often difficult to determine. Roy (1985) proposes the following three categories of methods:

(1) unique synthesis criterion approach disregarding any incomparability,

(2) outranking synthesis approach, accepting incomparability, and

(3) interactive local judgement approach with trial-error iterations.

The classification of the MCDA approaches that is adopted in this chapter has been proposed by Pardalos et al. (1995). It distinguishes four categories:

(1) multiobjective mathematical programming,

(2) multiattribute utility theory,

(3) outranking relations approach, and

(4) preference disaggregation analysis.

- **Multiobjective mathematical programming**

Multiobjective mathematical programming (MMP) is an extension of well-known single objective mathematical programming framework. It involves the optimization of a set of objectives expressed in the form of linear or non-linear functions of some decision variables. The optimization of these objectives is performed subject to constraints imposed either by the decision environment or by the decision maker. Formally, a mathematical programming problem has the following form:

Max/Min $\{f_1(\underline{x}), f_2(\underline{x}), \ldots, f_n(\underline{x})\}$

Subject to:

$\underline{x} \in B$

where:

$\underline{x}$ is the vector of the decision variables,

$f_1, f_2, ..., f_n$ are the objective functions to be optimized,

B is the set of feasible solutions.

The conflicting nature of the objectives in real world decision problems makes impossible their simultaneous optimization. Thus, the decision maker cannot obtain an optimum solution with respect to all the objective functions, but has to consider finding a satisfying one. The determination of this satisfying solution depends on the decision maker's preferences, judgment and decision policy. The procedure that leads to the determination of a satisfying solution is interactive and iterative; it involves the search of all efficient solutions to identify the one that meets the decision makers preferences and decision policy. A solution is called efficient or Pareto optimal if it is not dominated by any other solution with respect to all the specified objectives. Generally, the procedure employed by MMP techniques is the following. Initially an efficient solution is identified and it is presented to the decision maker. If the decision maker is not satisfied with this solution, he/she provides some preferential information indicating the way that the efficient set should be investigated. This preferential information may involve the definition of some reference points or the determination of the objectives that should be improved and the tradeoffs that the decision maker is willing to undertake with respect to other objectives. This preferential information provides a guide for a new search of the efficient set, and a new solution is obtained. The same iterative procedure continues until an efficient solution, that meets the decision makers' preferences, is obtained.

Several methods have been proposed to perform the aforementioned solution procedure. Their differences involve mainly the form of the interaction with the decision maker and the efficient solution generation procedure. More details on these methods can be found in the books of Zeleny (1982) and Steuer (1986).

An alternative approach to address multiobjective programming problems is through goal programming. In contrast to MMP techniques, which seek to optimize each objective separately, the aim of the goal programming approach is to optimize a function of the deviations from some pre-specified ideal points. These points are determined by the decision maker as some ideal values of the objectives that are involved in the considered problem. Thus, the original objectives of the problem are transformed into constraints and the optimization of the deviations from the specified ideal points results indirectly to the optimization of the initial objectives. The general form of a goal programming formulation is the following:

Max/Min $g\left(d_i^+, d_i^-\right)$

Subject to:

$f_i\left(\underline{x}\right) + d_i^+ - d_i^- = c_i$

$\underline{x} \in B$

$d_i^+, d_i^- \geq 0$

where:

f_i is the i objective of the problem,

c_i is the ideal value of the f_i objective,

d_i^+, d_i^- are the deviations from the specified ideal values c_i,

g is a function of the deviations.

The simplicity of the goal programming approach has made it quite popular among researchers in the study of real world problems including financial engineering. Spronk (1981) provides a comprehensive discussion of the goal programming approach and its applications to financial planning.

The multiobjective/goal programming paradigm is well adapted to financial engineering and the optimization perspective often employed within this field. However, in contrast to the traditional single-objective approaches employed in financial engineering, multiobjective and goal programming techniques enable the financial engineers to introduce in their analysis not only the profit maximization perspective, but all additional aspects that are relevant to the considered as well. Most of the applications of this approach to financial engineering problems involve the construction of portfolios and financial planning (a list of these applications is given later on).

- **Multiattribute utility theory**

The multiattribute utility theory (MAUT) is an extension of the classical utility theory. Its aim is to represent/model the decision maker's preferences through an utility function $u(\underline{g})$, aggregating all the evaluation criteria: $u(\underline{g}) = u(g_1, g_2, ..., g_n)$, where $\underline{g}$ is the vector of the evaluation criteria $g_1, g_2, \ldots, g_n$. Utility functions are non-linear monotone functions of the criteria's values, indicating the value of the alternatives in the global preference system of the decision maker. The most studied form of utility function, from a theoretical point of view, is the additive form:

$$u(\underline{g}) = p_1 u_1(g_1) + p_2 u_2(g_2) + \ldots + p_n u_n(g_n),$$

where,

$u_1, u_2, \ldots, u_n$ are the marginal utility functions defined on the scales of criteria,

$p_1, p_2, \ldots, p_n$ are the weights of the criteria.

The additive utility function is a generalization of the simple weighted average where all u_i are monotone linear functions. A significant assumption that underlies the use of the additive utility function involves the condition of preferential independence of the evaluation criteria. Within a set $\underline{g}$ of evaluation criteria, a subset $\underline{g}'$ is considered to be preferentially independent if the preferences among the alternatives that only differ with respect to the criteria set $\underline{g}'$, do not depend upon the rest of the criteria. When the preferential independence condition does not hold, then the use of the multiplicative utility function is more appropriate:

$$u(\underline{g}) = \frac{\prod_j \left[k u_j(g_j) + 1 \right] - 1}{k},$$

where,

k is a scaling constant.

The book of Keeney and Raiffa (1993) provides a comprehensive discussion of utility theory and the underlying assumptions of the several types of utility functions.

The development of the utility function is developed through the direct interrogation of the decision maker, who specifies the weights of the evaluation criteria as the tradeoffs between them, and the form of the marginal utility functions. Several techniques have been presented in the international literature to facilitate the definition of the marginal utility functions by the decision maker; the midpoint value technique is the most widely used one (Keeney and Raiffa, 1993).

On the basis of the utilities of the alternatives that are determined through the developed utility function, the decision maker can rank them from the best alternatives (alternatives with the higher utility) to the worst ones (alternatives with the lower utility), classify them into appropriate classes through the definition of appropriate utility thresholds, or select the alternative with the higher utility as the best one.

The books of Zeleny (1982) and Keeney and Raiffa (1993) provide a comprehensive discussion of MAUT, its axiomatic foundations, and the forms of utility functions that are commonly employed in decision making problems, both, under certainty and uncertainty.

The fact that the utility theory constitutes a core breakthrough in the field of economics and finance, makes apparent the significant implications of the extension of the traditional mono-criterion utility approach to a multiattribute one, for modeling the financial engineers' decision policy and attitude.

- **Outranking relations**

The outranking relations approach was developed in Europe with the presentation of the ELECTRE methods (ELimination Et Choix Traduisant la REalité) by Roy (1968). The outranking relations techniques operate into two stages. The first stage involves the development of an outranking relation among the considered alternatives, while the second stage involves the exploitation of the developed outranking relation to rank the alternatives, sort them into homogenous classes or choose the best alternatives.

The outranking relation is a binary relation that enables the decision maker to assess the strength of the affirmation that an alternative α outranks an alternative b. The strength of such an affirmation increases if there are enough arguments (coalition of the criteria) to confirm that α is at least as good as b, while there is no strong evidence to refuse this statement. The development of the outranking relation depends upon the preferential information provided by the decision maker. This information differs among the several methods that have been developed, but in most cases it involves the specification of the weights of the evaluation criteria as well as some other technical and non-technical parameters such as the preference, indifference, and veto thresholds. The preference threshold is defined as the minimum difference on the evaluations of two alternatives on an evaluation criterion above which a strict preference of an alternative over the other can be established. The indifference threshold is the maximum difference on the evaluations of two alternatives on an evaluation criterion below which there is some degree of indifference between the two alternatives. Finally, the veto threshold is the minimum difference between the evaluations of two alternatives *a* and *b* on a specific criterion, which can take away all the credibility of the affirmation "*a* is at least as good as *b*" no matter what the performances of the alternatives on the rest of the criteria are. The definition of these parameters enables the examination of whether there is a sufficient majority of criteria for which *α* is better than *b* (concordance) and if the unfavorable deviations for the rest of the criteria (discordance) are not too high. In this case it is possible to conclude that alternative *α* outranks alternative *b*.

Once the outranking relation is constructed, the second stage of the process is to exploit this outranking relation to obtain a ranking or sorting of the alternatives or to select some of them as the most appropriate ones. A significant feature of the exploitation procedure is that it enables the decision maker not only to identify whether an alternative is preferred to another, but also to identify incomparable alternatives (i.e., cases where the performances of two alternatives on the evaluation criteria differ significantly, thus making impossible their comparison). The identification of such situations is possible due to the fact that the developed outranking relation is neither transitive nor complete. The exploitation procedure can result either to a complete ordering of the considered alternatives from the best to the worst ones, or to a weak ordering represented into an outranking graph such as the one presented in Figure 1.4. Each node of this graph corresponds to an alternative, while the arcs represent the existence of an outranking relation among two alternatives. Thus, in the example of Figure 1.4, the arc between alternatives *a* and *b* and its direction, imply that alternative *a* outranks alternative *b*. The core of this graph is a set of alternatives for which there is no outranking relation between them, and each one of these alternatives outranks at least one alternative not belonging to this set. In graph of Figure 1.4 the core consists of alternatives *a* and *d*, since there is no outranking relation between them (there is no arc), while furthermore both *a* and *d* outrank at least one of the rest of the alternatives (*a* outranks *b* and *c*, while *d* outranks *c*). The elements of the core constitute the best alternatives that should be considered by the decision maker.

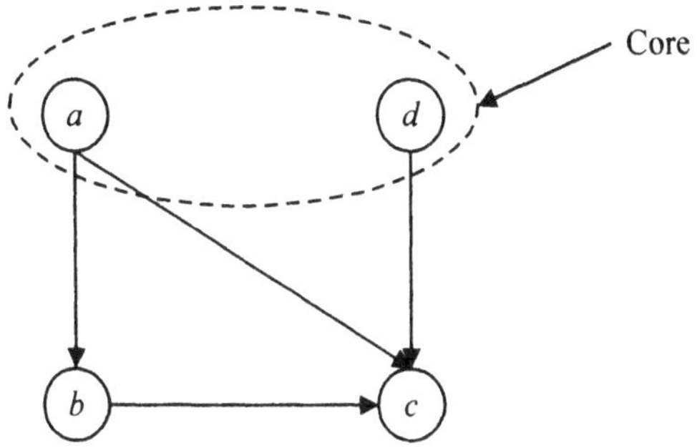

Figure 1.4. An example of an outranking graph

Some of the most widely known outranking relations methods include the family of the ELECTRE methods (Roy, 1991) and the family of the PROMETHEE methods (Brans and Vincke, 1985). A detailed presentation of all outranking methods can be found in the works of Vincke (1992) and Roy and Bouyssou (1993).

- **Preference disaggregation analysis**

The preference disaggregation approach refers to the analysis (disaggregation) of the global preferences (judgement policy) of the decision maker in order to identify the criteria aggregation model that underlies the preference result (ranking or classification/sorting). Similarly to MAUT, preference disaggregation analysis uses common utility decomposition forms to model the decision maker's preferences. Nevertheless, instead of employing a direct procedure for estimating the global utility model (MAUT), preference disaggregation analysis uses regression–based techniques (indirect estimation procedure).

More specifically, in preference disaggregation analysis the parameters of the utility decomposition model are estimated through the analysis of the decision maker's overall preference on some reference alternatives, which may involve either examples of past decisions or a small subset of the alternatives under consideration. The decision maker is asked to provide a ranking or a classification of the reference alternatives according to his/her decision policy (global preferences). Then, using regression-based techniques the global preference model is estimated so that the ranking or classification specified by the decision maker can be reproduced as consistently as possible through the developed decision model. A comprehensive bibliography on preference disaggregation methods can be found in the works of Jacquet-Lagrèze and Siskos (1983) and Pardalos et al. (1995).

The preference disaggregation analysis is based on the simple finding that generally, in real world situations, decision makers are either unable or unwilling to provide, in a direct way, specific information regarding their preferences including weights or tradeoffs. Even if this is possible, the procedure that will be employed to elicit such information from the decision maker is time consuming. This may forestall its practical applications in real decision problems where decisions have to be taken in real time.

On the contrary, instead of describing the procedure that leads to the final decision, it would be easier for the decision maker to provide the analyst with the actual decision he/she would take considering the specific characteristics and conditions of the problem at hand. For instance, when a portfolio analyst must evaluate some securities in order to decide which are appropriate to be included in a portfolio, the past evaluations that the analyst has made can be used. These evaluations can either have the form of an ordinal scale (ranking or classification), or ratio scale (how many times a security is preferred compared to another security; cf. Lam and Choo, 1995). Furthermore, it is even possible to consider more detailed information that the decision maker can provide, for instance the ranking of the securities on each evaluation criterion combined with the ranking of the criteria according to their significance (Cook and Kress, 1991).

The purpose of gathering such information from the decision maker is to have some representative examples of the decisions that he/she takes. These examples reflect the decision policy and the preferences that the decision maker has implicitly used in making the decision. Consequently, through the analysis of such decision instances, the analyst can derive useful information concerning the global preference system of the decision maker.

Decision makers when making decisions evaluate each alternative over a set of factors, criteria, attributes or points of view that affect the overall evaluation of the alternatives. Then, these partial evaluations are aggregated to derive the final decision. Following the same approach, the aim of the preference disaggregation analysis is to disaggregate the overall decision into the partial evaluations of each one of the evaluation criteria. The disaggregation should be performed in such a way so that the aggregation of the partial evaluations will lead to the overall evaluation provided by the decision maker. If this is not possible, then the deviations that occur should be minimized.

In such a disaggregation process it is clear that the form that the partial evaluations will have as well as the selection of the model which will be used to aggregate the partial evaluations are two key issues. Similarly to MAUT, the aggregation models employed within the context of preference disaggregation analysis have the form of utility functions. The aim of preference disaggregation analysis is to estimate the marginal utilities of each evaluation criterion so that their aggregation using either an additive or a multiplicative utility function results in an evaluation of the alternatives which is consistent with the decision maker's preferences and judgement policy. This estimation is achieved through mathematical programming techniques with the objective being the optimization of a measure of consistency. Multiplicative utility functions can generally be more appropriate for modeling decision makers' preferences in real world decisions taking into account possible interactions among the decision makers' preference on several criteria (Oral and Kettani, 1989). However, their estimation results in non-linear mathematical programming problems (non-linear constraints) that are computationally intensive and difficult to solve. Consequently, in practice additive utility functions are commonly used instead of multiplicative ones, since they provide a simple but powerful approach for modeling decision makers' preference in multiple criteria decision making problems.

The most well-known preference disaggregation methods include the family of the UTA methods initially developed by Jacquet-Lagrèze and Siskos (1982). Their applications in financial engineering have been extensive in order to develop evaluation models (a list of relevant studies is provided later on).

6.3.2 Problem type oriented classification

Except for the functional and methodological differences among the four aforementioned MCDA approaches, their differences, with regard to the types of decision problems that they address, should also be pointed out. Real world decision problems can be categorized into two groups:

- Problems where the decision maker must evaluate a finite set of alternatives in order to select the most appropriate one, to rank them from the best to the worst, to classify them into predefined homogeneous classes, or to describe them. Typical examples involve the selection among different investment projects, personnel evaluation (ranking problem) and financial distress prediction (classification problem; i.e., discrimination between healthy and financially distressed firms). Within the context of the MCDA framework, such problems are referred to as discrete MCDA problems.
- Problems where there is an infinite set of alternatives, thus the decision maker must construct the most appropriate one according to his/her goals or objectives. Recourse allocation problems are typical examples of this kind. For instance, a portfolio manager faces the problem of constructing a portfolio of securities according to his specific investment policy and objectives. Different combinations of securities can result to numerous portfolios. Thus, it is impossible to define an exhaustive set of portfolios for evaluation and selection of the most appropriate one. Instead, the portfolio manager must construct the most appropriate portfolio through the determination of the amount of capital that should be invested in each security. Within the context of the MCDA framework, such problems are referred to as continuous MCDA problems.

The study of discrete MCDA problems requires the development of a framework to aggregate all evaluation criteria into a single evaluation model of some form. This can be achieved using MAUT, outranking relations or preference disaggregation analysis. On the other hand, in continuous MCDA problems MAUT, outranking relations and preference disaggregation analysis are not directly applicable since there are not any specific alternatives to be evaluated. Such problems are addressed using MMP or goal programming techniques. This does not mean that discrete MCDA techniques are of no use to solve continuous MCDA problems. On the contrary, several interactive MMP techniques at each iteration of the solution process, they construct some efficient solutions, which must be evaluated by decision maker in order to elicit indirectly the necessary preferential information that will guide the solution process. The constructed set of efficient solutions is a finite set of alternatives. Thus, discrete MCDA techniques can be used to support the decision maker in evaluating the efficient solutions that are obtained and to select the most appropriate one. A typical example of this approach is the ADELAIS decision support system that employs MMP techniques as well as the UTA method (a discrete MCDA method; Jacquet-Lagrèze and Siskos, 1982) in order to address multiobjective linear programming problems (Siskos and Despotis, 1989).

Figure 1.5, illustrates the classification described above of the MCDA approaches according to the types of decision problems that they address. The solid lines connecting the four MCDA approaches to the two types of problems indicate direct applicability, while dotted lines indicate indirect applicability in the way discussed above.

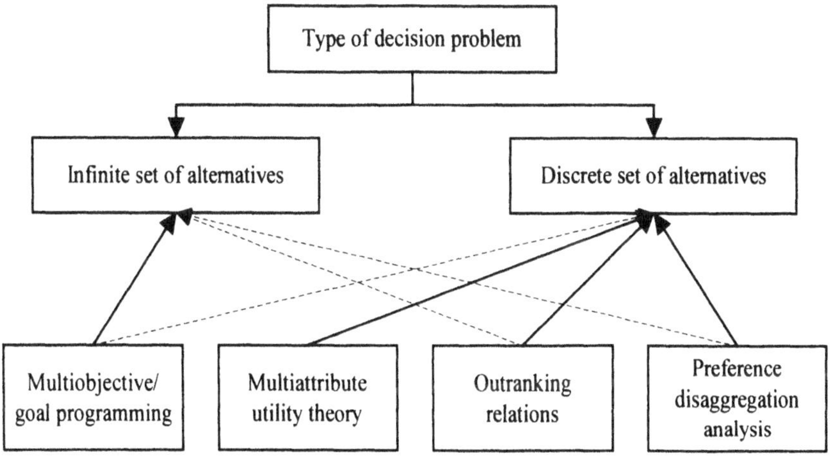

Figure 1.5. MCDA approaches classification according to the types of problems that they address

6.4 MCDA contributions to financial engineering

MCDA is well adapted to the multidimensional nature of financial risks and it has already contributed in a significant manner in the solution of several financial risk management problems such as venture capital investment, business failure risk, credit granting, bond rating, country risk, evaluation of the performance and viability of organizations, choice of investments, financial planning and portfolio management. Table 1.2 reports some of the applications of MCDA in these fields of financial engineering and financial risk management (list not exhaustive) categorized according to the four MCDA approaches presented above.

Table 1.2. MCDA applications in financial engineering (Source: Zopounidis, 1999b)

		Multiobjective mathematical programming	Multiattribute utility theory	Outranking relations	Preference disaggregation analysis
Corporate mergers and acquisitions			Slowinski and al. (1997)		Zopounidis and Doumpos (1998b)
Bankruptcy risk assessment			Slowinski and Zopounidis (1995), Dimitras et al. (1998), Greco et al. (1998)	Zollinger (1982), Andenmatten (1995), Dimitras et al. (1995)	Zopounidis (1987), Zopounidis et Doumpos (1997)
Country risk evaluation		Mondt and Despontin (1986)	Tang and Espinal (1989)	Clei (1994)	Cosset et al. (1992), Oral et al. (1992), Cook et Hebner (1993), Anastassiou and Zopounidis (1997), Doumpos et al. (1998)
Evaluation of performance of organizations	Insurance companies			Mareschal and Mertens (1993), Pardalos et al. (1997)	
	Banks			Mareschal and Mertens (1990, 1992)	Zopounidis et al. (1995a), Michalopoulos et al. (1998)
	Firms		Diakoulaki et al. (1992), Jablonsky (1993), Lee et al. (1995)	Mareschal and Brans (1993), Bergeron et al. (1996)	Zopounidis et al. (1992), Siskos et al. (1994), Zopounidis et al. (1996), Zopounidis and Doumpos (1998a)
Financial planning		Vinso (1982), Eom et al. (1987-88), Goedhart and Spronk (1995)			
Venture capital			Riquelme and Rickards (1992), Muzyka et al. (1996)		Siskos and Zopounidis (1987), Zopounidis (1994)
Investments		Lin (1978), Bhaskar (1979), Khorramshahgol and Okoruwa (1994)	Evrard and Zisswiller (1982), Kivijärvi and Tuominen (1992)	Danila (1980), Ribarovic and Mladineo (1987), Zopounidis (1993a)	
Portfolio selection and management		Lee and Chesser (1980), Colson and de Bruyn (1989), Zopounidis et al. (1995b), Hurson and Zopounidis (1995, 1997)	Saaty et al. (1980)	Martel et al. (1988, 1991), Khoury et al. (1993), Hurson and Zopounidis (1995, 1997)	Zopounidis (1993b), Zopounidis et al. (1995b), Hurson and Zopounidis (1995, 1997)

Most of these financial problems have been studied in the past using mainly multivariate statistical analysis techniques (factor analysis, discriminant analysis, logit and probit analyses, etc.) as well as optimization approaches. Although these techniques acknowledge the existence of multiple factors that affect financial decision making, they fail to comprise the decision makers' preferences, while they often fail to provide the support required (in some models the parameters do not have any physical or economic meaning). This fact led financial and operations researchers to the exploitation of the capabilities of alternative techniques. Among these alternative techniques, as the above list of studies indicates, MCDA has found several applications.

Overall, the main advantages that MCDA methods provide in financial engineering, could be summarized in the following aspects (Zopounidis, 1999a).

- *Structuring complex financial decision problems*

The complexity that is evident in financial engineering problems necessitates that financial engineers proceed with the careful and proper structure of the problem at hand, before continuing on with the solution process. Problem structure is one of the key issues in the application of MCDA methods. The continuous interaction between the MCDA tools with the actual decision makers and the trial and error process that is often involved during this interaction, enable financial engineers to identify inconsistencies, deficiencies and possible limitations on the structure of the problem. In this interactive way the financial engineers gain insight on the special features of the problem that they face, which facilitates the problem structure process.

- *Introducing both quantitative and qualitative criteria in the decision making process*

Financial theory address financial engineering problems within an economic perspective, which is based heavily on quantitative analysis involving profit or shareholders' wealth maximization. Financial engineers, however, acknowledge that qualitative factors are vital evaluation criteria, often posing constraints on the solutions that could be obtained. In fact, in some cases, the quantitative variables may be the result of some qualitative factors. For instance, the poor organization of a firm will affect its operating expenses and consequently its profitability. However, the incorporation of qualitative criteria in the financial decision making process, through the classical optimization approach is difficult if not impossible. An approach that is commonly employed to overcome this problem is to quantify the qualitative factors through the introduction of a numerical measurement scale. However, such quantification changes the nature of the considered qualitative factors. It depends heavily on the numerical scale that is employed and consequently it can be misleading. Instead, the MCDA approach provides financial engineers with a variety of methods, able to handle both quantitative and qualitative factors, without necessitating any changes on the qualitative scales that are employed. This capability provides financial engineers with an approach to study comprehensively the considered problem, from all aspects including non-quantifiable ones.

- *Argumentation on financial decisions*

Unlike other fields, in financial engineering the development of a solution to a problem is often not enough for the problem to be addressed. The implementation of the obtained solution necessitates that the financial engineer understands the process that led to this solution, so that he/she can argue upon its suitability to address the considered problem. The decision support orientation of MCDA methods provides the means to overcome this issue. MCDA methods' primary focus is on the modeling of the decision maker's preferences and decision making policy, thus enabling him/her to participate actively in all stages of the financial decision making process. In this way, through an iterative and interactive procedure, the decision maker gets familiar with the MCDA methods used to solve a financial engineering problem as well as with the special features of the problem that he/she is facing. This direct intervention of the decision maker in the decision making process, provides him/her with all the necessary support that is required to argue upon the decisions taken, thus ensuring that they are properly implemented.

- *Introducing sophisticated and realistic scientific methods in the field of financial engineering.*

Except for its scientific interest financial engineering is also a field with significant practical interest. Actually, the methodologies and models that are developed should not only be scientifically sound and sophisticated, but they should also be able to comprise the reality in order to be practically applicable. Of course MCDA methods are not the only sophisticated approach to study financial decision problems. Actually, several quite sophisticated optimization, statistical and econometric techniques have already been introduced in financial decision making (Dahl et al., 1993a,b; Mulvey et al., 1997). However, such techniques are often based on specific assumptions that can hardly represent reality, while the weakening of these assumptions results to the development of complicated and computationally intensive models. On the other hand, MCDA methods combine successfully sophistication and realism, while in general, most of them are computationally tractable and easy to implement in daily practice, which requires real-time decision support. Of course, one could argue that sophistication and realism do not ensure effectiveness. Nevertheless, the results of several research studies applying MCDA methods in financial management show that these methods enhance the financial decision making process, while in many cases they are compared favorably to alternative methodological tools including multivariate statistical analysis, econometrics and optimization techniques.

In conclusion, MCDA methods seem to have a promising future in the field of financial engineering, because they offer a highly methodological and realistic framework to financial decision making problems. Nevertheless, their success in practice depends heavily on the development of computerized systems implementing multicriteria methods. Financial institutions as well as firms acknowledge the multidimensional nature of financial decision problems; the results of the study by Bhaskar and McNamee, 1983, that were discussed above, confirm this finding. Nevertheless, they often use optimization, statistical or econometric approaches to address their financial problems, since several software packages (e.g., SAS, LINDO, SPSS, etc.) that implement such approaches are easily available in relatively low cost, even though most of these software packages are developed for general use and are not specifically designed for financial decision making problems. Consequently, the use of MCDA methods to support real-time financial decision making, calls upon the development of integrated user-friendly multicriteria decision support systems that will be specifically designed to address financial problems. The development and promotion of such systems is a key issue towards the successful application of MCDA methods in financial engineering. As the advances in other fields progress rapidly, the integration of MCDA with other disciplines is of particular interest in order to improve the support provided to financial decision makers.

Following this research direction, the subsequent sections of this book discuss comprehensively the integration of MCDA with the decision support systems, expert systems and artificial intelligence technologies in general leading to the multicriteria knowledge-based decision support systems framework.

Chapter 2

DECISION SUPPORT SYSTEMS

1. DECISION SUPPORT SYSTEMS: GENERAL FRAMEWORK AND MAIN FEATURES

In some decision problems finding a proper solution is a straightforward procedure of repetitive character that can be fully automated using an algorithmic approach. Such cases are referred to as well-structured problems. However, in most managerial problems this is not the case. This is also true in the case of financial engineering. Most financial engineering problems cannot be addressed using a straightforward, fully automated algorithmic approach. The decisions that must be taken on financial engineering problems are directly related to the constantly changing business environment. Thus, even if the objective of the decision remains the same, the way to address a specific financial engineering problem must be adapted to the decision environment conditions. Furthermore, the method that can be used to derive the appropriate decision is not unique. Actually, financial engineering problems can be addressed through a variety of approaches that, most likely, will result to different and often not equivalent solutions. Even in the case of financial engineering decisions that have a repetitive nature (for instance, the evaluation of investment instruments, such as stocks, bonds, treasury bills, etc., to construct a portfolio) it is impossible to fully automate the decision process. Such problems are referred to as ill-structured problems.

Addressing ill-structured problems in daily practice is quite a cumbersome situation. Especially, in the field of financial engineering, the limited time, the plethora of factors that are involved and the changing financial/economic environment, necessitate the development and implementation of computer systems that will not only enable information processing, but they will also enable the user (financial engineer) to perform sophisticated analyses of the available information so as to support the decision making process, in real-time if possible. Traditional management information systems are mainly involved with the former issue (i.e., information processing), while the later issue falls within the realm of decision support systems.

Decision support systems (DSSs) constitute an application of the capabilities provided by computer science to support decision making in ill-structured and complex decision problems, where no straightforward solution methodology can be applied. Klein and Methlie (1995) define a DSS as "a computer system that provides information regarding a given domain of application, in order to support a decision maker in making decision effectively in complex and ill-structured (non-programmable) tasks".

Support is a key notion in the DSSs framework. The efficiency of decision making is ameliorated through the distinction between the tasks that can be performed by the computers and the tasks that should be performed by the decision maker. This distinction takes advantage of the capabilities of the modern computers' technology, while enabling the decision maker to use its experience and knowledge on evaluating the results obtained through the analytical models. In this way, the high processing capabilities of modern computers enable information and data management as well as the performance of computationally difficult tasks. On the other hand, the decision maker decides himself the way that the analysis should be performed. The evaluation/interpretation of the obtained results rests on his/her knowledge and experience rather than on some inference procedures performed by the computer. Therefore, the DSSs' framework provides support to the decision maker rather than replacement by an automated computer system.

On the basis of the above discussion, the basic characteristics of a DSS can be summarized in the following five issues (Er, 1988; Sprague and Carlson, 1982; Sprague and Watson, 1976):

1. Their major objective is to support the decision making process in complex and ill-structured problems.
2. They integrate decision analysis techniques with data access and management.
3. Their design and development is focused on user-friendliness so that decision makers that are not familiar with the sophisticated decision analysis methods or with the computer technology can take full advantage of the capabilities that DSSs provide.
4. They have the flexibility to adapt to the changing decision environment as well as to possible changes/adjustments in the decision making policy and the preferences of the decision maker.
5. They operate in an interactive way to enable real-time decision making.

2. DSSs' STRUCTURE

The basic structural components of a DSS are the following: (Methlie, 1987; Sprague and Carlson, 1982):

1. The database: this part of the DSS comprises all the necessary information and data required to perform the analysis of the problem at hand. Data management, i.e., data entry, access, update, storage, retrieval, etc., is performed through the database management system (DBMS).
2. The model base: similarly to the database, the model base of a DSS is a collection of decision analysis tools that are used to support decision making. The model base and the database are directly related so that the models are fed with the necessary information and data. The model base management system (MBMS) is responsible for handling the model base including the storage and retrieval of models that are developed, their update and adjustment.
3. The user interface: this is one of the key components of a DSS, with respect to the successful implementation of the system in practice. The form of the user interface defines the level of flexibility of the system and its user-friendliness. The user interface is responsible for the communication of the user with the system. A special part of the user

interface, the dialog generation and management system (DGMS) is specifically designed to manage this communication.

Figure 2.1 presents the general structure of a DSS and the interactions among its major structural parts.

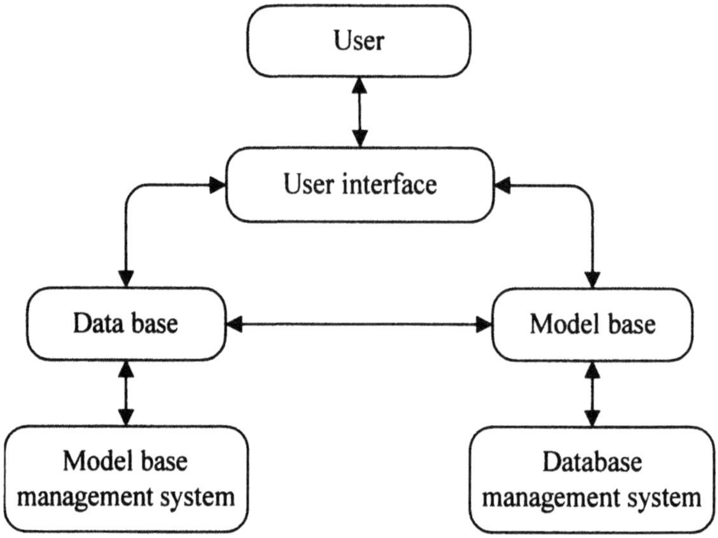

Figure 2.1. DSSs' structure

2.1 The user interface

The interaction between the DSS and the user is a significant factor of the successful implementation of the system. Even if a DSS incorporates advanced and sophisticated decision analysis techniques and excellent database management capabilities, the user can only take advantage of these tools if he/she can easily communicate and interact with them. Otherwise, it will be difficult for the user to understand how the system should be used, how to perform the appropriate analysis and derive the required results. The appropriate design of the user interface ensures that these communication issues are addressed in the most efficient way from the users' point of view. Of course, a well-designed user interface itself does not ensure the ultimate success of the system, but it is an essential prerequisite of success.

The advances made over the last decade in the computer technology and the development of advanced operating systems based on a graphical user interface have provided the basic means for the appropriate user interfaces in DSSs. The most frequently used types of communication are the following:

- *Questions-answers*

In this form of user interface, the DSS communicates with the decision maker by posing questions regarding the tasks that the system should perform. The responses of the decision maker to the imposed questions define the information and data that will be analyzed, the decision analysis procedures that the system will implement and the presentation form of the results. This type of communication is usually performed through natural language, and it is appropriate in cases where the decision maker is not familiar with the system or with the specific features of the problem that he/she faces.

- *Command-based user interface*

This is the oldest type of user interface used even from the very beginning of the DSSs technology. The decision maker communicates with the system through a command language that determines the actions and tasks to be performed by the system. This form of user interface has been very popular in the past among DSSs' developers, due to the lack of graphical support by the computer technology. It is still being used, however, even today (in combination with other forms of communication) to provide increased flexibility to the system, and to enable the decision maker to take full control of its operation. These two features are the basic advantages of a command-based user interface. Its major shortcoming is the experience and the knowledge that the decision maker must have in order to use the command language of the system. The more complex the command language is the more difficult is for the decision maker to become familiar with it as well as with the functionality of the system.

- *Menu and window-based user interface*

This is the most common form of user interface used in DSSs over the last decade. Its widespread application is facilitated by the development of computer operating systems that employ a graphical user interface. In contrast to the previous two types of communication the decision maker can select the tasks and the analyses to be performed by the system through menus and buttons. Multiple windows combining graphics, text and tables are used to display the information that the user requests and the results of the system. Through the mouse the user can easily shift through the windows, thus enabling the simultaneous presentation of a larger volume of information to the decision maker. The major disadvantage of this type of communication is the limited flexibility that it provides to the decision maker. Indeed, the decision maker can select among the tasks and functionalities of the system that correspond to the specific selections that the decision maker can make through the menus, buttons or other objects that appear on the computer screen. Thus, the ability to customize the functionalities of the system is limited. To overcome this shortcoming several DSSs combine a menu/window-based interface with a command language. Such a combination enables both novice and experienced users to take full advantage of the capabilities that the system provides. Novice users are facilitated through the menu/window-based interface that does not require significant experience on the use of the system. As such users gain experience on the use of the system and become more and more familiar with it, they can use the command language to customize, according to their needs, some key features that the system provides, usually with regard to model development and management.

Through the user interface the decision maker can perform all the main support functions of a DSS including information access, display and manipulation, model access and management, report generation, evaluation of alternative solutions, etc. Actually, the interface is the layer between the decision maker and the DSS's resources and it is responsible for transferring the decision maker's actions (commands, choices) to the appropriate part of the system to perform the task that the decision maker asked for.

2.2 The database

The database includes the information and data required to perform an analysis through the DSS. The database except for its role as a data management tool, it also serves as a link between the user interface and the model base. The user inputs data in the database of the DSS through the user interface. The data are stored in the database and the decision analysis tools of the model base retrieve the necessary information from the database to perform the analysis.

For the representation, organization, and storage of the information and data in the database of a DSS, several techniques have been developed and implemented (Sprague and Carlson, 1982).

1. Record model: this is the oldest and probably the most popular data representation and organization technique. In this case the data are represented through a set of records, each one of which consists of several fields that include all the necessary information regarding the specific record. For instance, a database regarding credit applications may include several records corresponding to each applicant. These records may include fields representing the name of the applicant, his/her debt obligations, his/her assets, the collateral that he/she offers, etc.
2. Relational model: a relational database includes only information regarding the relations among data, using fields that are related to each other. Every relation can be considered as a two-dimensional table, whose rows are records and columns are fields (the columns are often called attributes). The fields except for the information that they include on each record, they also include a domain that defines the allowed values for the field.
3. Hierarchical model: in this case, the data are organized in a hierarchical way from the most general and abstract ones to the most specific ones. Every level of the hierarchy consists of a set of records, according to which the next level of the hierarchy is defined. Thus, the relations among the data are organized through a hierarchical structuring.
4. Network model: this is a generalized case of the hierarchical model. The network consists of a set of records connected through links that represent the relation among the connected records. Thus, in contrast to the hierarchical model, the network model enables a record to take part in more than one relations.

2.3 The model base

The model base constitutes the "heart" of a DSS. It is the part of the system that is responsible for performing the actual analysis of the decision problem that is addressed and for obtaining the appropriate results that will support the decision making process. Actually the user interface and the database are supportive parts of the DSSs, necessary for the operation of the system. They do not provide results; they just facilitate the information manipulation and management process, as well as the form of user-system interaction. The results and the decision support that the decision maker expects from the use of a DSS are obtained from the model base. In that regard, the model base is the major distinguishing characteristic of the DSSs framework as opposed to other forms of information systems.

The model base is nothing else but a collection of models and decision analysis techniques that facilitate the solution of a decision problem. These tools may include models related to the operational, tactical or strategic support of the decision making process. They can vary from the most complex models to the smallest and simplest ones, used often to support other models.

The model base is directly linked to the user interface so that the user can control the operation and the use of the models. Furthermore, the user interface provides the necessary means for presenting the results obtained through the decision models in the most appropriate way to the decision maker, thus facilitating the derivation of useful conclusions regarding the decisions that should be taken.

Except for the link between the model base and the user interface, a link with the database is also necessary. This link enables the model base to acquire the required data and information from the model base. Furthermore, this direct link between the model base and the database enables the real-time update of the models as well as their restructuring, in cases where there are significant changes in the available data.

The model base management system is responsible for controlling the operation of the model base. The most significant tasks performed by the model base management system involve model formulation, model validation and model restructuring/update (Sprague and Watson, 1976).

- *Model formulation*

This is the first step of the data exploitation process involving the transformation of the available input data into useful information to support decision making. Model formulation involves the definition of the form that such a transformation should have. This is crucial for the subsequent process. Improper model formulation will most likely lead to inappropriate analysis and ultimately to misleading results.

Several DSSs provide specific forms of models that are applicable to the decision problem for which they have been designed to address. The decision maker selects among the pre-specified forms according to the analysis that he/she wants to perform. Except for this fixed form of models, most DSSs also provide decision makers with the ability to define themselves the model's form to be used in the analysis, using a command language. This is a very useful feature that increases significantly the system's flexibility, enabling the decision maker to construct customized models that best meet his/her preferences, decision policy, the problem context and the changing conditions of the business environment.

- *Model development*

Once the form of the decision model is specified, the decision maker must estimate its parameters, so that the model becomes operational. The estimation of the model's parameters can be performed in a variety of ways depending upon the form of the model and the available information. In some cases the decision maker must specify some technical or economic parameters of the model (this is often the case in mathematical programming formulations), while if enough information is available regression-based techniques can also be used.

Providing support in the parameter estimation process is one of the most essential tasks performed by the model base management system. The provided support involves among others:

- access to statistical, econometric and operations research techniques,
- interactivity throughout the parameter estimation process,
- sensitivity and robustness analyses,
- hypotheses testing,

- model validation (e.g., cross-validation tests, measures of goodness of fit, etc.),
- visualization of the results of the estimation procedure.

- *Model restructuring and update*

Formulating a model and estimating its parameters does not mean that the model can always be used in decision making without any further reconsideration, at least in problem domains that evolve dynamically. This is the case in the field of financial engineering. The context of financial engineering decision problems evolves constantly following the changing economic, socio-political and technological conditions that govern the global business environment. These changes affect the way that a financial engineering problem is addressed in a variety of ways. For instance, the changes encountered in the decision environment may require the consideration of additional factors in the analysis, they may impose a change in the interrelationships of the factors already considered or even lead to a change of the objective of the analysis.

All these impacts that a changing decision environment imposes on the decision analysis process should be accommodated by the models used to perform this analysis. Such an accommodation can be performed in two ways: the decision models that are used are either restructured or updated. Model restructuring refers to the change of the underlying form of the model. Restructuring is necessary in cases where the changes in the decision environment or in the objective of the decision are so significant that they cannot be addressed any longer by the form model. This cannot even be done when its parameters are re-estimated. On the other hand, model update refers only to the re-estimation of the parameters of the model to accommodate any new information that becomes available. This is a necessary procedure that the decision maker should undertake any time the new information changes the way the considered factors are related to each other and to the ultimate objective of the analysis.

3. DSSs APPLICATIONS IN FINANCIAL ENGINEERING

The decision process in the field of financial management involves the analysis of a large volume of data and information. Therefore, the need for accessing large databases and performing computations in real-time is vital. The applicability of the DSSs' technology to these kinds of tasks has already led many researchers to the implementation of DSSs in most of the fields of financial management, such as:

- financial planning (Eom et al., 1987-88; Hayen, 1982; Jenkins, 1973; Sprague, 1972),
- financial analysis (Mareschal and Brans, 1991; Siskos et al., 1994; Zopounidis et al., 1992),
- portfolio management (Gerrity, 1971; Singh and Cook, 1986; Zopounidis et al., 1995),
- banking (Langen, 1989; Mareschal and Mertens, 1992; Sprague and Watson, 1976).

An extended review of the applications of DSSs in several areas of decision making, found in the international literature, has been presented by Eom and Lee (1990). Er (1988) discusses in detail the main characteristics and components of DSSs, describes some problems encountered in their implementation involving business and management areas and presents the future trends of DSSs. Radermacher (1994) presents the scope of DSSs through the discussion of the notion of decision and related cognitive concepts and describes the potential of DSSs in improving the decision making process. Eom et al. (1993) carried out a bibliographic research to identify the various subfields of DSS research, the contributing disciplines of DSS and the subsets of functional management (financial management, marketing management, etc.) which have influenced the development of specific DSSs. Pomerol (1993) described the main features of the existing DSSs incorporating MCDA approaches in order to explain their weaknesses and suggested necessary developments and research to meet in reality the decision makers' needs.

In order to illustrate the potentials that DSSs provide to financial engineering, the subsequent section presents two examples of recently developed DSSs that incorporate most of the features discussed previously in this chapter. Both the FINCLAS and the INVESTOR systems that are presented employ MCDA approaches in assessing credit risk and constructing stock portfolios, respectively.

4. ILLUSTRATIONS FROM CREDIT RISK ASSESSMENT AND PORTFOLIO MANAGEMENT

4.1 Credit risk assessment: The FINCLAS system

4.1.1 Problem domain

Credit granting is a significant area of financial management which is of major interest to practitioners, financial and credit analysts of firms, and credit institutions. On a daily basis credit/financial analysts have to investigate an enormous volume of financial and non-financial data of firms, perform an in depth analysis, estimate the corresponding credit risk, and finally make crucial decisions regarding the financing of firms. At the same time, considerable attention has been devoted in this field from the theoretical and academic point of view. Financial and operational researchers, mainly during the last three decades, have tried to relate the characteristics of a firm (financial ratios and strategic variables) to its credit risk. According to this relationship the components of credit risk are identified and decision models are developed to assess credit risk and the corresponding creditworthiness of firms as accurately as possible.

Decisions regarding credit risk assessment concern the evaluation of the firms' financial and non-financial characteristics (strategic ones) in order to make "optimal" decisions. These decisions incorporate a tradeoff between the potential risk of loss against the probability of profits from granting credit (Srinivasan and Kim, 1987; Srinivasan and Ruparel, 1990). Actually, credit granting decisions are usually made by credit and financial analysts by sorting (classifying) the firms into categories according to their creditworthiness (i.e. creditworthy and insolvent firms).

During the credit evaluation process there are two major problems which are usually encountered (Bergeron et al., 1996).

1. The first one concerns the plethora of factors which should be examined. Factors which affect the assessment of credit risk include the financial characteristics of firms, strategic variables of qualitative nature which affect the general operation of the firm and its relation with the market and even macroeconomic factors (i.e. inflation, interest rates, growth rate, etc.). The credit analysts have to identify the most relevant factors for credit risk evaluation and focus their further analysis on the examination of these factors.
2. The second major problem concerns the aggregation of the factors which have been selected in the previous phase, in order to make a final decision. Usually, factors affecting credit risk assessment lead to conflicting results and decisions. The credit/financial analysts when performing credit risk analysis, they implicitly consider the tradeoffs between the conflicting criteria, according to their global preference system. In this way, they conclude an appropriate aggregation of the partial evaluations of firms on each one of the evaluation criteria and derive the "optimal" decision.

This complexity of the credit granting process has necessitated the construction of credit scoring models, based on the sorting approach, which can be used by financial and credit analysts both as evaluation systems of new firms seeking financing as well as screening tools of the firms which are included in the loan portfolio of a bank or a credit institution (Lane, 1972; Altman et al., 1981; Grablowsky and Talley, 1981; Srinivasan and Kim, 1987; Srinivasan and Ruparel, 1990).

4.1.2 General structure of the FINCLAS system

The FINCLAS system (Zopounidis and Doumpos, 1998a) is the outcome of an attempt to integrate powerful methodologies from the preference disaggregation approach of MCDA with the DSSs' technology. This is done to provide financial/credit analysts with a user-friendly but powerful tool to study financial classification decision problems efficiently in real time.

The structure of the system is similar to the general structure of a decision support system as proposed by Sprague and Carlson (1982). The basic modules of the system include the database, the model base (financial and multicriteria model base) and the user interface (Figure 2.2). There is a complete interaction and integration of these modules. The database management and the model base management are closely related to the friendly window-based user interface of the system. The latter enables the financial/credit analyst to access and handle easily the data of the firms and to exploit the financial modeling tools as well as the MCDA methodologies which are incorporated in the model base.

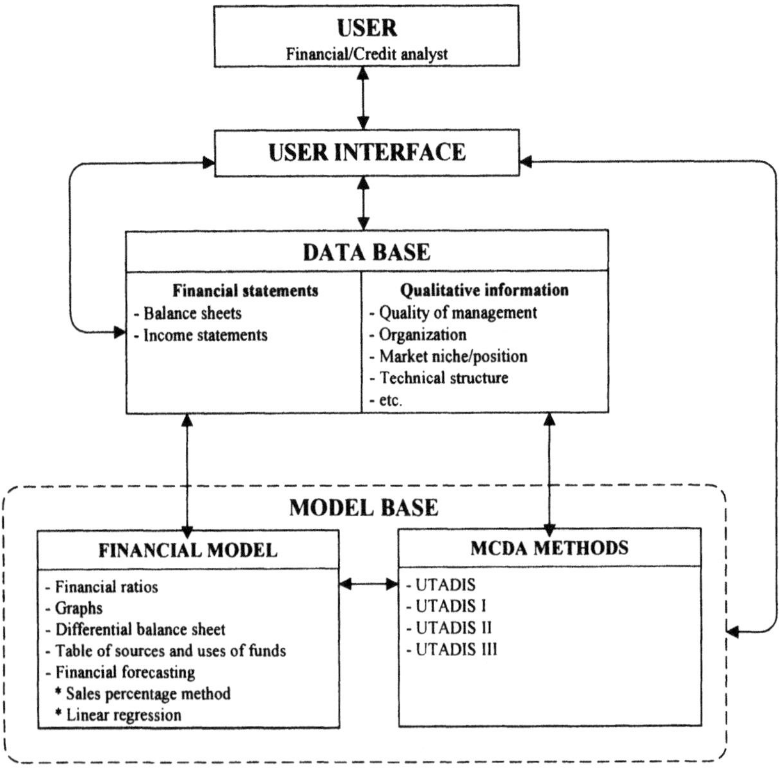

Figure 2.2. Structure of the FINCLAS system (Source: Zopounidis and Doumpos, 1998a)

4.1.3 The database

To perform a detailed analysis of corporate performance and viability, two types of information are required: financial data and non-financial data regarding key factors for the operation of the firm such as its management and organization, its technical structure, its market niche/position, the market trend, etc. This information is included in the database of the FINCLAS system.

The financial data of firms are drawn from their financial statements (i.e. the balance sheet and the income statement) for a five year period which is commonly considered as a pertinent time period to derive reliable estimations on the evolution of the basic financial characteristics of a firm. The financial data are further used by the financial model base of the system for the calculation of several financial ratios (profitability ratios, solvency and liquidity ratios, managerial performance ratios), which are used as evaluation criteria for the classification of the firms. No specialized knowledge is needed to insert and handle the financial data of the firms in the database of the system. The system using a user-friendly spreadsheet type of communication (Figure 2.3) enables the financial/credit analyst to perform easily the basic database management activities, such as editing, storage and retrieval of data.

As shown in Figure 2.3 the user interface of the FINCLAS system has the general form of a Windows-based application. On the top of the screen there are several menus as well as the toolbar, which can be used through the mouse in order to perform the tasks and the analyses that the system implements. The main part of the screen consists of three tables. The big table, in the center, is used to input the financial data of the firms. Above this table, there is another one used to present some general information on the evaluation criteria that are employed by the system (financial ratios and qualitative variables), such as the most and the least preferred values of the criteria and the type of the criteria. Those criteria for which higher values indicate higher preference (e.g., profitability ratios) are noted as "increasing", while criteria for which higher values indicate lower preference (e.g., debt ratios) are noted as "decreasing". The third table to the right part of the screen is used to present the classification of the firms according to their credit risk (in the example of the screen presented in Figure 2.3 class 1 corresponds to firms of low credit risk, while class 2 corresponds to the high-risk class).

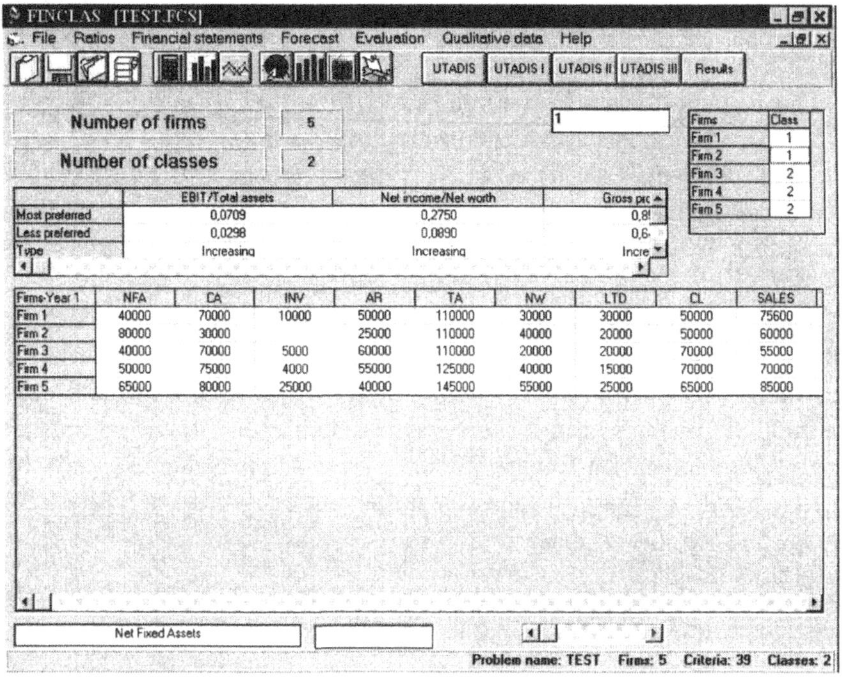

Figure 2.3. Basic screen of the system (data base)

In addition to the financial data of the firms, qualitative information is also included in the database of the FINCLAS system. This information involves the quality of management, the technical structure of the firm, its market position, its organization, the special know-how that the firm possesses concerning its production methods, the market trend, etc. These variables affect both the long-term and short-term operation of the firm, and they can be of even greater significance than the financial characteristics of the firms for the evaluation of their credit risk. A different module of the database of the system is used to input such type of information to the system (Figure 2.4). The modeling of these qualitative criteria is generally up to the decision maker that uses the system. However, an indicative form of modeling, in the case of the manager's work experience and the market position of the firms, could be the following:

Manager's work experience

Negative experience	→	Managers' work experience is not satisfactory
No experience	→	Managers' work experience is medium
Positive experience up to 5 years	→	Managers' work experience is satisfactory
Positive experience 5-10 years	→	Managers' work experience is very satisfactory
Positive experience more than 10 years	→	Managers' work experience is perfect

Market position

Strong competition, firm's weak position	→	Market position is not satisfactory
Strong competition, established and competitive firm	→	Market position is medium
Moderate competition, firm's strong position	→	Market position is satisfactory
Weak competition, firm's leadership position	→	Market position is very satisfactory
Single position, monopoly	→	Market position is perfect

4.1.4 Financial model base

The financial model base module of the FINCLAS system provides the financial/credit analyst with an arsenal of well-known financial modeling tools including advanced graphical illustrations of the evolution of the financial ratios of the firms for the time period under consideration, the structure of the balance sheet and the income statement, statistical information (analysis) regarding the special characteristics of each class of firms (mean, variance, etc.), the table of sources and uses of funds, and financial forecasting methods such as the sales percentage method and linear regression. These tools are necessary in order to perform an initial, descriptive financial analysis of the firms under consideration.

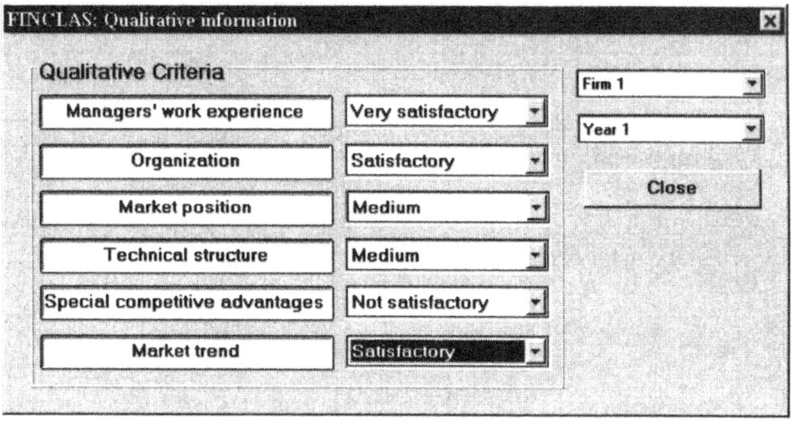

Figure 2.4. Qualitative data input

- *Graphical illustrations*

The financial model base of the FINCLAS system includes 30 financial ratios, which enable the financial/credit analyst to perform an extensive analysis of the financial characteristics of firms, concerning their financing, investment, dividend and credit policies. Following the methodology proposed by Courtis (1978), these ratios are categorized in three major groups: (a) profitability ratios, (b) solvency ratios (including liquidity), and (c) managerial performance ratios. Based on the financial data of the firms, the financial ratios are computed for a five year period (a shorter period can also be considered in case of lack of data).

The financial model base of the system provides a variety of graphical illustrations of the evolution of financial ratios (Figure 2.5) as well as of the structure of the balance sheet (Figure 2.6) and the income statement (Figure 2.7). This type of descriptive analysis is commonly used by financial/credit analysts as a preliminary, elementary but useful examination of the financial characteristics of firms.

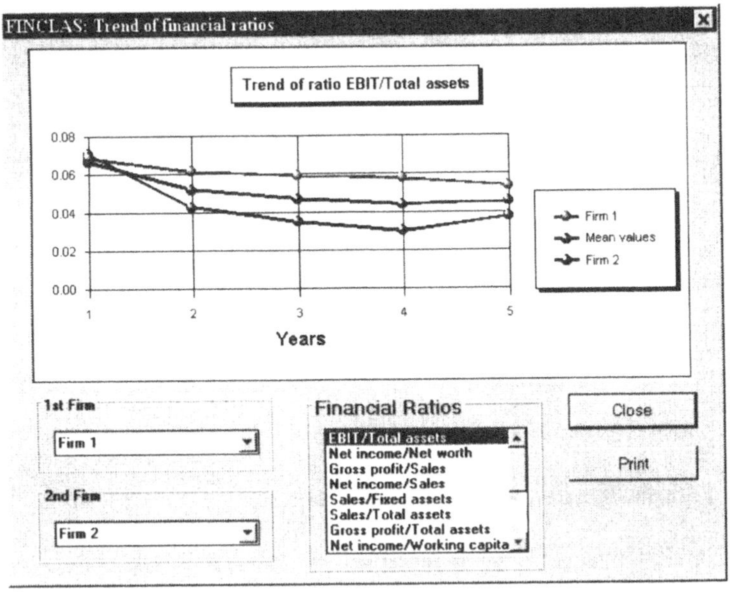

Figure 2.5. Trend of financial ratios

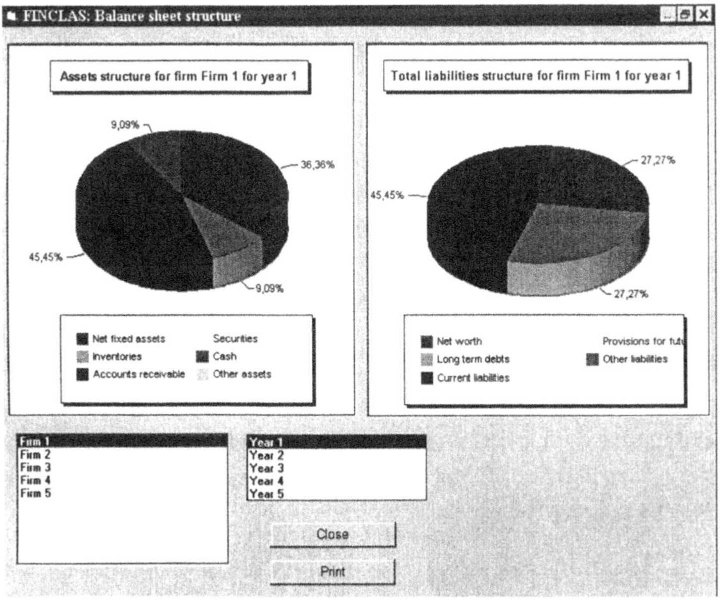

Figure 2.6. Structure of the balance sheet

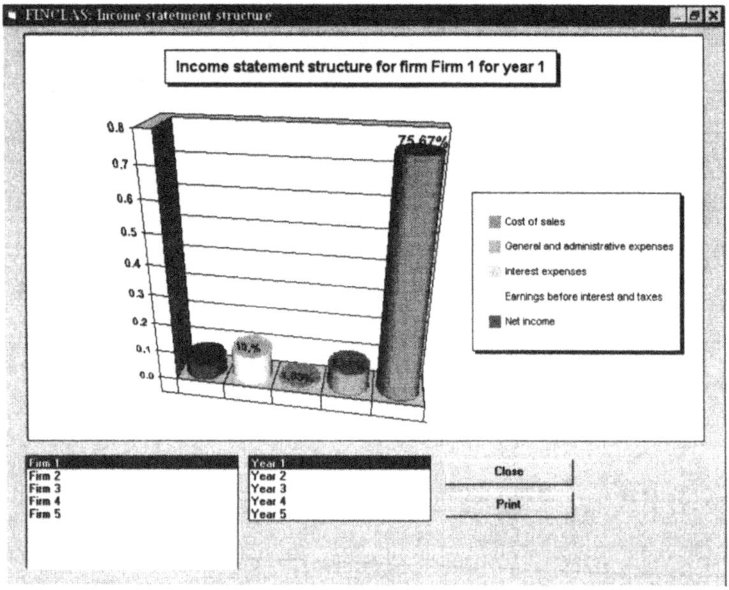

Figure 2.7. Structure of the income statement

- *The table of sources and uses of funds*

The table of sources and uses of funds constitutes a tool for the dynamic analysis of the inflows and the outflows of the firm and their uses that affect its financial position, in order to examine the investment and financing policy of a firm. Any decrease in assets, or increase in total liabilities and stockholders' equity constitutes a source of funds, while any increase in assets, or decrease in total liabilities and stockholders' equity constitutes a use of funds. Therefore, based on the changes in the accounts of the balance sheet for two successive years, and using some additional information (i.e. purchases and sales of fixed assets, depreciation policy, possible increase in capital stock by incorporation of retained earnings, etc.), the construction of the table of sources and uses of funds is accomplished (Figure 2.8).

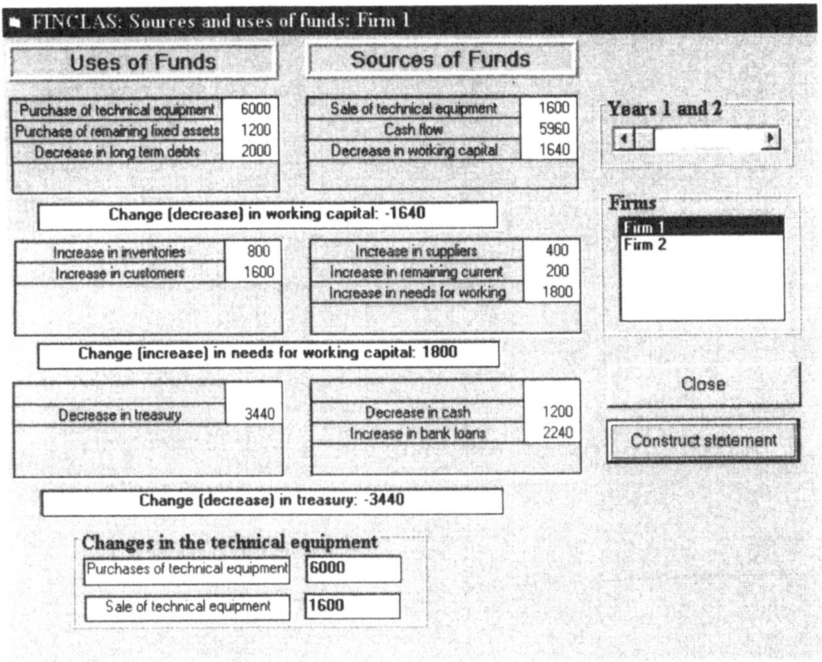

Figure 2.8. Table of sources and uses of funds

- *Financial forecasting methods*

The sales percentage method and linear regression, are two simple financial forecasting methods which are commonly used in corporate finance. The aim of the sales percentage method is to forecast the external financing required for a given increase in sales, as well as the percentage of the increase in sales that should be financed by external funds, according to the changes of the accounts of the balance sheet with regard to the increase in sales (Figure 2.9). On the other hand, the linear regression method can be used to forecast the accounts of the balance sheet with regard to the sales (Figure 2.10).

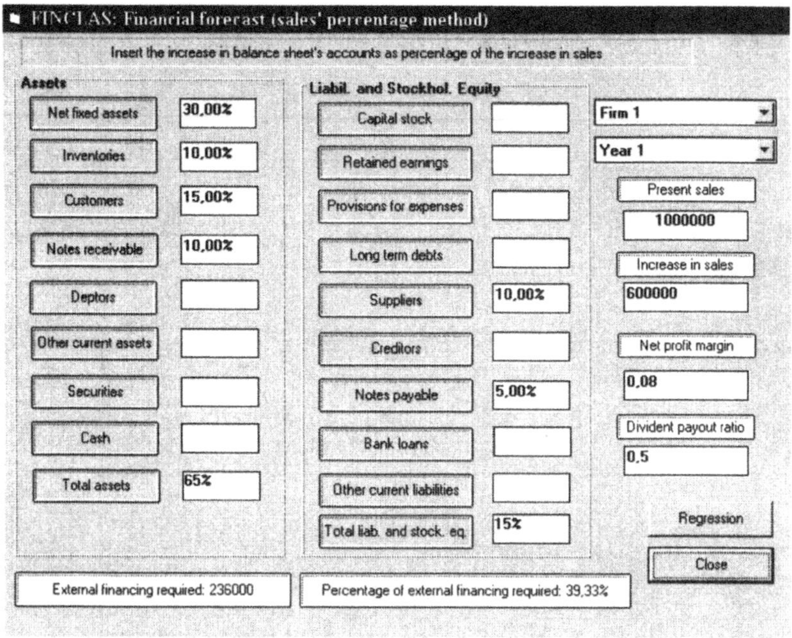

Figure 2.9. Sales percentage method

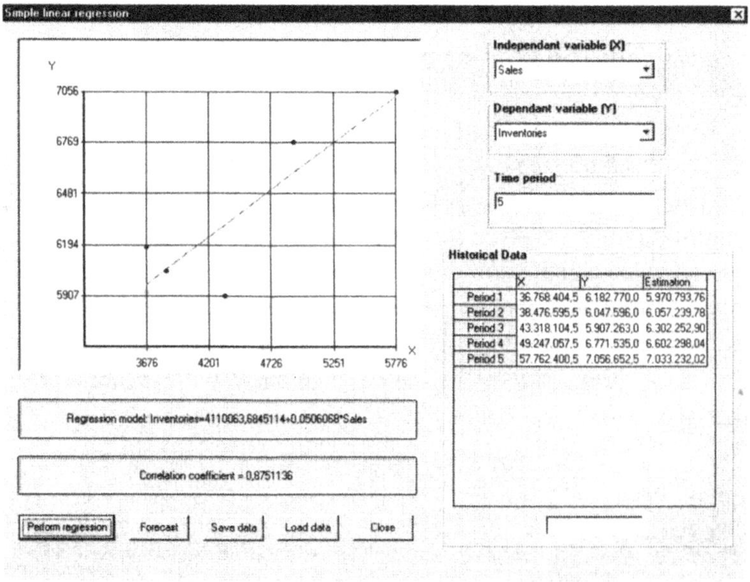

Figure 2.10. Linear regression analysis

4.1.5 Preference disaggregation sorting methods

Although all the aforementioned financial modeling techniques can provide useful information on the basic financial characteristics and policy of a firm, more sophisticated tools are required to support financial/credit analysts in making a reliable estimation regarding the credit risk level of firms. For this purpose, an arsenal of MCDA methods is also included in the model base of the system. These methods originate from the preference disaggregation approach (Jacquet-Lagrèze and Siskos, 1982; Zopounidis, 1999a). The preference disaggregation approach refers to the analysis (disaggregation) of the global preferences of the decision maker to deduce the relative importance of the evaluation criteria and develop the corresponding preference model as consistently as possible with the global preferences of the decision maker. This is achieved through ordinal regression techniques based mainly on linear programming formulations.

More specifically, the model base of the FINCLAS system incorporates the UTADIS method (UTilités Additives DIScriminantes; Jacquet-Lagrèze and Siskos, 1982; Jacquet-Lagrèze, 1995; Zopounidis and Doumpos, 1997), and three of its variants, referred as UTADIS I, UTADIS II and UTADIS III (Doumpos and Zopounidis, 1998; Zopounidis and Doumpos, 1997). The UTADIS method originating from the family of UTA methods (Lacquet-Lagrèze and Siskos, 1982; Despotis et al., 1990), is an ordinal regression method, based on the preference disaggregation approach of MCDA. Given a predefined classification of the alternatives (i.e. firms) in classes, the objective of the UTADIS method is to estimate an additive utility function and the utility thresholds that classify the alternatives in their original classes with the minimum classification error. The estimation of both the additive utility function and the utility thresholds is accomplished through linear programming techniques. A detailed description of the method and its variations is presented in the Appendix of this chapter.

In addition to the classification of the alternatives (firms, loan applications, investment projects, portfolios, etc.) the financial/credit analyst through the UTADIS method and any of its variants can determine the competitive level between the alternatives of the same class (i.e. which are the best and the worst) according to their global utilities.

Figure 2.11, illustrates the presentation of the classification results obtained through the preference disaggregation methods in the FINCLAS system. The original and the estimated class are presented as well as their global utilities, the utility thresholds which distinguish the classes, the weights of the evaluation criteria, the total number of misclassifications, and the accuracy rate. The developed additive utility model can be stored so that it can be used to evaluate new firms which are inserted in the data base of the system (extrapolation).

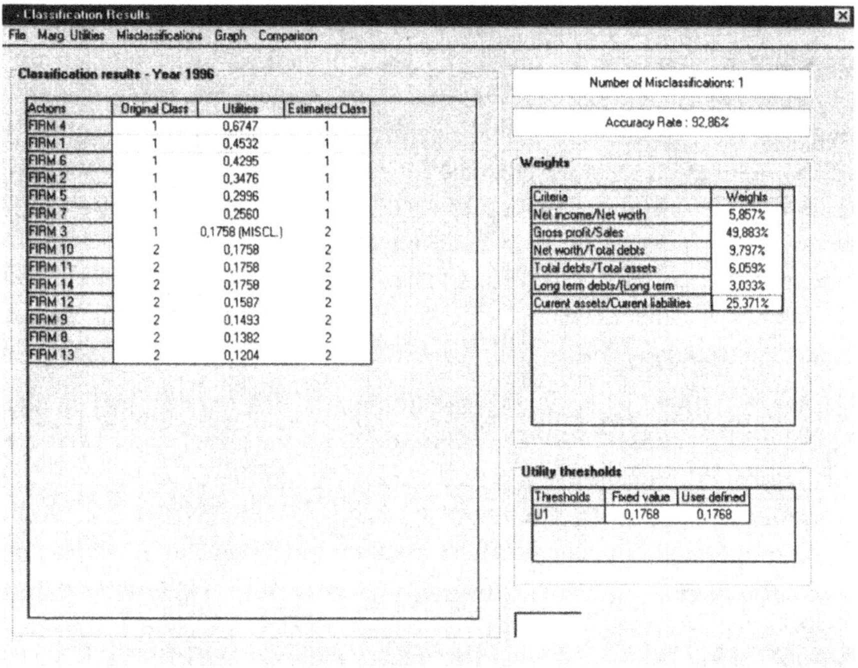

Figure 2.11. Presentation of the classification results using the UTADIS methods

Figure 2.12 presents the marginal utilities of the evaluation criteria estimated by the UTADIS method or its variants. The values of the marginal utilities show the relative significance of the evaluation criteria (the relative importance of each criterion in the classification model). The decision maker selects the criterion, for which he is interested to see its marginal utilities, using a list of all the evaluation criteria used to develop the additive utility model. Marginal utilities of the selected criterion are represented in a graph. The horizontal axis of the graph represents the possible values of the criterion (criterion range) and the vertical axis represents the utilities of the selected criterion.

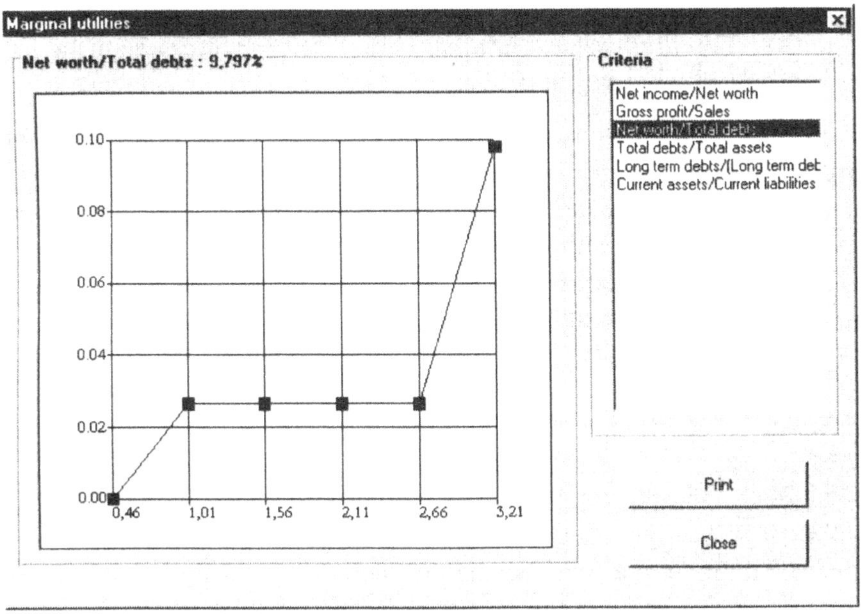

Figure 2.12. Graphical presentation of marginal utilities

4.2 Portfolio management: The INVESTOR system

4.2.1 Problem domain

Portfolio management is one of the most essential problems in the modern financial market theory. It involves the construction of a portfolio of securities (stocks, bonds, treasury bills, etc.) that maximizes the investor's utility. The process leading to the construction of such a portfolio consists of two major steps. In the first step the decision maker (investor, portfolio manager) has to evaluate the securities that are available as investment instruments. The vast amount of available securities, especially in the case of stocks, makes this step necessary, in order to focus the analysis on a limited number of the best investment choices. Thus, during this evaluation stage the decision maker selects a small number of securities, which constitute the best investment opportunities. On the basis of these selected securities, in the second step of the process, the decision maker must decide on the amount of the available capital that should be invested in each security, thus constructing a portfolio of the selected securities. The constructed portfolio should be in accordance with the decision maker's investment policy.

The portfolio theory assumes that the decision maker's judgment and investment policy can be represented by a utility function that is implicitly used by the decision maker in making his investment decisions. Thus, the maximization of this utility function will lead to the construction of a portfolio that is as consistent as possible with the decision maker's expectations and investment policy. However, it is quite difficult to determine explicitly the form of this utility function. The founder of portfolio theory, Nobelist Harry Markowitz, has developed a framework according to which the decision maker's utility is a function of two variables, the expected return of the portfolio and its risk (Markowitz, 1952; 1959). Thus, he formulated the maximization of the decision maker's utility as a two-objective problem involving the maximization of the expected return of the portfolio and the minimization of the corresponding risk. To consider the return and the risk, Markowitz used two well-known statistical measures, i.e., the mean to estimate the return of the portfolio (the mean of all possible returns) and the variance to measure its risk. On the basis of this mean-variance framework, Markowitz has developed a mathematical framework based on quadratic programming techniques to identify the efficient set of portfolio, i.e., the portfolios that are not dominated by any other portfolio in terms of their return and risk. Given the risk aversion policy of the investor, it is possible to select the most appropriate portfolio from the efficient set.

This pioneer work of Markowitz motivated financial researchers to develop new portfolio management techniques and significant contributions have been made over the last decades. The most significant of the approaches that have been proposed for portfolio management include the capital asset pricing model (CAPM; Shapre, 1964), the arbitrage pricing theory (APT; Ross, 1976), single and multi index models, as well as several optimization techniques. The book of Elton and Gruber (1995) provides a comprehensive discussion of these approaches, while the review of Pardalos et al. (1994) is focused on the applications of optimization methodologies to portfolio selection and management.

4.2.2 Structure of the INVESTOR system

The INVESTOR system (Zopounidis, 1998b) is a DSS designed and developed to support the portfolio management process regarding the construction of portfolios of stocks. The basic characteristic of the system is the combination of portfolio theory models, multivariate statistical methods and MCDA techniques for stock evaluation and portfolio construction. The structure of the system is presented in Figure 2.13.

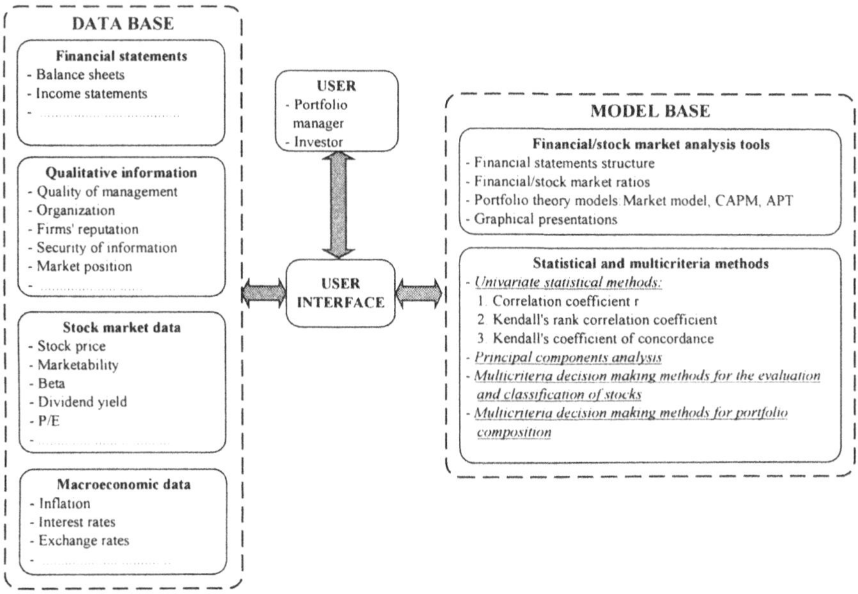

Figure 2.13. Structure of the INVESTOR system (Source: Zopounidis, 1998b)

4.2.3 The database

Performing an integrated portfolio analysis requires the consideration of several information of diversified nature. This information includes:

- *Financial information*

Gathering and analyzing the corporate financial data is a crucial process for portfolio selection and management in order to determine whether the firms are in a sound financial position or not, to identify their strengths and weaknesses, as well as their future development perspectives. These issues constitute some key factors that can influence the stock market performance of the firms. The database of the INVESTOR system includes financial information drawn from the balance sheets and the income statements of the firms for a period of five years to enable the analyst to consider the evolution of the financial position of the firms.

- *Stock market information*

While the aforementioned financial information is useful in determining the financial position of the firms, it is not adequate to perform an analysis of their stock market performance. This necessitates the consideration of information related to the stock market behavior of the firms, such as their stock price, their marketability, their capitalization, etc. This information constitutes the basis for calculating several ratios related to the stock market performance and behavior of the firms, such as the price/earnings ratio, the dividend yield, the price/book value ratio, etc., which are key factor often considered in portfolio construction. The stock market related data are inserted in the database of the INVESTOR system on a daily basis to enable real-time portfolio management decision making.

- *Qualitative information*

In combination with the aforementioned quantitative information (financial and stock market) some qualitative features of the considered firms are also essential in determining the stocks that should be included in a portfolio. The management of the firms, their organization, their reputation in the market, their position in their business sector, the innovation and know-how levels, etc., are some crucial factors that are directly related to the performance of the firms. These factors are often much more important to investors than some quantitative figures. The INVESTOR system enables the portfolio manager/analyst to introduce this significant information in the analysis in order to derive integrated conclusions regarding his/her investment decisions.

- *Macroeconomic factors*

All types of information described above are related only to the performance of the firms and their stock market behavior. However, an investment decision regarding portfolio construction is inevitably affected by the economic conditions within which a stock market operates. Factors such as the inflation, the interest rates and the exchange rates among others are directly related to the performance of the stock market as a whole. The recent crises have clearly demonstrated the effect of the rapidly changing economic environment to the operation of stock markets worldwide. Therefore, introducing such information to the portfolio selection and management process enables the analyst to consider the risk of investing in a specific stock market, which combined with the analysis of the performance and the stock market behavior of the firms leads to an integrated analysis of the alternative investment decisions.

Figure 2.14 illustrates the window-based user interface of the INVESTOR system during data entry and management.

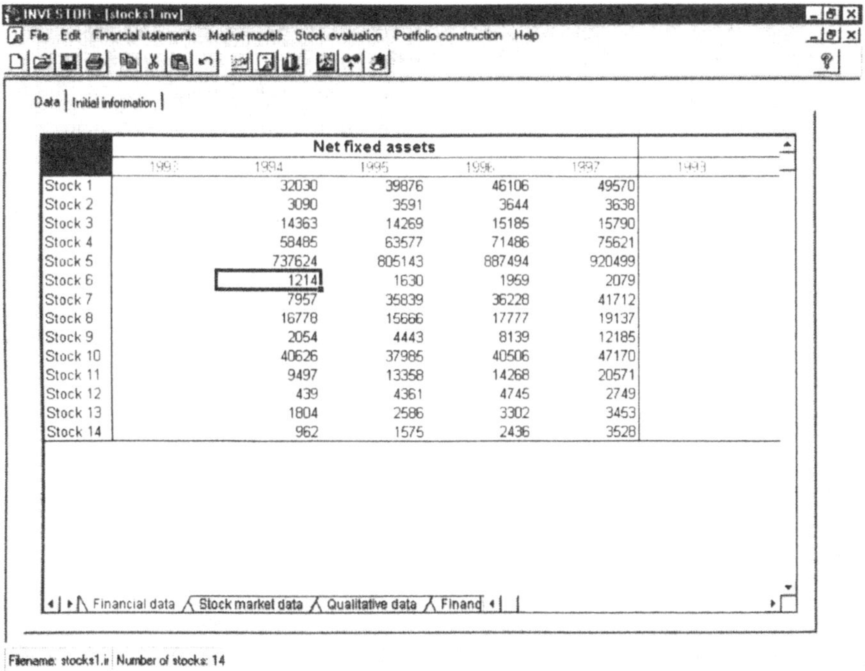

	Net fixed assets					
	1993	1994	1995	1996	1997	1998
Stock 1		32030	39876	46106	49570	
Stock 2		3090	3591	3644	3638	
Stock 3		14363	14269	15185	15790	
Stock 4		58485	63577	71486	75621	
Stock 5		737624	805143	887494	920499	
Stock 6		1214	1630	1959	2079	
Stock 7		7957	35839	36228	41712	
Stock 8		16778	15666	17777	19137	
Stock 9		2054	4443	8139	12185	
Stock 10		40626	37985	40506	47170	
Stock 11		9497	13358	14268	20571	
Stock 12		439	4361	4745	2749	
Stock 13		1804	2586	3302	3453	
Stock 14		962	1575	2436	3528	

Figure 2.14. User interface during database management

4.2.4 The model base

The model base of the INVESTOR system includes a variety of analysis techniques that can be used to evaluate the available information and to derive conclusions with respect both to the selection of stocks to be included in the portfolio and to the composition of this portfolio. These analysis tools can be categorized into two major categories: (i) financial and stock market analysis techniques and (ii) statistical and multicriteria analysis techniques.

- *Financial and stock market analysis techniques*

This part of the model base of the INVESTOR system is responsible for performing some elementary tasks that facilitate a financial and stock market analysis of the considered firms. Some of the key features of this part of the model base include:

- Common size financial statements (balance sheet and income statement) to identify the relationship among the key financial accounts of the firms to their total assets and their sales (e.g., debt/total assets, net worth/total assets, current assets/total assets, net fixed assets/total assets, cost of sales/sales, net income/sales, interest expenses/sales, etc.).
- Calculation of financial and stock market ratios according to the information inserted in the database, which are used as criteria in the stock evaluation and portfolio composition procedures (e.g., return on investment, return on assets, quick and current ratios, price/earnings ratio, marketability, beta coefficient, etc.).
- Several graphical presentation involving the evolution of the financial and stock market data and the corresponding ratios.
- Implementation of well-known stock market models, including the market model, the capital asset pricing model (CAPM) and the arbitrage pricing theory (APT) to estimate the expected return of the stocks. The form of these models is the following.

Market model: $R_{it}=a_i+\beta_i R_{Mt}+u_{it}$

where: R_{it} = the return of stock i during period t,

R_{Mt} = the return of the market portfolio M during period t,

β_i = the beta coefficient (systematic risk),

u_{it} = the non-systematic risk,
a_i = the expected return R_{it} when R_{Mt}=0.

CAPM: $E(R_i)=R_f+[E(R_M)-R_f]\beta_i$
where: $E(R_i)$ = the expected return of stock i,
R_f = the return of a risk-free asset,
$E(R_M)$ = the expected return of the market portfolio,

APT: $R_i=E(R_i)+\sum b_{ik}F_k+\varepsilon_i$

where: F_k = the k factor affecting the return of the stock,
b_{ik} = the sensitivity of stock i on factor k,
ε_i = the risk factor for stock i (non-systematic risk).

- *Statistical and multicriteria analysis techniques*

This second part of the model base includes all the advanced analysis techniques that are required to derive integrated conclusions on the portfolio selection and management problem. The tools that are included can support the analysis of the information included in the database, and the selection of the evaluation criteria that should be considered in the portfolio analysis process, using univariate and multivariate statistical techniques, as well as the analysis of the stocks' performance and the construction of a portfolio of limited number of selected stocks, using multicriteria analysis techniques. More specifically the tools included in this part of the model base and their functionality are the following:

- Univariate statistical measures such as the correlation coefficient, the Kendall's coefficient of concordance and the Kendall's rank correlation coefficient (Siegel, 1956) to estimate the stability of the beta coefficient of the stocks (systematic risk) over the considered time period. The Kendall's rank correlation coefficient τ measures the degree of correlation between two sets of ranks consisting of N objects (i.e., the rankings of N stocks according to their beta coefficient over two consecutive years). On the other hand, the Kendall's coefficient of concordance W measures the relation among several rankings (i.e., the rankings of the stocks according to their beta coefficient over a multi-year time period). The calculation of these coefficients is performed as follows:

$$\tau = \frac{S}{\frac{1}{2}N(N-1)} \text{ and } W = \frac{P}{\frac{1}{12}K^2(N^3 - N)}$$

where:

N = the number of objects (beta values of the stocks) ranked on years t and t–1,

S = the observed sum of +1 and –1 scores for all pairs of comparisons,

K = the number of rankings (i.e., the number of years),

P = the sum of observed deviations from the sum of ranks.

– Principal components analysis to analyze the financial and stock market characteristics of the stocks on the basis of the financial and stock market ratios. Principal components analysis is a multivariate statistical analysis technique of descriptive nature that enables the portfolio analyst/manager/investor to identify the ratios that best describe the performance and behavior of the stocks as well as to group the stock depicting similar characteristics into homogenous groups. Figure 2.15 illustrates the scatterplot of principal components analysis presented through the INVESTOR system).

– Discrete and continuous multicriteria analysis techniques to evaluate the considered stocks and compose a portfolio that meets the decision maker's investment policy and objectives.

The implemented discrete MCDA methods include the family of the UTADIS methods, used also in the FINCLAS system described above. The UTADIS methods enable the development of utility models, of an additive form, representing the decision maker's investment policy and judgment. The developed utility models are used to classify the considered stocks into predefined classes according to the selected evaluation criteria. Figure 2.16 illustrates a classification of stocks into three classes according to a model developed through the UTADIS method. This classification/utility approach provides a distinction of the stocks which have high stock market and financial performance, from those stocks which are in an intermediate situation, and those that do not have a positive stock market perspective. Of course, additional classes of stocks can be introduced in the analysis if necessary. In this way the portfolio manager is able to identify a wide spectrum of possible alternatives (stocks) which constitute the best investment opportunities according to his/her decision policy. At the same time the estimated global utility of each stock can be used as an index to evaluate the competitive level between the stocks of the same class.

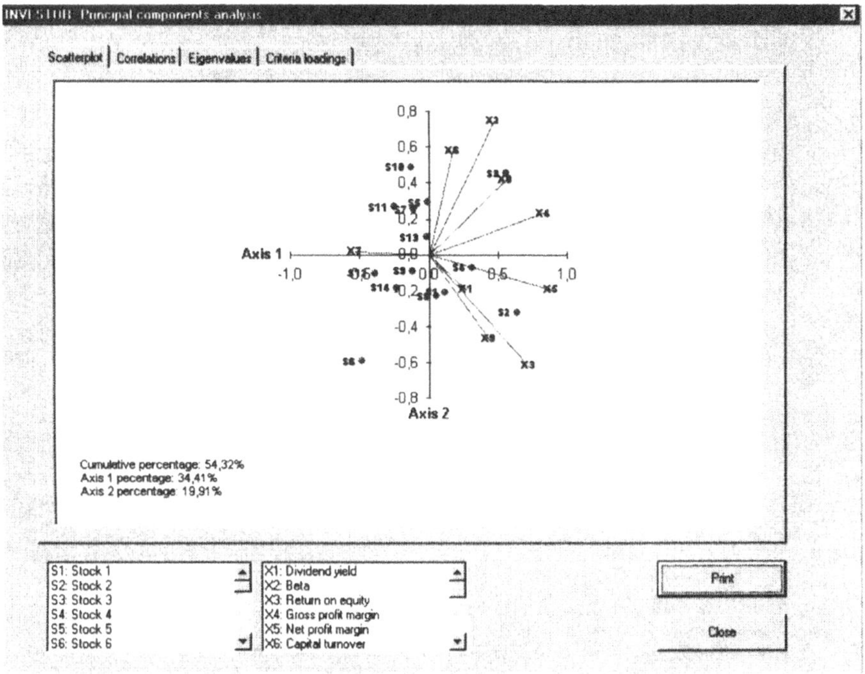

Figure 2.15. Presentation of principal components analysis results

On the basis of the classification obtained through the family of the UTADIS methods, the investor/portfolio manager can select a limited number of stocks to include in the portfolio that should be constructed (best investment opportunities). The construction of the portfolio consisting of the selected stocks is accomplished through continuous MCDA techniques including multiobjective and goal programming, which are appropriate for optimizing a set of objective functions subject to some constraints. In portfolio management the objective functions represent the investor/portfolio manager's objectives on some evaluation criteria (return, beta, marketability, etc.), while constraints can be imposed to ensure that the constructed portfolio meets some basic aspects of the investment policy of the investor/portfolio manager. For instance, the investor/portfolio manager can introduce constraints on the amount of capital invested in stocks of specific business sectors, the amount of capital invested on high risk or low risk stocks, to determine a minimum level of return or a maximum level of risk, etc. Once, such details are determined, an interactive and iterative optimization procedure is performed that leads to the construction of a portfolio of stocks that meets the investor/portfolio manager's investment policy and preferences. The results presented through the screen of Figure 2.17 involve the proportion of each stock in the constructed portfolio, the performance of the portfolio on the specified evaluation criteria (attained values) as well as the rate of closeness (achievement rate) of the performance of the portfolio as opposed to the optimal values on each evaluation criterion (the higher this rate is the closer is the performance of the portfolio to the optimal one for each criterion).

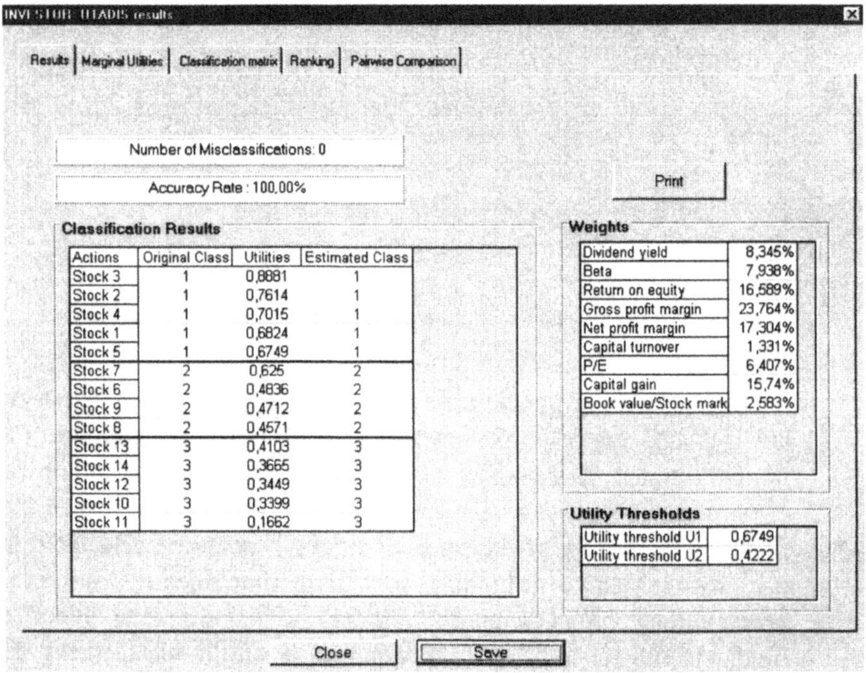

Figure 2.16. Classification of the stocks in the INVESTOR system using the UTADIS methods

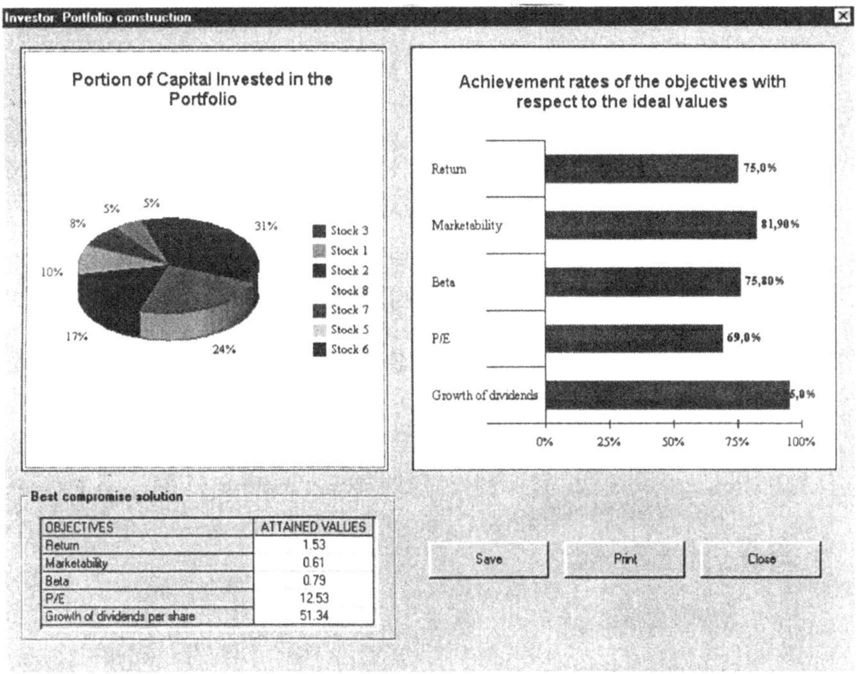

Figure 2.17. Results of the portfolio construction process using continuous MCDA methods

5. DSSs' CONTRIBUTION AND LIMITATIONS

The above discussion on the characteristics and features of the DSSs' framework, along with the presentation of the FINCLAS and the INVESTOR systems is indicative of the kind of support that a DSS provides in addressing complex financial engineering problems. However, it is important to clearly identify the main contributions and limitations that one could expect from the implementation of DSSs in real-world financial engineering practice. In terms of the contribution of the DSSs technology, it is possible to identify the following aspects (Turban, 1993):

- DSSs provide the necessary means for dealing with semi-structured and unstructured problems of high complexity, such as many problems from the field of financial engineering. Except for providing access to data and model bases that DSSs provide, they support all the stages of the decision process, i.e. the structuring of the problem, the selection of the proper alternative solution and finally the implementation of the decision.

- The support provided by DSSs may respond to the needs and the cognitive style of different decision makers, combining the preferences and the judgment of every individual decision maker with the information derived from analytical decision models.

- The time and the cost of the whole decision process is significantly reduced. The decision maker through the use of DSSs can handle (storing, retrieval, update, etc.) easily a large volume of information and data concerning the problem under consideration. Furthermore, DSSs provide the means to analyze this information using sophisticated techniques and methods.

- The support that is provided by DSSs responds to the needs of various managerial levels, ranging from top managers and executives to simple staff managers.

- DSSs facilitate the learning process of the decision maker. Through the continuous use of a DSS, the decision maker is able to analyze all the new relevant information that becomes available while furthermore he/she gets familiar with the sophisticated decision analysis tools that are incorporated in the system. Finally, the use of these tools enables the decision maker to all the important aspects of the considered financial engineering problem, even those that he/she overlooked in his/her daily practice.

Although DSSs proved to be an effective tool for every decision maker who wants to improve the quality and the effectiveness of his decisions, their application reveals several possible problems. The main problems can be summarized in the following three aspects (Er, 1988; Klein and Methlie, 1995):

- The operation of every DSS is governed by specific assumptions. In cases where the decision maker is not familiar with these assumptions, then the use of a DSS may lead to incorrect conclusions and estimations.

- The judgment and the interpretation of the derived results of a DSS is made by the decision makers, assuming that they have the necessary theoretical knowledge to understand the assumptions of the system, and to interpret the derived results in the most appropriate manner. In case the user/decision maker does not have the appropriate background and knowledge on the methodological tools employed by the DSS, this may lead to the improper use of these tools and to inappropriate decisions as well.

- Many DSSs are not compatible with each other, they force decision makers to retype data and make unnecessary efforts that lead to significant loss of time. Problems also arise from the lack of compatibility of several DSSs with existing databases and computer networks.
- The basic features of DSSs have to be standardized so that they can be used by more decision makers, taking in the same time into account the preferences of each separate decision maker.
- Finally, it should be noted that many of the DSSs which have been designed in the past, are based only on the examination of quantitative factors. Despite the fact that some form of quantitative analysis is always used in any financial engineering problem, there are several significant aspects of qualitative nature regarding the financial decisions. The inability of traditional quantitative analysis techniques such as optimization, statistics, econometrics, to consider qualitative information in an appropriate way, often leads to the exclusion of qualitative factors analysis. This results in the loss of valuable information that can improve the decision making process in financial engineering.

APPENDIX: THE UTADIS METHOD AND ITS VARIANTS

The UTADIS method originating from the family of UTA methods (Lacquet-Lagrèze and Siskos, 1982; Despotis et al., 1990) is an ordinal regression method based on the preference disaggregation approach of MCDA. Given a predefined classification of the alternatives (i.e. firms, stocks, securities, investment projects) in classes, the objective of the UTADIS method is to estimate an additive utility function and some utility thresholds in order to classify the alternatives in their original classes with the minimum classification error. The estimation of both the additive utility function and the utility thresholds is accomplished through linear programming techniques. A detailed description of the method and its variations is presented below.

Let $g_1, g_2, ..., g_m$ be a consistent family of m evaluation criteria, and $A=\{a_1, a_2, ..., a_n\}$ a set of n alternatives to be classified in q ordered classes $C_1, C_2, ..., C_q$ which are defined *a priori* in the following way:

$$C_1 \ \boldsymbol{P} \ C_2 \ ... \ C_{q-1} \ \boldsymbol{P} \ C_q$$

where, $\boldsymbol{P}$ denotes the strict preference relation between the classes.

In the proposed preference disaggregation approach based on the UTADIS method, the classification model is a utility function of the following additive form:

$$U(a)=\sum_{i=1}^{m} u_i[g_i(a)]$$

where $U(a)$ is the global utility of an alternative $a \in A$ and $u_i[g_i(a)]$ is the marginal utility of an alternative $a \in A$ on the evaluation criterion g_i.

To classify the alternatives in their original classes the necessary utility thresholds $u_1, u_2, \ldots, u_{q-1}$ ($u_1 > u_2 \ldots u_{q-2} > u_{q-1}$) have to be estimated (the utility threshold u_k distinguishes the classes C_k and C_{k+1}, $\forall k \leq q-1$). Comparing the global utilities of an alternative a with the utility thresholds, the classification of this alternative is achieved as follows:

$$U(a) \geq u_1 \quad \Rightarrow a \in C_1$$

....

$$u_k \leq U(a) < u_{k-1} \quad \Rightarrow a \in C_k$$

....

$U(a) < u_{q-1} \qquad \Rightarrow a \in C_q$

The aim of the UTADIS method is to estimate the additive utility model and the utility thresholds so that the misclassification errors are minimized. The misclassification errors are considered using two error functions $\sigma^+(a)$ and $\sigma^-(a)$. In cases where an alternative a is classified by the decision maker in class C_k, while according to its global utility it is classified in class C_{k+i} (i>0), then the misclassification error is $\sigma^+(a) = u_k - U(a)$. This error represents the amount of utility that should be added to the global utility of the alternative a so that it can be correctly classified. Similarly, in cases where an alternative a is classified by the decision maker in class C_k, while according to its global utility it is classified in class C_{k-i} (i>0), then the misclassification error is $\sigma^-(a) = U(a) - u_{k-1}$. This error represents the amount of utility that should be subtracted from the global utility of the alternative a so that it can be correctly classified.

The marginal utilities of the evaluation criteria have piece-wise linear form (Figure 2.18). For each evaluation criterion g_i the range $G_i = [g_{i*}, g_i^*]$ of its values is defined. The values g_{i*} and g_i^* of criterion g_i represent the least and the most preferred ones respectively. If for a criterion g_i, higher values are preferred (increasing preference), then the most preferred value is considered to be the highest value of this criterion for all the alternatives belonging to A. Similarly, the least preferred value is considered to be the lower value of the criterion for the alternatives belonging to A. The least and the most preferred values for criteria for which lower values are preferred, can be determined in exactly the opposite way.

The range G_i is divided into $a_i - 1$ equal subintervals $G_i^j = [g_i^j, g_i^{j+1}]$, j=1, 2, ..., a_i-1 (Figure 2.18). The number of these subintervals can be specified by the decision maker or it can be determined by the analyst so that there is at least one alternative falling into each subinterval. Each point g_i^j can be calculated using linear interpolation through the following equation:

$$g_i^j = g_{i*} + \frac{j-1}{a_i - 1}\left(g_i^* - g_{i*}\right)$$

The aim is to estimate the marginal utilities in each of these points. Suppose that the evaluation of an alternative a on criterion i is

$g_i(a) \in [g_i^j, g_i^{j+1}]$. Then, the marginal utility of the alternative action a, $u_i[g_i(a)]$, can be approximated through linear interpolation:

$$u_i[g_i(a)] = u_i(g_i^j) + \frac{g_i(a) - g_i^j}{g_i^{j+1} - g_i^j}\left[u_i(g_i^{j+1}) - u_i(g_i^j)\right]$$

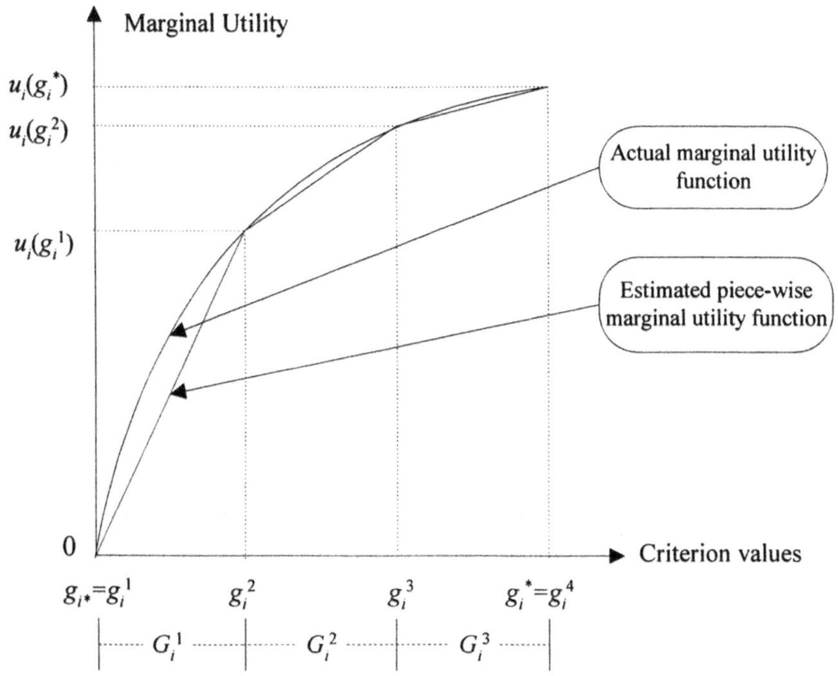

Figure 2.18. The piece-wise linear form of the marginal utility functions (criterion with increasing preference)

A basic assumption of the UTADIS method is that the preferences of the decision maker are monotone (increasing or decreasing) functions on the scale of the evaluation criteria. To achieve the monotonicity of the preferences the following constraint must be satisfied:

$$u_i(g_i^{j+1}) - u_i(g_i^j) \geq 0, \quad \forall i$$

These monotonicity constraints can be converted into non-negativity constraints which are handled easier using linear programming formulations. Therefore, the following transformations are applied:

$$\left.\begin{aligned} & w_{ij} = u_i\left(g_i^{j+1}\right) - u_i\left(g_i^j\right) \geq 0 \;\; \forall i, j \\ & u_i\left(g_{i*}\right) = 0 \\ & u_i\left(g_i^j\right) = \sum_{k=1}^{j-1} w_{ik} \end{aligned}\right\}$$

Using these formulations, the estimation of the marginal utilities and the utility thresholds can now be achieved by solving the following linear program (LP1):

$$\text{Minimize } F = \sum_{a \in C_1} \sigma^+(a) + \ldots + \sum_{a \in C_k} [\sigma^+(a) + \sigma^-(a)] + \ldots + \sum_{a \in C_q} \sigma^-(a)$$

s.t.

$$\sum_{i=1}^{m} u_i[g_i(a)] - u_1 + \sigma^+(a) \geq 0 \qquad \forall a \in C_1$$

$$\left.\begin{aligned} & \sum_{i=1}^{m} u_i[g_i(a)] - u_{k-1} - \sigma^-(a) \leq -\delta \\ & \sum_{i=1}^{m} u_i[g_i(a)] - u_k + \sigma^+(a) \geq 0 \end{aligned}\right\} \qquad \forall a \in C_k$$

$$\sum_{i=1}^{m} u_i[g_i(a)] - u_{q-1} - \sigma^-(a) \leq -\delta \qquad \forall a \in C_q$$

$$\sum_{i=1}^{m} \sum_{j=1}^{a_i - 1} w_{ij} = 1$$

$$u_{k-1} - u_k \geq s \quad k = 2, 3, \ldots, q-1$$

$$w_{ij} \geq 0, \; \sigma^+(a) \geq 0, \; \sigma^-(a) \geq 0$$

The threshold δ is used to ensure the strict inequality $U(a) < u_{k-1}$, $k=2, 3, \ldots, q$, while s is used as a threshold denoting the strict preference between the utility thresholds that distinguish the classes ($s > \delta > 0$).

After the solution F^* of this linear program has been obtained, a post optimality stage is carried out in order to identify, if possible, other optimal or near optimal solutions corresponding to error values lower than $F^* + k(F^*)$. $k(F^*)$ is a small proportion of F^*, which could provide a more consistent representation of the decision maker's preferences. Therefore, the error objective is transformed into a new constraint of the type:

$$\sum_{a \in C_1} \sigma^+(a) + \ldots + \sum_{a \in C_k} [\sigma^+(a) + \sigma^-(a)] + \ldots + \sum_{a \in C_q} \sigma^-(a) \leq F^* + k(F^*)$$

Through the post optimality analysis a range is determined for both the marginal utilities and the utility thresholds, within which there is an optimal or near optimal solution. In this way the sensitivity analysis of the marginal utilities of the criteria is achieved, and at the same time one can have an idea of the sensitivity of the utility thresholds.

Using the UTADIS method, the minimization of the total misclassification error is achieved in terms of the distances of the misclassified alternatives from the utility thresholds using the two error functions $\sigma^+(a)$ and $\sigma^-(a)$. However, this objective may lead to place some correctly classified alternatives very close to the utility thresholds, resulting in poor generalizing (predicting) ability of the model. Therefore, a more appropriate approach would be to minimize the total misclassification error and at the same time to maximize the distances of the global utilities of the alternatives from the utility thresholds. This is the aim of the first variant of the UTADIS method, referred as UTADIS I. The new linear programming formulation is the following (LP2):

$$\text{Minimize } F = p_1 \sum_a [\sigma^+(a) + \sigma^-(a)] - p_2 \sum_a [d^+(a) + d^-(a)]$$

s.t.

$$\sum_{i=1}^{m} u_i[g_i(a)] - u_1 + \sigma^+(a) - d^+(a) = 0 \qquad \forall a \in C_1$$

$$\left.\begin{aligned} &\sum_{i=1}^{m} u_i[g_i(a)] - u_{k-1} - \sigma^-(a) + d^-(a) = -\delta \\ &\sum_{i=1}^{m} u_i[g_i(a)] - u_k + \sigma^+(a) - d^+(a) = 0 \end{aligned}\right\} \qquad \forall a \in C_k$$

$$\sum_{i=1}^{m} u_i[g_i(a)] - u_{q-1} - \sigma^-(a) + d^-(a) = -\delta \qquad \forall a \in C_q$$

$$\sum_{i=1}^{m}\sum_{j=1}^{a_i-1} w_{ij} = 1$$

$$u_{k-1} - u_k \geq s \quad k=2, 3, \ldots, q-1$$

$$w_{ij} \geq 0, \sigma^{+}(a) \geq 0, \sigma^{-}(a) \geq 0, d^{+}(a) \geq 0, d^{-}(a) \geq 0$$

where d^+ and d^- are the distances of the global utilities from the utility thresholds. p_1 and p_2 are weighting parameters of the two objectives in the UTADIS I method that involve the minimization of the classification errors and the maximization of the distances of the global utilities of the correctly classified alternatives from the utility thresholds. These parameters must be set such that $p_1 > p_2$, otherwise the classification error variables σ^+ and σ^- will be pushed towards their upper bound to allow the increase of the distance variables d^+ and d^-, thus leading to the development of a meaningless additive utility function.

The post optimality stage is carried out similarly to the UTADIS method. The only difference is that the objective function of LP2 is now converted into two separate constraints:

$$\sum_{a}[\sigma^{+}(a)+\sigma^{-}(a)] \leq F_1^{*} + k(F_1^{*})$$

$$\sum_{a}[d^{+}(a)+d^{-}(a)] \geq F_2^{*} - k(F_2^{*})$$

where F_1^* and F_2^* are the optimal values for the total misclassification error and the total amount of distances respectively, obtained by solving LP2, and $k(F_1^*)$ and $k(F_2^*)$ are small portions of F_1^* and F_2^*.

Both methods, UTADIS and UTADIS I, minimize the number of misclassified alternatives in an indirect manner, assuming that minimizing the misclassification errors (in terms of distances) the number of misclassifications will also be minimized. However, this is not always the case. A more direct approach would be to minimize the number of the misclassified alternatives using a variant of the UTADIS method (referred as UTADIS II). In this case the linear program LP1 is transformed into an integer programming one, by substituting the error variables $\sigma^{+}(a)$ and $\sigma^{-}(a)$ with the binary variables $M^{+}(a)$ and $M^{-}(a)$, which indicate whether an alternative a is misclassified or not. This is achieved through the following linear program:

$$\text{Minimize } F = \sum_{a \in A} M^+(a) + M^-(a)$$

s.t.

$$\sum_{i=1}^{m} u_i[g_i(a)] - u_1 + M^+(a) \geq 0 \qquad \forall a \in C_1 \qquad (1)$$

$$\left.\begin{aligned} &\sum_{i=1}^{m} u_i[g_i(a)] - u_{k-1} - M^-(a) \leq -\delta \qquad (2) \\ &\sum_{i=1}^{m} u_i[g_i(a)] - u_k + M^+(a) \geq 0 \qquad (3) \end{aligned}\right\} \forall a \in C_k$$

$$\sum_{i=1}^{m} u_i[g_i(a)] - u_{q-1} - M^-(a) \leq -\delta \qquad \forall a \in C_q \qquad (4)$$

$$\sum_{i=1}^{m} \sum_{j=1}^{a_i - 1} w_{ij} = 1$$

$$u_{k-1} - u_k \geq s \quad k = 2, 3, \ldots, q-1$$

$$w_{ij} \geq 0,\ s > 0,\ \delta > 0,\ M^+(a), M^-(a) \in \{0,1\}$$

Taking into consideration the fact that $U[g(a)] \in [0,1]$ and $u_k \in (0,1]$ ($\forall a \in A$, k=1, 2, …, $q-1$), the difference between the global utility of an alternative and the utility thresholds is always lower than 1. Consequently, the three following cases hold.

1. If an alternative is classified by the decision maker in class C_k while its global utility is lower than the utility threshold u_k, then adding to its global utility an amount equal to $M^+(a)=1$ will certainly lead to the correct classification of this alternative and the constraints (1) and (3) are satisfied.
2. If an alternative is classified by the decision maker in class C_k while its global utility is lower than the utility threshold u_{k-1}, then subtracting from the global utility an amount equal to $M^-(a)=1$ will certainly lead to the correct classification of this alternative and the constraints (2) and (4) are satisfied.

3. On the other hand, if an alternative is correctly classified according to its global utility, then $M^+(a)$ and $M^-(a)$ will be set equal to 0 since all the constraints (1)–(4) are satisfied.

According to these remarks if $M^+(a)$=0 and $M^-(a)$=0, then the alternative a is correctly classified by the additive utility model to its original class, otherwise if $M^+(a)$=1 or $M^-(a)$=1 then the alternative a is misclassified. A drawback of this formulation is that although the binary variables $M^+(a)$ and $M^-(a)$ indicate whether an alternative is correctly classified or not, in cases of misclassification the magnitude of the misclassification error is not taken into consideration (e.g. if an alternative is misclassified by one or more classes). For instance, according to this formulation, two misclassifications of the type $C_k \rightarrow C_{k+1}$ and $C_k \rightarrow C_{k+2}$ will have the same impact on the objective function of minimizing the number of misclassifications. This issue should be studied further in the near future in order to develop a formulation that considers the magnitude of the misclassification errors. Moreover, it should be noted that the computational difficulties of this mixed-integer linear program make it applicable only for small-scale problems.

Combining this formulation with the objective of maximizing the distances of the correctly classified alternatives from the utility thresholds (UTADIS I), results to another variant of the UTADIS method, which is referred as UTADIS III. The aim of UTADIS III is to minimize the number of classifications and maximize at the same time the distances of the correctly classified alternatives from the utility thresholds. The LP formulation used to achieve this objective is similar to the LP formulation of the UTADIS I method. The only difference is that similarly to the UTADIS II method, the misclassification errors $\sigma^+(a)$ and $\sigma^-(a)$ are transformed into two binary variables $M^+(a)$ and $M^-(a) \in \{0,1\}$. The new LP formulation is the following:

$$\text{Minimize } F = p_1 \sum_a [M^+(a) + M^-(a)] - p_2 \sum_a [d^+(a) + d^-(a)]$$

s.t.

$$\sum_{i=1}^{m} u_i[g_i(a)] - u_1 + M^+(a) - d^+(a) = 0 \qquad \forall a \in C_1$$

$$\left.\begin{aligned}&\sum_{i=1}^{m} u_i[g_i(a)] - u_{k-1} - M^-(a) + d^-(a) = -\delta\\&\sum_{i=1}^{m} u_i[g_i(a)] - u_k + M^+(a) - d^+(a) = 0\end{aligned}\right\} \quad \forall a \in C_k$$

$$\sum_{i=1}^{m} u_i[g_i(a)] - u_{q-1} - M^-(a) + d^-(a) = -\delta \qquad \forall a \in C_q$$

$$\sum_{i=1}^{m} \sum_{j=1}^{a_i - 1} w_{ij} = 1$$

$u_{k-1} - u_k \geq s \quad k = 2, 3, \ldots, q-1$

$w_{ij} \geq 0$, $M^+(a)$ and $M^-(a) \in \{0,1\}$, $d^+(a) \geq 0$, $d^-(a) \geq 0$

Chapter 3

EXPERT SYSTEMS

1. GENERAL FRAMEWORK

The presentation of the DSSs' framework in the previous chapter demonstrated that computer science and information technology have been established as useful means to perform computationally difficult tasks. Except for this trend, however, researchers have also explored the capabilities of computer science and information technology towards developing systems that can perform reasoning tasks similar to the ones of human beings.

Artificial intelligence is a scientific field that addresses the development of intelligent systems through which computers can perform some tasks in a way similar to the human brain, such as inference for problem solving, natural language processing, speech recognition, etc. Until today, despite the significant amount of research on artificial intelligence, the obtained results with respect to the ultimate objective of artificial intelligence, have not reached the expected level yet. Of course, significant progress has been made over the last 20 years, but still the simulation of the operation of human brain remains a goal yet to be reached.

Despite some disappointment caused by the failure to meet the early expectations of artificial intelligence researchers, new fields of research emerged with promising results and potentials for improving decision making. Among these fields expert systems (ESs) are one of the most significant ones. ESs provide an approach to address decision making problem through the representation of expert's knowledge and the simulation of human reasoning. These features of ESs have led to their extensive application in several decision making fields including finance. Eom and et al. (1993) provide a comprehensive bibliography of these applications.

2. ESs' DEFINITION AND BASIC CHARACTERISTICS

Any information system that implements knowledge management and inference processes is a knowledge-based system. Systems that acquire this knowledge from experts of the problem domain that they address, are called expert systems (ESs). Thus, the problem solving procedure and the knowledge implemented in an ES are a representation of the heuristics and the knowledge/experience of expert analysts in the considered decision making field that constitutes the problem domain of the ES. A formal definition of an ES is the following: an ES is a computer information system that employs knowledge and inference procedures to solve decision making problem in a way similar to the one used by a human expert (Ford, 1985; Klein and Methlie, 1995; Turban, 1993).

This brief introduction on the ESs' technology identifies two of the major characteristics of ESs:

1. Their development is based on the description of the problem solving procedures employed by human experts.
2. They focus on the representation of experts' knowledge and experience.

These two characteristics of ESs result to the third major feature of the ESs' technology. ESs incorporate "swallow" knowledge that enables them to perform efficiently in specific, well-defined problem domains, but they cannot be used to address problems for which they do not have the appropriate knowledge. For instance, an ES developed for stock evaluation using the knowledge of stock market analysts should be able to perform as good as they are in their delay practice. However, the special-purpose knowledge of the system makes it an inappropriate tool if the user wants to evaluate other form of securities. On the other hand, the procedure that is used to exploit the experts' knowledge is independent of the decision problem that is considered and consequently it can be used in any problem domain. Generally, the problem domain for which an ES will be developed must fulfill the following requirements:

1. The decisions must be based on a well-defined set of evaluation criteria.
2. The performance of the considered alternatives on the evaluation criteria must be determined, or at least the domain of criteria values should be defined.
3. The procedure that leads to the decision according to the evaluation criteria should be determined.

The representation of experts' knowledge in an ES constitutes one of the main benefits of the ESs' technology; it enables knowledge transfer from the expert analysts to the actual decision makers who do not always have the experts' experiences and knowledge. Thus, decision makers can use ESs to derive decisions on the basis of the reasoning and the expertise of expert analysts of the problem domain that is considered.

In general, an ES can perform two major tasks: (1) it can derive conclusions of a specific problem domain, (2) and it can provide explanations on the way that these conclusions were derived. The conclusions may involve a decision, a recommendation, or a diagnosis for the decision problem under consideration. All possible outcomes of the analysis conducted by the ES are predetermined in advance; the ES does not "construct" the outcome (decision, diagnosis, recommendation) that fits the given information. Instead, the ES using the experts' knowledge that it incorporates, matches the known information on the considered problem with the set of the possible conclusions in order to select the most appropriate conclusion.

The procedure that is used to derive a conclusion is based on a structured interactive dialog with the decision maker so that the necessary information is obtained. This interactive communication is fully controlled by the ES; the decision maker can only affect the procedure through his/her responses to the questions imposed by the ES. Thus, in contrast to the DSSs framework where the decision maker controls the analysis process, ESs provide limited capabilities to the decision maker on controlling the way that the decision problem at hand should be examined.

Of course, the derivation of a decision is not the final step of the decision analysis process conducted by an ES. The decision maker should also be able to support the decision taken through the appropriate argumentation. In the ESs' framework this support is achieved through the explanations provided on the conclusions drawn. The most common form of explanations that ESs provide involves the way that a specific conclusion was derived. In this type of explanation, the ES presents all the reasoning procedure that it employed towards deriving its overall conclusion. The second most common form of explanations involves the reasons for which a specific information is requested by the decision maker. Finally, a third type of explanations which is of special interest for ESs developers involves the tracing of the inference procedure used by the ESs in deriving conclusions; this enables the examination of the inference procedure to detect possible inconsistencies, errors and generally any form of defect that may result to improper conclusions by the ES.

3. ESs STRUCTURE

According to Turban (1993), an ES comprises four main parts:

1. the knowledge base,
2. the inference engine,
3. the user interface,
4. the knowledge acquisition system and the knowledge engineer.

Figure 3.1 presents the structure of an ES and the interrelationship between its structural parts.

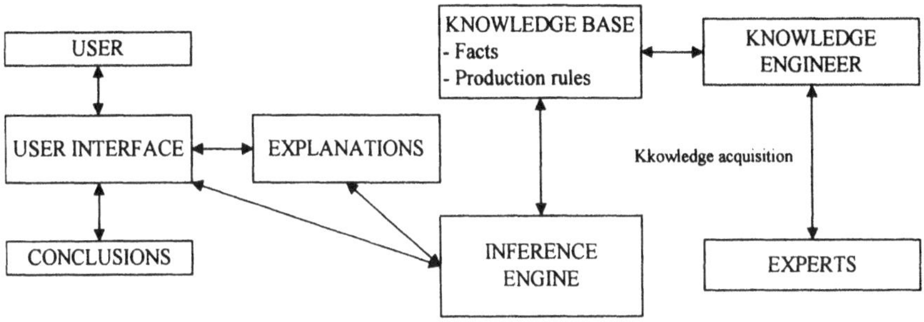

Figure 3.1. ESs' structure (Source: Turban, 1993)

The knowledge base includes the knowledge regarding the decision problem that is considered. This knowledge that is acquired by experts, is represented in the appropriate form so that it can be exploited by the ES. The knowledge is acquired through the knowledge acquisition system and the knowledge engineer who supervises the knowledge acquisition process.

The inference engine is responsible for exploiting the knowledge represented in the knowledge base of the ES in order to derive conclusions and to provide explanations.

The role of the user interface in the ESs' framework is similar to its role in the DSSs' context. The user interface is responsible for the communication of the decision maker with the ES and for presenting the results of the system and its explanations.

The subsequent subsections discuss in more details the functionality of each of these parts of the ESs' architecture.

3.1 The knowledge base

The knowledge base is one of the distinguishing characteristics of ESs as opposed to the DSSs' framework and other types of information systems. It involves the knowledge regarding the problem domain under consideration, including the description of the experts' behavior in addressing the problem, the description of objects related to the problem domain, the restrictions imposed by the decision environment, the relations between objects and the heuristics solution procedures employed by experts. The main forms of knowledge representation include production rules, semantic networks and frames.

- **Production rules**

Production rules are the most commonly used form of knowledge representation within the ESs framework. A production rule has the following form:

IF *conditions*

THEN *conclusions*

The first part of the rule involves the necessary conditions that should be fulfilled so that the rule is satisfied. Each rule can have one elementary condition or a set of elementary conditions connected with the operators AND, OR and NOT. The second part of the production rule involves the conclusions that will be derived if the conditions' part is fulfilled. The conclusions may involve decisions, recommendations, further actions that should be undertaken by the ES, numerical estimations, the presentation of a report or the inquiry for further information, etc.

Despite the fact that "IF-THEN" statements are commonly used in any programming environment, this does not mean that any software that implements a series of such statements is an ES. There is a fundamental difference between conventional "IF-THEN" programming statements and production rules. In conventional programming techniques an "IF-THEN" statement is activated only if the programmer directs the control flow to it. On the contrary, in rule-based ES a production rule is executed whenever there is enough information available to fulfill its condition part; it is a data-driven approach (Leinweber, 1988).

Each production rule represents a part of the knowledge of the ES and is independent of other rules. This enables the modification of the set of production rules by adding new rules or deleting existing ones. Such modifications, however, should always be followed by the appropriate consistency checks to ensure that the changes are consistent with the existing knowledge and production rules, thus avoiding the use of rules that lead to conflicting results.

Except for this modularity that production rules provide, they have two additional advantageous features: (i) they are easily understandable, and (ii) they have a self-explanatory capability that makes them a very useful tool in providing explanations regarding the reasoning that led the ES to a specific conclusion.

On the other hand, the major disadvantage of using production rules to represent the experts' knowledge is that quite often this knowledge is too complex to be represented through a compact set of rules. As the number of rules increases the computational time required to process the knowledge base increases dramatically. In such cases of large rule sets, to retain the efficiency of the ES it is necessary to consider the integration of the rule-based approach with other forms of knowledge representation or with additional knowledge management techniques. The most common approach that is usually employed to improve the efficiency of large sets of production rules is to break down the problem domain into sub-problems and organize the rules appropriately into smaller sets, each one of which addresses a specific aspect of the problem at hand. Thus, each subset of production rules corresponds to one of the sub-problems that are defined. Such an organization of the rule sets does not only improve the performance of the ES, but it also provides increased feasibility in performing changes in the rules and facilitates their easy maintenance.

In combination with the organization of rules into appropriate sets it is quite common to use a specific form of rules to control more efficiently the inference process. These rules are known as meta-rules (Pinson, 1989; 1992; Turban 1993). On the basis of the available information, the meta-rules can be used to direct the knowledge base search procedure towards specific sets of rules and even to alter the existing production rules.

- **Semantic networks**

Except for the production rules, semantic networks are another quite popular knowledge representation technique used in ESs' development (Turban, 1993; Duchessi and Belardo, 1987; Mui and McCarthy, 1987). The goal of semantic networks in knowledge representation is to provide a structured organization of facts about the objects involved in the problem domain.

Semantic networks have the structure of a traditional network. Their nodes represent objects, concepts or situations related to the considered problem, while the links among the nodes represent the relationship between these facts. The most common forms of relationships that are represented through semantic networks are the "IS-A" relationship and the

"HAS-A" relationship. An example of a semantic network for the description of the concept "security" is presented in Figure 3.2.

The constructed semantic network has a hierarchical structure that enables the organization of the knowledge from the most general and abstract concepts to the most specific ones. This kind of structure constitutes the major advantage of semantic networks. Each level of the network has all properties of its preceding levels, thus enabling the transitivity of knowledge properties from the most general concepts to the most specific ones.

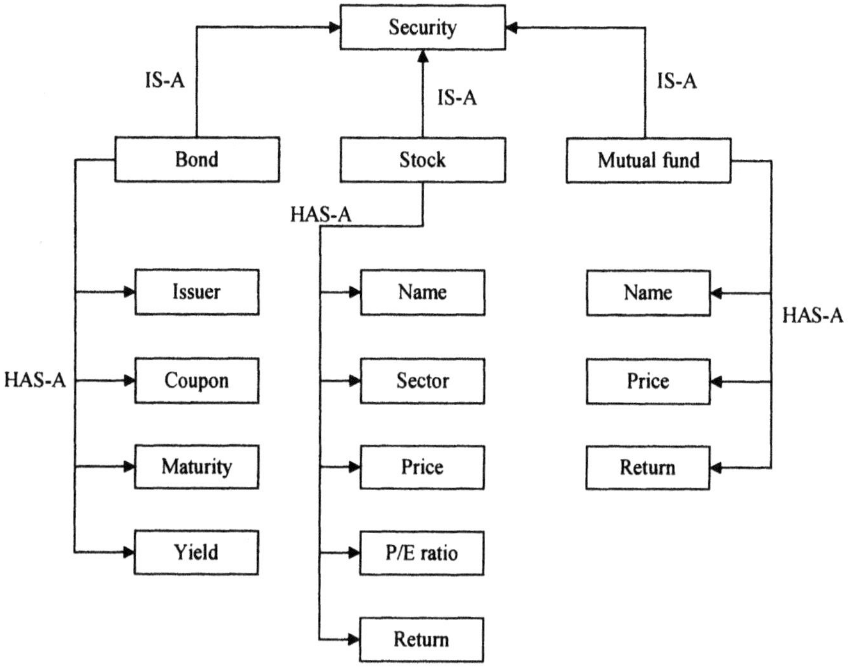

Figure 3.2. Example of a semantic network describing the concept "security"

The ability of semantic networks to enable the representation of complex relationship between the concepts and objects involved in the considered problem domain constitutes their major advantage over other representation forms. However, as the complexity of the existing/represented relationship increasing, the search of the network to locate a specific object/concept for inference purposes can be a quite difficult procedure. In such cases of high complexity it is also rather difficult to provide explanations on the conclusion drawn by the ES. This is due to the fact that it involves a detailed tracing of the way that the semantic network is employed to derive the obtained conclusion.

- **Frames**

Frames are the second most popular knowledge representation technique used in the ESs' framework (Minsky, 1975). A frame is a data structure that comprises all the knowledge on an object. Actually, frames are an application of the object-oriented programming approach to knowledge representation in artificial intelligence and ESs.

Each frame consists of slots and facets. A slot is a set of characteristics/attributes describing the object/concept to which the frame refers to. Each slot consists of several facets that include information on the attribute that the slot describes. This information may involve the value of the attribute, its domain, the type of the attribute (quantitative, qualitative) the actions that should be performed when the value of the attribute is sought, etc.

Similarly to semantic networks, hierarchical structuring of knowledge is a key issue in representing knowledge through frames. More specifically, frames are organized hierarchically so that the frames of the higher levels of the hierarchy represent the more abstract concepts, while the frames of the lower levels of the hierarchy represent the more specific concepts. The frames are linked in this hierarchy with relationships similarly to the semantic networks approach. The relationships used in representing knowledge through frames are the "IS-A" relationship and the "INSTACE-OF" relationship. Figure 3.3 presents a hierarchy of frames describing the concept "security".

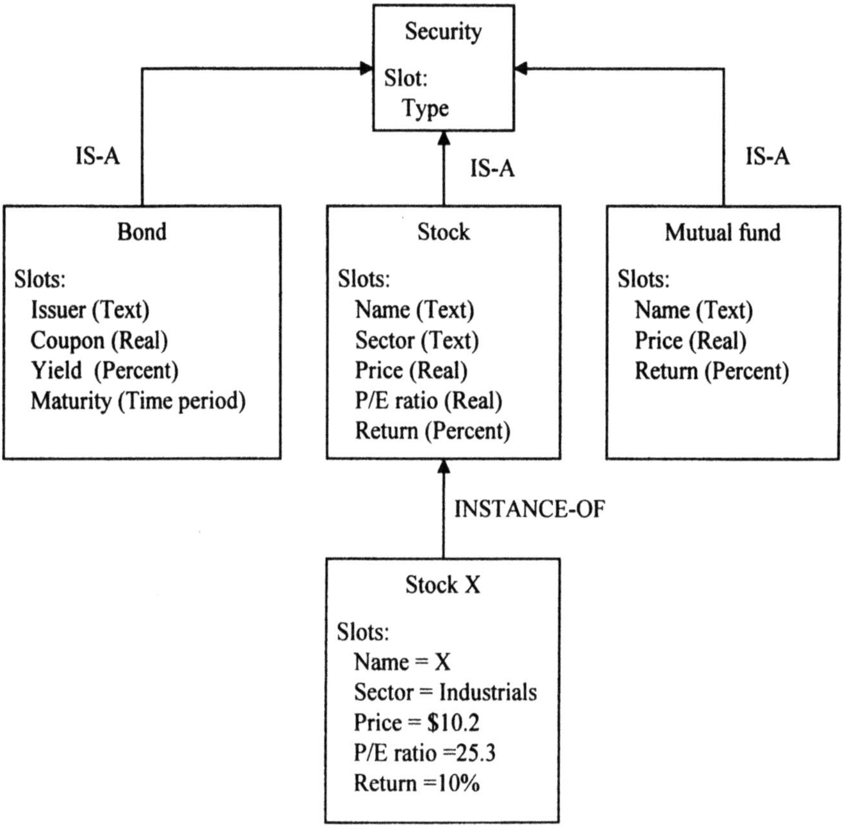

Figure 3.3. Hierarchy of frames for the description of the concept "security"

3.2 Knowledge acquisition and the knowledge engineer

One of the major obstacles encountered during the ESs' development process is the acquisition of the domain knowledge from the experts and the representation of this knowledge in the most appropriate and applicable form. Acquiring knowledge from the experts is a very difficult and time-consuming process, since experts are often inaccessible due to time constraints. They are unenthusiastic and usually there is a lack of communication between the knowledge engineer and the expert.

The expert is the person that possesses all the specific knowledge that is required to address a decision problem along with the appropriate experience on the methodological approaches used to derive decisions. The expert provides his/her knowledge on the way that the ESs should address the considered decision problem.

The acquisition of expert's knowledge for ESs' development is performed by the knowledge engineer. The knowledge engineer acts as a facilitator in the knowledge acquisition process, while he/she is also responsible for the appropriate codification and representation of the acquired knowledge in the knowledge base of the ES. The knowledge engineer communicates with the expert to acquire the knowledge that the expert has. Once the knowledge is acquired the knowledge engineer is responsible for the selection of the appropriate knowledge representation form as well as for the codification of the knowledge to the ES.

The knowledge acquisition process consists of five stages (Hayes-Roth et al., 1983):

1. Determination of the problem domain and its characteristics: in this first step of the process, the knowledge engineer specifically defines the problem that the ES should address. The problem can be decomposed into smaller parts and the sources that can provide the necessary information are identified.
2. Determination of the concepts: after the determination of the problem domain, the concepts that are employed to describe the objects involved are identified along with their interrelationships.
3. Knowledge structuring: in this third stage the knowledge engineer cooperates with the experts to acquire the knowledge that is necessary to address the considered decision problem. Once the knowledge has been acquired, it is represented in the knowledge based of the ES through the appropriate representation technique (production rules, frames, semantic networks, etc.).
4. Implementation: after the knowledge acquisition process is completed and the appropriate representation technique is selected, the knowledge engineer is responsible for the codification of the acquired knowledge in the knowledge base of the ES. In the same stage some refinements of the acquired knowledge can be performed.
5. Validation: this last stage of the process involves the validation of the knowledge inserted in the knowledge base of the ES. This is achieved by applying the ES to some representative examples of hypothetical decision situations. The conclusions drawn by the ES

are presented to the experts used during the knowledge acquisition process, so as to identify any errors and make the appropriate corrections.

Often the application of this knowledge acquisition process in practice is time consuming and even difficult to follow. The direct interrogation of the experts to acquire the necessary knowledge is restricted by the willingness of the experts to provide such information to the knowledge engineers as well as by the ability of the knowledge engineers to elicit the information from the experts and represent it appropriately in the knowledge base of the ES. To overcome these problems several researchers have proposed the use of machine learning techniques based on an inductive approach (inductive learning, cf. Holland et al., 1986; Michalski, 1983). The goal of this approach is to elicit knowledge using examples of decisions taken by the experts and to represent it in the form of production rules, so that the developed rules can reproduce the decisions taken by the experts as accurately as possible. The automatic generation of the production rules through such an inductive approach provides a significant support to ESs developers in order to reduce the time, cost and effort required to acquire knowledge from experts. The experts can evaluate the rules developed through the employed inductive approaches in order to ensure that these rules do not only comply with the decision examples used to develop them, but they also have the generalizing ability necessary to address all practical situations. Some of the most well known inductive learning approaches include the algorithms ID3 and C4.5 developed by Quinlan (1983), the recursive partitioning algorithm (Cronan et al., 1991), and the rough set theory (Pawlak, 1982).

3.3 The inference engine

The knowledge included in the knowledge base of an ES must be exploited through an inference procedure in order to derive conclusions. The inference engine is responsible for this task. The inference engine includes the methodologies that are used to infer conclusions according to the knowledge base of the ES. Actually the inference engine can be thought as the "brain" of the ES.

The procedures used by the inference engine to derive the appropriate conclusions are based on simple logic. For instance, given a fact A, and the production rule "If A then B", the inference engine will conclude on whether B is true or false. Performing a sequence of such elementary conclusions, the inference engine can derive overall conclusions on the problem that is considered. Each time a new elementary conclusion is reached, it is added to the set of information available so that new conclusions can be derived.

There are two main inference approaches used by an inference engine to exploit the knowledge base: forward chaining and backward chaining (Turban, 1993). Forward chaining is data driven approach, in the sense that the available data and information guide the inference process and the search of the knowledge base. In forward chaining, on the basis of the initial available information, the inference engine searches the knowledge base for production rules whose condition part is fulfilled by the available information. The information drawn from the conclusions of such rules is then added to the available information, thus forming a new set of available information that guides the subsequent inference process. Once enough information is available, the final conclusion can be derived. Generally, the forward chaining approach can be considered as an aggregation approach of the available information through the knowledge base so that an overall conclusion can be obtained.

In contrast to the data driven orientation of forward chaining, backward chaining is goal driven, in the sense that the inference process is guided by the ultimate conclusion (goal) that should be derived rather than by the available information. In this case the inference process starts with the goal of the search of the knowledge base, and all rules whose conclusions part involves this goal are identified. Then, the conditions part of such rules become the new goals of the search of the knowledge base. This backward approach is actually a disaggregation of the goal to be reached into the elementary conclusions that must be derived to decide upon the ultimate goal. The disaggregation proceeds up to the level where no further decomposition can be performed and the user must provide some information to the ES.

To illustrate both inference procedures consider a simple example involves the conclusion on the financial soundness of a firm X. Suppose that its return on equity (ROE) is 15%, its return on investment (ROI) is 10%, its debt to equity ratio (DE) is 50% and its quick ratio (QR) is 1.3. An example set of production rules describing the relation between the financial soundness of a firm and these ratios is the following:

Rule 1: **If** ROE ≥ 10% **and** ROI ≥ 5% **then** Profitability = High

Rule 2: **If** DE ≤ 70% **then** Debt burden = Low

Rule 3: **If** Debt burden = Low **and** QR ≥ 1 **then** Solvency = High

Rule 4: **If** Profitability = High **and** Solvency = High **then** Financial soundness = Satisfactory

Given the available information on the four financial ratios, the inference engine using the forward chaining will search the knowledge base to find a production rule whose condition part can be verified by the available information. In this example the initial available information verifies rules 1 and 2, since the condition part of the two other rules involves unknown information on the debt burden, profitability and solvency. The first rule found, verified by the available information, is applied. Then, rule 1 is applied and according to its conclusion part firm X's profitability is estimated to be high. Thus, the new set of available information for the firm involves its ROE, ROI, DE and QR ratios along with its profitability. This information verifies only rule 2, according to which it is concluded that the debt burden of the firm is low. The new information set is (ROE, ROI, DE, QR, Profitability, Debt burden), which verifies rule 3 and the solvency of the firm is evaluated to be high. Finally, since both profitability and solvency have been sought, rule 3 can be applied to conclude on the financial soundness of the firm which is the ultimate objective of the inference process. Figure 3.4 presents the procedure used by the forward chaining approach in this example.

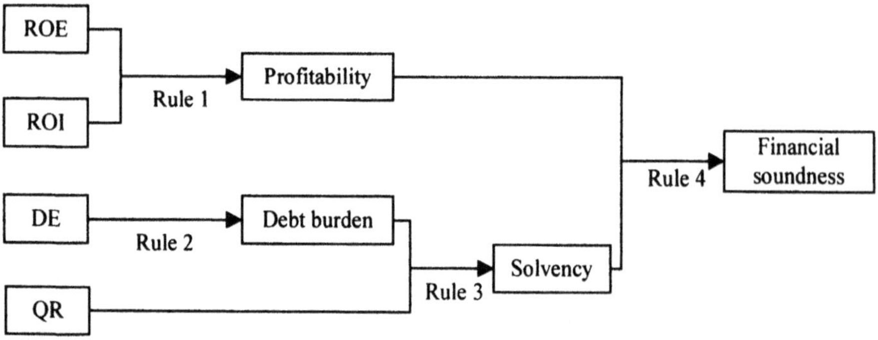

Figure 3.4. The forward chaining inference process

In contrast to the forward chaining inference, backward chaining first seeks for a production rule whose conclusion part involve the ultimate objective of the inference procedure. In the above example the objective is to derive a conclusion on the financial soundness of the considered firm. The only rule that includes financial soundness in its conclusion is rule 4. According to the condition part of rule 4 in order to conclude on the financial soundness of a firm its profitability and solvency should be sought, both of which are unknown for the firm of this example. Suppose the search procedure begins with profitability, the first elementary condition of rule 4. Thus, the new objective of the search of the knowledge base is to conclude on the profitability of the considered firm. Rule 1 is the only rule that includes profitability in its conclusions. This rule is verified by the available information, thus profitability is now known (high). Now the search proceeds with the examination of the second information that is required to conclude on the financial soundness of firm X, that is solvency. Solvency is included in the conclusion part of rule 3. The conditions of this rule involve the quick ratio, which is known, and the debt burden, which is unknown. Thus, the search proceeds with the evaluation of the debt burden of the firm on the basis of rule 2, which is verified by the available information. Now both solvency and profitability are known, thus rule 4 can be used to derive an estimation on the financial soundness of the firm. Figure 3.5 presents the procedure used by the forward chaining approach in this example.

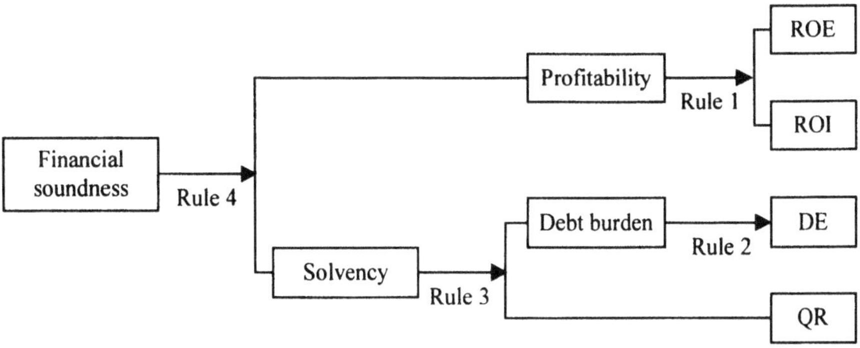

Figure 3.5. The backward chaining inference process

Expect for these deductive approaches that an inference engine implements to derive conclusions on the basis of the acquired experts' knowledge, another essential functionality of the inference engine involves the management of the uncertainty and fuzziness that is often encountered in real-world decision making. There are several approaches to address this issue, including probability theory (Bayesian inference) and fuzzy set theory. The latter has found several applications in ESs' development and over the last two decades several ESs have been designed based on fuzzy rules. Such rules associate a degree of possibility ranging between 0 and 1 with their conclusion part, which enables the determination of the possibility that an outcome included in the conclusion of rule can be true given the information described in the conditions of the rule. The strong theoretical foundations, the significant ongoing research on fuzzy sets theory, and the appealing potentials that it provides in handling fuzziness has been the main factors for its widespread application.

Another very popular approach within the ESs' community to handle uncertainty is based on inexact reasoning techniques, among which the most commonly implemented one involves the use of certainty factors. Certainty factors are a measure of uncertainty associated to a fact, ranging between -1 and 1. If the certainty factor associated to a fact is close to 1, then there is strong evidence that the fact is true. On the other hand, if the certainty factor is close to –1, then there is strong evidence that the corresponding fact is not true. The use of certainty factors in rule-based ESs is accomplished through the use of an approach similar to that of fuzzy sets, based on the maximum (for conjunction) and minimum (for disjunction) operators. Each elementary condition of a rule is associated to a certainty factor. Depending on the nature of the condition part (conjunction or disjunction of elementary conditions) the maximum and minimum operators are applied to determine the certainty factor of the condition part. This certainty factor is combined with the certainty factor of its conclusion part using the multiply operator. Finally, the certainty factor of a series of production rules can be determined using similar operators (maximum, minimum, multiply) or alternative combination techniques. In order to derive a conclusion on the overall objective of the knowledge-base search, a cut-off point is determined. If the overall certainty factor exceeds this cut-off point a conclusion is drawn, otherwise it is considered that there is not enough information to derive a secure conclusion.

3.4 The user interface

Similarly to the DSSs framework, a key issue in the success of an ES is the way that the system communicates with the user/decision maker. The user interface is responsible for the form of this communication. In the ESs' context the user interface presents the results of the system to the decision maker along with the explanations that justify these results. Furthermore it provides access to the knowledge base enabling the decision maker to examine the knowledge of the system to perform modifications if necessary.

Overall, the quality of the user interface depends on the communication and presentation means that are employed, the knowledge that the decision maker should have in order to use the system as well as the complexity of the task that should be performed by the decision maker in order to derive the necessary conclusions through the system.

4. ESs APPLICATIONS IN FINANCIAL ENGINEERING

Many essays can be found in the international literature concerning the implementation of the ESs' technology in the financial management field. Some of the most significant essays concerning the implementation of ESs in several fields of financial engineering and financial management in general, such as portfolio management, accounting, assessment of bankruptcy risk, credit granting, financial analysis, bond rating, investments and financial marketing are presented in Table 3.1.

Table 3.1. ESs' applications in financial engineering

Portfolio management	Suret et al. (1981) Pau and Giannoti (1986) Shane et al. (1987) Tam et al. (1991) Lee and Jo (1999)
Accounting	Michaelsen (1984) Elliot and Kielich (1985) Hansen and Messier (1986) Steinbart (1987)

Table 3.1. ESs' applications in financial engineering (continued)

Assessment of bankruptcy risk	Elmer and Borowski (1988) Messier and Hansen (1988) Michalopoulos and Zopounidis (1993)
Credit granting	Ben-David and Sterling (1986) Shaw and Gentry (1988) Lévine and Pomerol (1989) Nikbakht and Tafti (1989) Butera et al. (1990) Cronan et al. (1991) Sangster (1995)
Financial analysis	Bouwman (1983) Mui and McCarthy (1987) Sena and Smith (1987)
Financial planning	Dirks et al. (1995)
Investments	Heuer et al. (1988) Myers (1988) Valentine (1988)
Bond rating	Kim and Lee (1995)
Financial marketing	Kastner et al. (1986) Mays (1987) Borch and Hartvigsen (1991)

A comprehensive bibliography of the applications of the ESs technology in several business areas, including finance, from 1975 through 1989, can be found in Eom et al. (1993), while O'Leary (1995) reports the contribution of artificial intelligence techniques in the fields of accounting, finance and management.

It is clear that researchers in the financial management field have already tried to exploit the ESs technology, to represent the knowledge of human experts in order to provide recommendations and to support the decision making process. The major part of the past work concerning the implementation of ESs in the assessment of corporate performance and viability, focused on the acquisition of the domain knowledge either through the experts or through the application of several inductive methods and the representation of this knowledge in the ES using production rules, networks or frames.

5. ILLUSTRATION OF ESs DEVELOPMENT AND IMPLEMENTATION: THE ES PART OF THE FINEVA SYSTEM

This section demonstrates the implementation of the ESs' technology in the development of an ES to evaluate corporate performance and viability. The developed ES is a module of the FINEVA system (FINancial EVAluation; Zopounidis et al., 1996a), a multicriteria knowledge-based decision support system for the assessment of corporate performance and viability. The system was developed to run on IBM compatible machines using the operating system MS WINDOWS 3.1 or higher. The software has been written using Microsoft's Visual Basic 3.0 Professional Edition, while the ES part of the system has been developed using the ES shell M4 (Cimflex Teknowledge, 1991).

The basic characteristic of the FINEVA system is the combination of an ES with a multivariate statistical method (principal components' analysis) and the multicriteria method UTASTAR (Jacquet-Lagrèze and Siskos, 1982; Siskos and Yannacopoulos, 1985), to estimate the corporate performance and the viability of firms. The discussion that follows concentrates on the development and implementation of the ES part of the system, while more details on the other parts of the system as well as its overall structure and operation will be given on Chapter 6.

Within the context of the FINEVA system, the role of its ES module is to provide an initial evaluation of the performance and viability of the firms on the basis of some financial ratios and qualitative criteria. The "heart" of the ES is the knowledge base, containing the domain knowledge from the field of financial analysis, concerning the assessment of corporate performance and viability. The knowledge acquisition and representation methodology used to develop the knowledge base is presented in the following sections.

5.1 Methodology of knowledge acquisition

The knowledge acquisition process employed during the development of the ES part of the FINEVA system was based on interviews with expert financial analysts, from the academic and banking fields as well as on the international literature concerning the assessment of corporate performance and viability. The aim was initially to identify and select the most appropriate criteria (financial ratios and qualitative criteria) for the evaluation of corporate performance and viability, in a second stage, to achieve the modeling of the selected criteria and in a third stage to determine the estimation process based on these criteria. Finally, there was a validation and refinement stage where the acquired knowledge was tested through several examples with the help of the experts. The knowledge acquisition process is presented in Figure 3.6 (Matsatsinis et al., 1997).

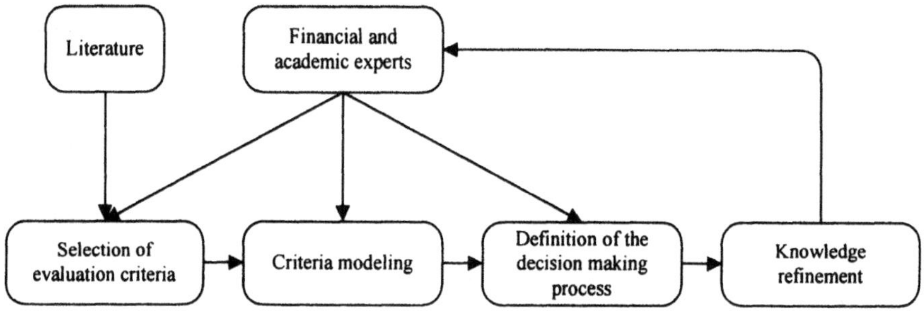

Figure 3.6. Knowledge acquisition process employed during the development of the ES part of the FINEVA system (Source: Matsatsinis et al., 1997)

An initial set of financial ratios and qualitative criteria were chosen from the international literature (Courtis, 1978; Lee, 1985; Zopounidis, 1987; Slowinski and Zopounidis, 1995) on the basis of their popularity and their relevance and contribution to the assessment of corporate performance and viability. The qualitative criteria were chosen based on previous experience from the banking sector (i.e. the ETEVA industrial and development bank in Greece; cf. Siskos et al., 1994). After a series of meetings with the expert financial analysts some additional financial ratios were proposed, while some others were considered as not necessary. Finally, with the agreement of all the experts, from the academic and banking fields, a set of sixteen financial ratios and six qualitative criteria was constructed to be used as decision criteria for the assessment of corporate performance. The financial ratios were categorized in three major groups, profitability ratios, solvency ratios, and managerial performance ratios, according to the methodology developed by Courtis (1978). Table 3.2 presents the final set of financial ratios and qualitative criteria, which are used as evaluation criteria for the assessment of corporate performance and viability.

Table 3.2. Evaluation criteria used in the FINEVA system

Code	Profitability ratios
A_1	Earnings before interests and taxes/Total assets
A_2	Net income/Net worth
A_3	Gross profit/Total assets
A_4	Net income/Gross profit
	Solvency ratios
B_1	Current liabilities/Total assets
B_2	Total liabilities/Total assets
B_3	Long term debt/(Long term debt + Stockholder's equity)
B_4	Current assets/Current liabilities
B_5	(Current assets – Inventories)/Current liabilities
	Managerial performance ratios
C_1	Interest expenses/Sales
C_2	General and administrative expenses/Sales
C_3	Accounts receivable × 365/Sales
C_4	Accounts payable × 365/Purchases of raw materials-accessories
C_5	Inventories × 365/Cost of sales
C_6	(Customers + Notes receivables) × 365/Sales
C_7	(Suppliers + Notes payable) × 365/Sales
	Qualitative criteria
D_1	Managers' work experience
D_2	Firm's market niche/position
D_3	Technical structure-facilities
D_4	Organization-personnel
D_5	Firm's special competitive advantages
D_6	Market flexibility

Each of the selected criteria was modeled using a five-point scale: non–satisfactory, medium, satisfactory, very satisfactory and perfect. The cut-off values for the financial ratios (Table 3.3) and the corresponding definitions of the qualitative criteria (Table 3.4), were determined by the experts, in such a way in order to represent their practical implementation.

Table 3.3. Modeling of financial ratios

IF	THEN	IS
$A_1 < 10\%$	Return on investment	Non–satisfactory
$10\% < A_1 \leq 20\%$	Return on investment	Medium
$20\% < A_1 \leq 30\%$	Return on investment	Satisfactory
$A_1 > 30\%$	Return on investment	Very satisfactory
$A_2 \leq 17.5\%$	Return on equity	Non–satisfactory
$17.5\% < A_2 \leq 20\%$	Return on equity	Medium
$20\% < A_2 \leq 23\%$	Return on equity	Satisfactory
$23\% < A_2$	Return on equity	Very satisfactory
$A_3 \leq 0\%$	Gross profit/Total assets	Non–satisfactory
$0\% < A_3 \leq 50\%$	Gross profit/Total assets	Medium
$50\% < A_3 \leq 75\%$	Gross profit/Total assets	Satisfactory
$A_3 > 75\%$	Gross profit/Total assets	Very satisfactory
$A_4 \leq 0\%$	Profit margin	Non–satisfactory
$0\% < A_4 \leq 50\%$	Profit margin	Medium
$50\% < A_4 \leq 100\%$	Profit margin	Satisfactory
$A_4 > 100\%$	Profit margin	Very satisfactory
$B_1 < 25\%$	Short term debt capacity	Very satisfactory
$25\% < B_1 \leq 50\%$	Short term debt capacity	Satisfactory
$50\% < B_1 \leq 75\%$	Short term debt capacity	Medium
$75\% < B_1 \leq 100\%$	Short term debt capacity	Non–satisfactory
$B_2 > 80\%$	Global debt capacity	Non–satisfactory
$60\% < B_2 \leq 80\%$	Global debt capacity	Medium
$40\% < B_2 \leq 60\%$	Global debt capacity	Satisfactory
$B_2 \leq 40\%$	Global debt capacity	Very satisfactory
$B_3 \leq 0.5$	Long term debt capacity	Satisfactory
$B_3 > 0.5$	Long term debt capacity	Non–satisfactory
$B_4 \geq 2$	Current ratio	Satisfactory
$B_4 < 2$	Current ratio	Non–satisfactory
$B_5 \leq 1$	Quick ratio	Non–satisfactory
$1 < B_5 < 1.5$	Quick ratio	Satisfactory
$B_5 \geq 1.5$	Quick ratio	Very satisfactory
$C_1 > 5\%$	Financial expenses	Non–satisfactory
$3\% < C_1 \leq 5\%$	Financial expenses	Medium
$2\% < C_1 \leq 3\%$	Financial expenses	Satisfactory
$C_1 \leq 2\%$	Financial expenses	Very satisfactory
$C_2 > 8\%$	General and administrative expenses	Non–satisfactory
$6\% < C_2 \leq 8\%$	General and administrative expenses	Medium
$4\% < C_2 \leq 6\%$	General and administrative expenses	Satisfactory
$2\% < C_2 \leq 4\%$	General and administrative expenses	Very satisfactory
$C_2 \leq 2\%$	General and administrative expenses	Perfect

Table 3.3. Modeling of financial ratios (continued)

IF	THEN	IS
$C_3 > C_4$	Accounts receivable turnover	Non–satisfactory
$C_3 \leq C_4$	Accounts receivable turnover	Satisfactory
C_5 increasing	Inventories turnover	Non–satisfactory
C_5 reducing or stable	Inventories turnover	Satisfactory
$C_6 \leq C_7$	Turnover of customers and notes receivable	Satisfactory
$C_6 > C_7$	Turnover of customers and notes receivable	Non–satisfactory

Table 3.4. Modeling of qualitative criteria

IF	IS	THEN
Managers' work experience	Negative experience	Non–satisfactory
	No experience	Medium
	Positive experience up to 5 years	Satisfactory
	Positive experience 5-10 years	Very satisfactory
	Positive experience more than 10 years	Perfect
Market niche/ position	Strong competition, firm's weak position	Non–satisfactory
	Strong competition, established and competitive firm	Medium
	Moderate competition, firm's strong position	Satisfactory
	Weak competition, firm's leadership position	Very satisfactory
	Single position, monopoly	Perfect
Technical structure-facilities	Old and inappropriate equipment, outdated production methods	Non–satisfactory
	Moderate technical structure, non-competitive production cost	Medium
	Relatively modernized equipment	Satisfactory
	Sound technical structure, full modernization scheme under way	Very satisfactory
	Excellent structure, modern production methods	Perfect
Organization/ personnel	Lack of organization/staff hiring policy	Non–satisfactory
	Moderate organization/staff hiring policy	Medium
	Moderate organization/staff hiring policy, willingness to improve	Satisfactory
	Good organization/staff hiring policy	Very satisfactory
	Excellent organization/staff hiring policy	Perfect
Firm's special competitive advantages	The firm does not possess expertise for its production methods	Non–satisfactory
	The firm possesses a small amount of expertise for its production methods	Medium
	The firm possesses a satisfactory level of expertise for its production methods	Satisfactory
	The firm possesses an exclusive expertise for its production methods	Very satisfactory
Market flexibility	The firm does not follow market trends, produces low-demand products	Non–satisfactory
	The firm has a limited flexibility	Medium
	The firm has a satisfactory flexibility	Satisfactory
	The firm follows market trends	Very satisfactory
	The firm is a leader in its production branch activity	Perfect

The major contribution of the experts concerned the definition of the evaluation process through the examination of the selected criteria. This complex task was carried out in a new series of meetings by the experts, where they were requested to express their evaluation methodology applied in practice when assessing corporate performance and viability. In this stage, decision tables were used to capture the experts' policy according to the evaluation criteria.

According to the decision tables, it was possible to build a detailed hierarchical decision tree, which clearly represents, in a graphical way, the whole decision process described by the experts. Figure 3.7 presents, a small portion of the whole decision tree. The same figure, also, depicts the structure of the constructed knowledge base. The first level of this hierarchical decision tree, at its left side, involves the modeling of the evaluation criteria, while the final level of the hierarchy, to the right side of the decision tree, involves the decisions drawn on the basis of the quantitative evaluation of the firms (financial ratios) and their qualitative evaluation (strategic variables).

The final stage of the knowledge acquisition process involved the refinement of the acquired knowledge. The validity of the acquired knowledge was checked on several representative examples. The derived results were presented to the experts and all the necessary changes and refinements were made according to the new supplementary recommendations and remarks.

5.2 Representation of knowledge

The acquired knowledge is represented in the knowledge base through production rules, in combination with some meta-rules (Pinson, 1989; 1992) necessary for the representation of the heuristics that the experts use in several practical cases to assess the performance of a firm as well as to reduce the time needed to reach the final estimation.

Based on the methodological knowledge represented in the decision trees and the explicit knowledge represented in the decision tables, a set of 1.693 production rules was constructed, representing over 13.000 possible combinations of the evaluation criteria (both financial ratios and qualitative criteria).

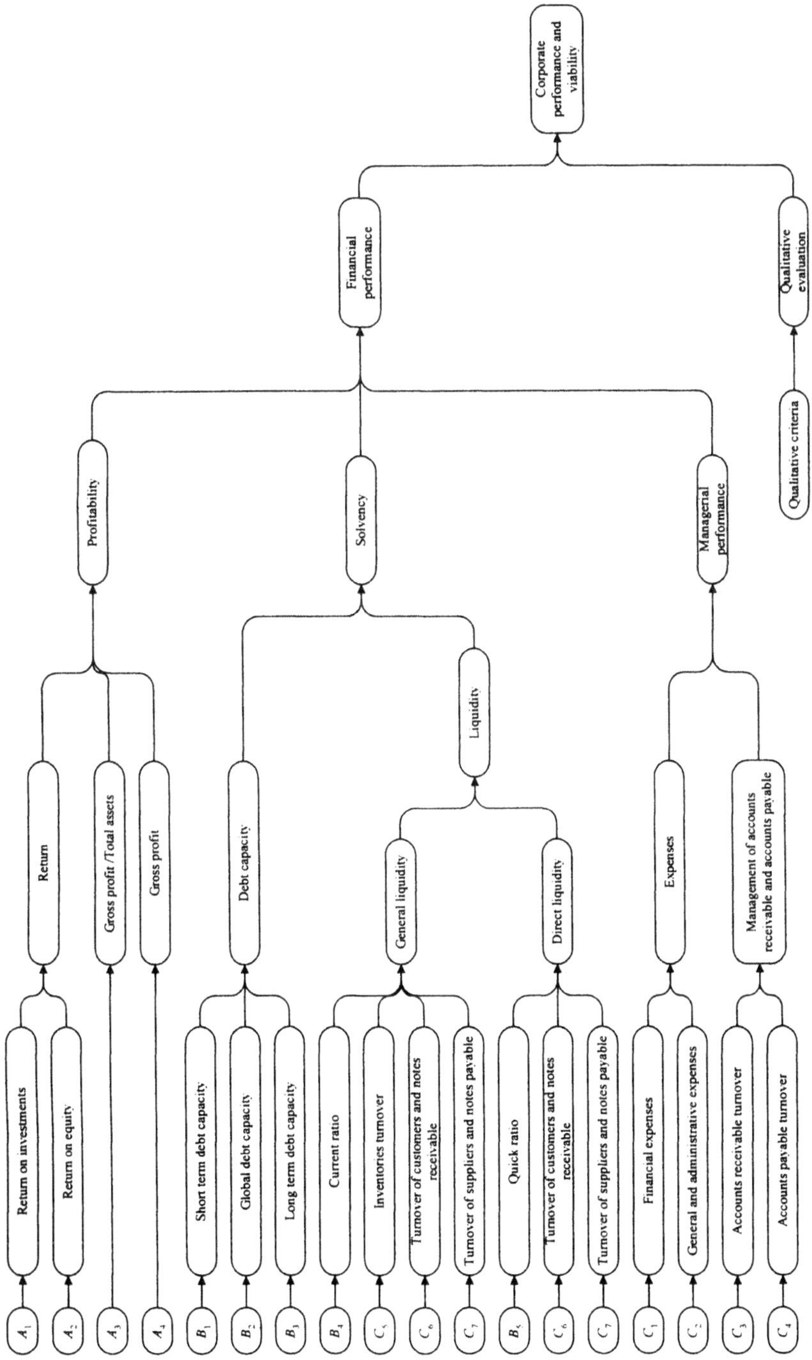

Figure 3.7. Decision tree representation of the evaluation process (Source: Matsatsinis et al., 1997)

One of the most important advantages of the constructed knowledge base is that it handles incomplete knowledge by ignoring the unknown information and continuing the inference and not by applying a probabilistic form. This is done without reducing the certainty of the conclusion reached. In cases of incomplete information, the decision makers try to draw conclusions based on the available data and information. The constructed knowledge base provides this capability to the decision makers, bearing in mind the fact that its purpose is to consult and to support the decision makers rather than to replace them.

5.2.1 Production rules

Some rule examples that represent the experts' methodology in the assessment of corporate performance are presented below. The first rule (rule 9) concerns the profitability of total assets and stockholder's equity, the second rule (rule 62) concerns the liquidity of a firm, the third rule (rule 75) concerns the expenses (financial, general and administrative), the fourth (rule 99) concerns the evaluation of a firm based on the financial ratios, the sixth (rule 626) concerns the evaluation of a firm based on the qualitative criteria and the last one (rule 1607) concerns the overall evaluation of a firm based on both the financial ratios and the qualitative criteria.

rule 9: **if** Return on equity = very satisfactory **and**
Return on investments = non–satisfactory **or**
Return on investments = medium
then Profitability = satisfactory.

rule 62: **if** Quick ratio = satisfactory **and**
Current ratio = non–satisfactory
then Liquidity = medium.

rule 75: **if** Financial expenses = medium **and**
General and administrative expenses = non–satisfactory **or**
General and administrative expenses = medium **or**
General and administrative expenses = satisfactory
then Expenses = medium.

rule 99: **if** Solvency = very satisfactory **and**
Managerial performance = satisfactory **and**

Profitability = satisfactory **or**
Profitability = very satisfactory
then Financial status = very satisfactory.

rule 626: **if** Managers' work experience = medium **and**
Firms market niche position = very satisfactory **and**
Technical structure = perfect **and**
Organization = medium **and**
Special competitive advantages = medium **and**
Market flexibility = non–satisfactory **or**
Market flexibility = medium
then Qualitative evaluation = medium.

rule 1607: **if** Financial status = very satisfactory **and**
Qualitative evaluation = satisfactory **or**
Qualitative evaluation = very satisfactory **or**
Qualitative evaluation = perfect
then Expert system evaluation = very satisfactory.

The complete representation of the experts' experience is achieved through the construction of several sets of production rules. Basically there are two major sets of rules: one concerns the evaluation of the financial soundness of the firms on the basis of their financial ratios, while the other involves the qualitative evaluation of a firm through the examination of the strategic variables. The first of these sets (evaluation of financial soundness) is divided into three subsets of production rules including a set of profitability rules, a set of solvency rules (including liquidity rules), and a set of managerial performance rules. Each of these subsets is further divided into smaller and more specific subsets of production rules (e.g. solvency rules include liquidity rules as well as debt capacity rules), following the knowledge base structuring presented in Figure 3.7.

5.2.2 Meta-rules

Through meta-rules it is possible to represent special cases that an expert financial analyst often faces using heuristics (Pinson, 1989; Turban, 1993). For example, in cases where the managers' work experience is non-satisfactory (negative work experience) then the expert assumes that the organization of the firm cannot be perfect. Thus, using a meta-rule, the corresponding value is excluded from the set of possible values of the criterion "organization". This heuristic is represented in the following meta-rule.

rule-1608: **if** *kbentry* (*L:legalvals* (organization) = [non–satisfactory, medium, satisfactory, very–satisfactory, perfect, unknown]) **and**
work-exp = non–satisfactory **and**
do (*add L:legalvals* (organization) = [non–satisfactory, medium, satisfactory, very–satisfactory, unknown])
then *set_legalvals* (organization).

This meta-rule initially checks the set of possible (legal) values of the criterion "organization". If the value "perfect" is included in the set of possible values for this criterion and the managers' work experience is non–satisfactory, then it defines a new set of possible values, excluding the value "perfect" (italics represent commands of the M4 expert system shell; cf. Cimflex Teknowledge, 1991).

5.2.3 Incomplete information

Sometimes it is impossible for the financial analysts to have all the necessary data needed to perform a complete assessment of corporate performance and viability. Even if this not the case, it would be desirable to let the decision maker choose the criteria he wants to be examined by the system. Until now such problems of limited information were faced by previous ESs through the introduction of certainty factors, providing conclusions in a probabilistic form. Each rule was associated with a certainty factor representing the confidence level of the expert in applying that rule (Shaw and Gentry, 1988). The objective of such ESs was to collect information that can lead to a conclusion with a certainty factor greater than a given threshold. The developed knowledge base faces the problem of limited data in a completely different manner. In such cases the system ignores the limited information and guides the inference of the ES to the corresponding set of rules which do not examine the unknown information. Of course the decision maker has to bear in mind two important aspects: firstly, the objective of the knowledge base is to support him in making a decision rather than replace him and secondly, the accuracy of the conclusion reached depends on the amount of the available data. The following meta-rule is used in cases where the evaluation of the firms' expenses is taken place. It is found that the financial expenses or the general and administrative expenses of a firm are unknown. The inference is then guided to the corresponding rule which does not take into account these financial ratios (italics represent commands of the M4 expert system shell, cf. Cimflex Teknowledge, 1991).

whencached (financial-expenses **is** unknown **or** general-and-administrative-expenses **is** unknown) = rule-1630.

5.3 An illustrative example

The example presented in this subsection is used to provide a comprehensive presentation of the inference process followed by the ES of the FINEVA system in evaluating the performance and the viability of firms. More details on this example can be found in the paper of Matsatsinis et al. (1997). Suppose that the ES of the FINEVA system is used to evaluate a firm X with characteristics presented in Table 3.5.

Table 3.5. Values of the criteria of firm X

Evaluation criteria	Values	Characterization
Return on equity	17.8%	Medium
Return on investments	28%	Very satisfactory
Profit margin	42.6%	Medium
Gross profit/Total assets	53.7%	Satisfactory
Short term debt capacity	42.9%	Satisfactory
Global debt capacity	38.9%	Very satisfactory
Long term debt capacity	0.48	Satisfactory
Current ratio	2.1	Satisfactory
Quick ratio	1.7	Satisfactory
Inventories turnover	Increasing	Satisfactory
Managers' work experience	Positive experience more than 5 years	Perfect
Firm's market niche/position	Moderate competition, firm's strong position	Satisfactory
Technical structure-facilities	Excellent structure, modern production methods	Perfect
Organization-personnel	Good organization/staff hiring policy	Very satisfactory
Special competitive advantages	The firm possesses a small amount of expertise for its production methods	Medium
Market's flexibility	The firm follows market trends	Very satisfactory

Once all the necessary data have been collected in the database of the system, the decision maker can use the ES part to get an initial evaluation of the performance and the viability of the firm that he wants to examine. The evaluation procedure of the ES starts by examining the financial status of a firm. This stage is automatically carried out by the ES, since the necessary information concerning the financial ratios can be drawn directly from the data base. The financial status of the firms is estimated through the evaluation of their profitability, solvency and managerial performance, according to the corresponding financial ratios and following the methodology used by experts and represented in the knowledge base. The evaluation of profitability and solvency of the firm X of our example is presented in Figures 3.8 and 3.9 respectively. As far as the managerial performance is concerned none of the corresponding financial ratios has been computed. Therefore the managerial performance is unknown and will not affect the evaluation of the firm.

Combining the evaluations concerning profitability and solvency (the managerial performance of the firm is not examined because of the lack of data), the overall financial status of the firm is estimated as presented in Figure 3.10.

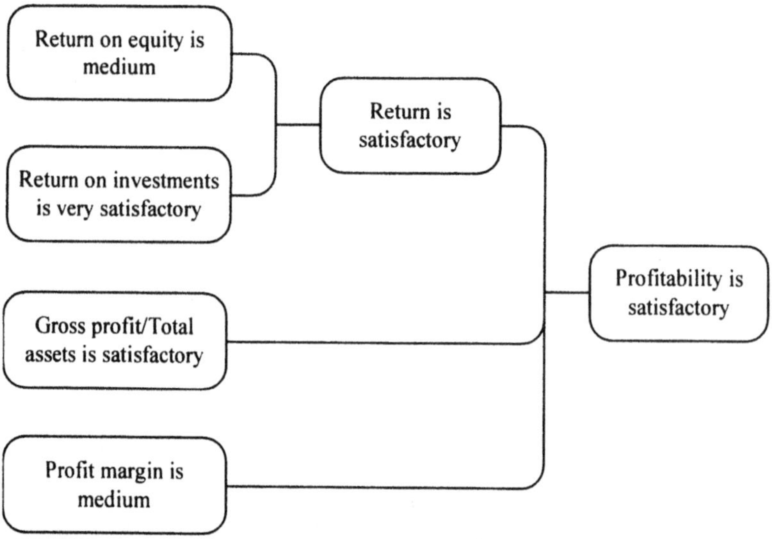

Figure 3.8. Evaluation of profitability

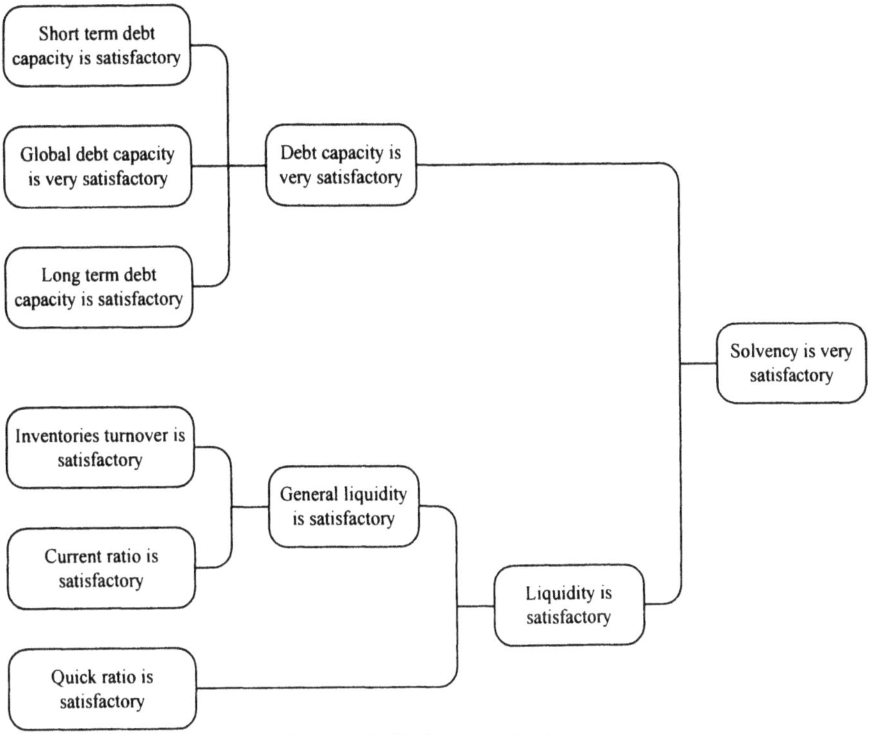

Figure 3.9. Evaluation of solvency

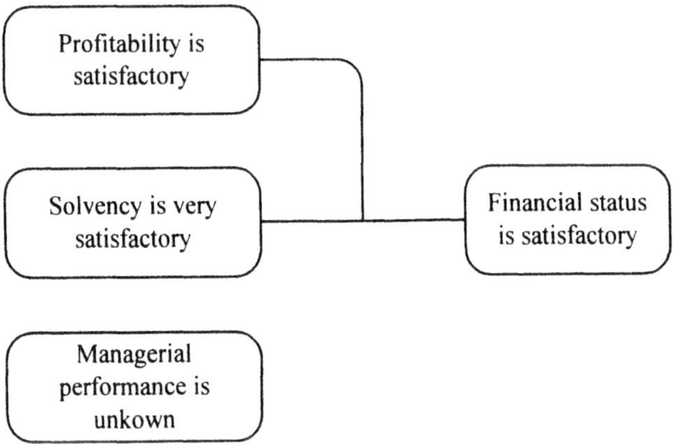

Figure 3.10. Evaluation of financial status

The second stage of the evaluation procedure involves the evaluation of the firm based on the qualitative criteria (Figure 3.11). If the decision maker is familiar with the modeling of the strategic variables, he can insert the corresponding information in the data base. In such cases this stage is also carried out automatically by the ES without posing any questions to the decision maker. In cases where the decision maker is not familiar with the modeling of the qualitative criteria, then the necessary information concerning the qualitative criteria is acquired through an interactive dialogue between the user and the ES (Figure 3.12). The ES poses questions to the user, together with the necessary explanations concerning all possible answers. In the case of Figure 3.12, the ES did not find any information in the database concerning the special competitive advantages of the examined firm. Thus, it poses the corresponding question to the decision maker. There are five possible answers: non–satisfactory, medium, satisfactory, very satisfactory and unknown. For each of these answers the corresponding explanations are provided in order to help the decision maker understand the modeling of the criterion. In this specific example, the ES explains that the special competitive advantages of a firm are non–satisfactory when the firm does not possess any expertise for its production methods, the special competitive advantages of a firm are medium when the firm possesses a small amount of expertise for its production methods, etc.

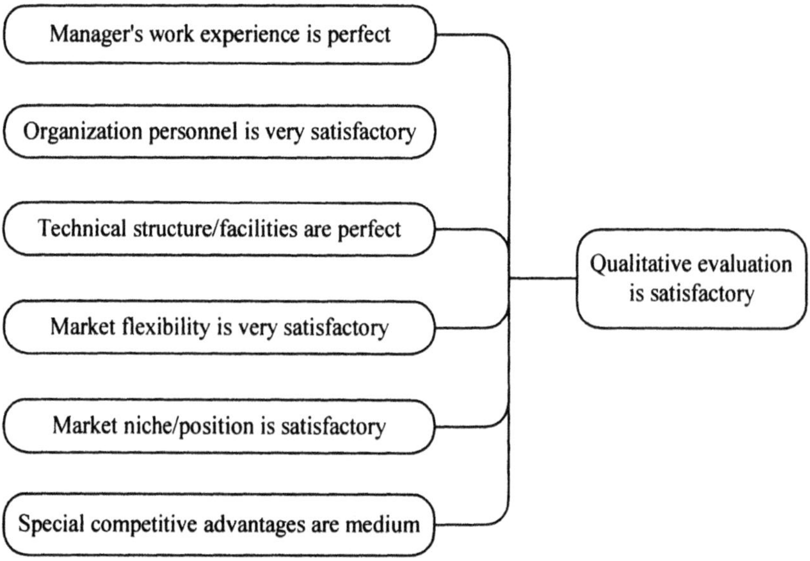

Figure 3.11. Qualitative evaluation of the firm X

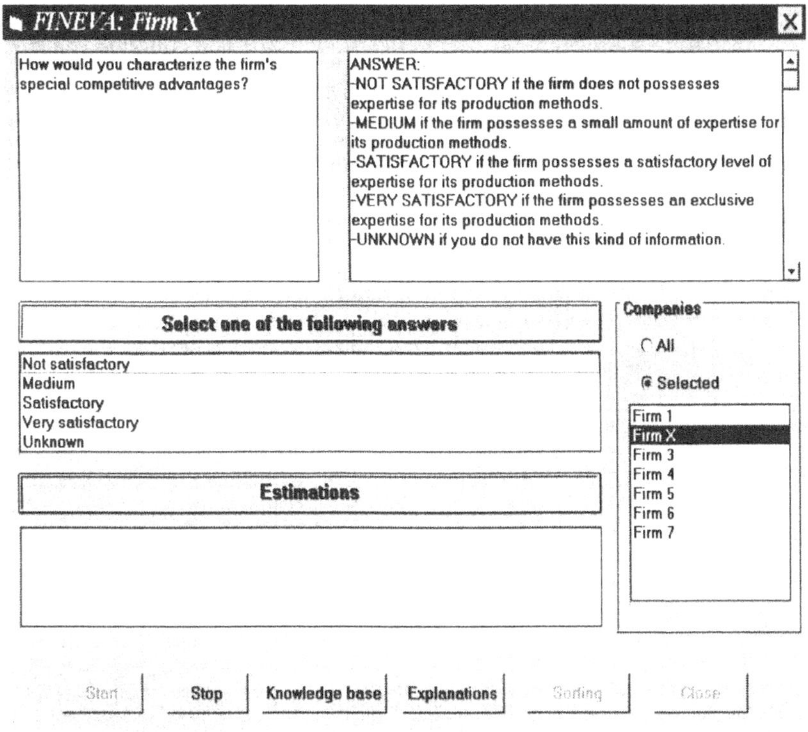

Figure 3.12. The communication between the decision maker and the ES

Combining the financial evaluation of the firm with the evaluation based on the qualitative criteria, the overall performance and viability of the firm is estimated (Figure 3.13).

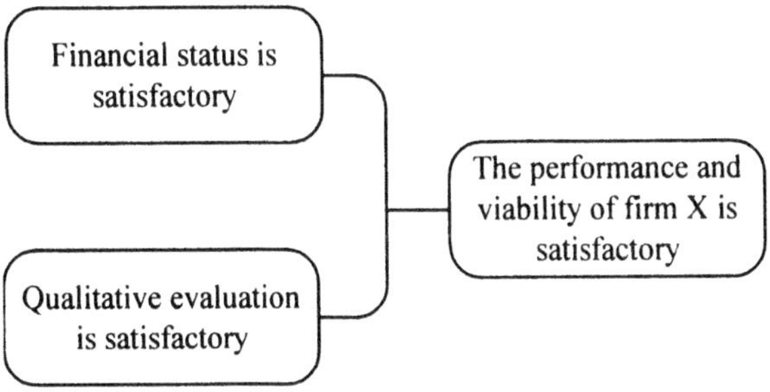

Figure 3.13. Final evaluation of the firm X

At any stage of the evaluation process by the ES the decision maker can ask for explanations either on a specific question or a conclusion. In the first case the ES will present the rule that it is trying to check and also any other rule that is currently under consideration and is related to the current search (Figure 3.14). In the second case the ES will present the rule that led to the final conclusion concerning the performance of a firm and all the elementary conclusions reached during the evaluation process (Figure 3.15).

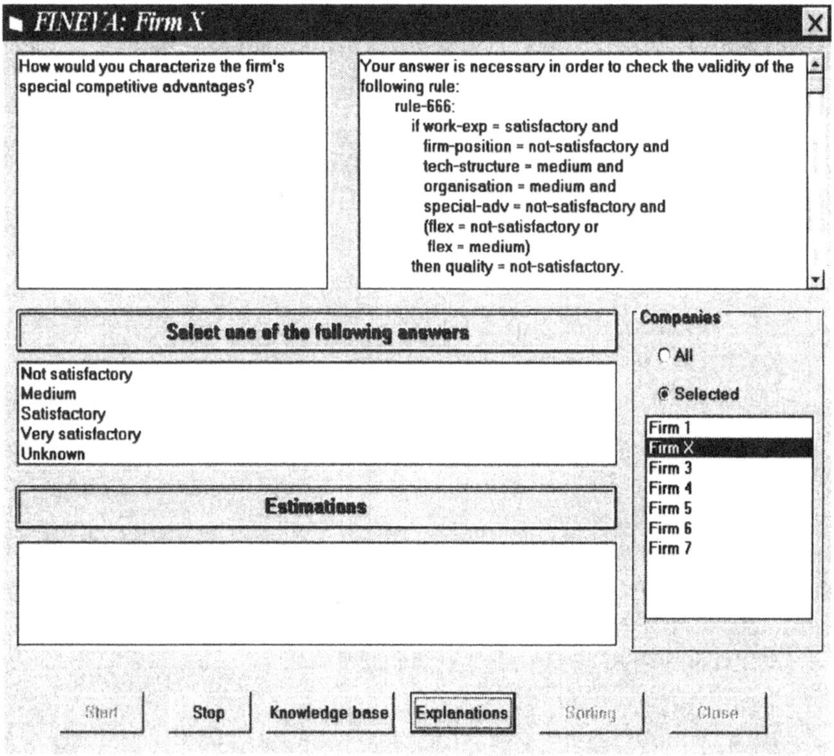

Figure 3.14. Explanations concerning a specific question posed by the expert system

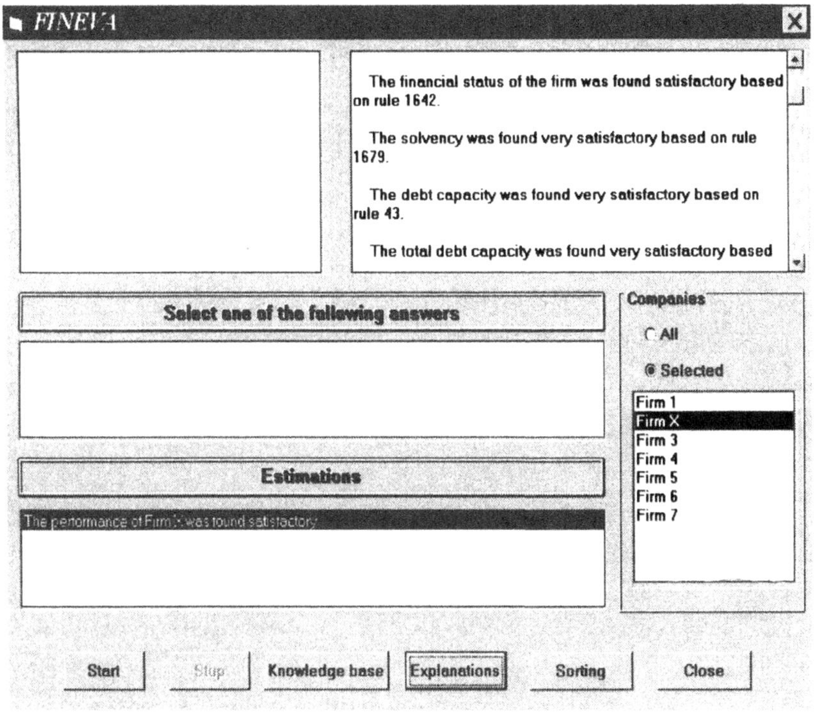

Figure 3.15. Explanations concerning the final estimation of the expert system

It is important to note that except for the expert system, the FINEVA system can provide estimations concerning the performance and the viability of the firms, based on the UTASTAR multicriteria method (Siskos and Yannacopoulos, 1985). The UTASTAR method is a preference disaggregation analysis technique used in the FINEVA system in order to develop a decision model, in the form of an additive utility function, which can be employed in evaluating the performance and the viability of firms. The results of such a model are used in order to rank the firms from the healthiest to the least viable ones, thus indicating the competitive level among the considered firms. Furthermore, the UTASTAR method can be employed in order to sort the firms into three classes according to their performance and viability. More details on the UTASTAR method and the way that is used in the FINEVA system are presented in Chapter 5.

6. ESs BENEFITS AND LIMITATIONS

The benefits of the ESs technology can be summarized in the following aspects (Klein and Methlie, 1995; Turban, 1993):

- ESs operate and draw estimations and conclusions using the knowledge and experience of human experts. Furthermore, the explanation capability of ESs can help the decision maker understand better the operation of the system, its assumptions as well as the inference that the system follows to draw certain conclusions.
- ESs draw conclusion much faster than humans, especially in complex problem domains where a large volume of information and data should be processed and analyzed.
- ESs provide the means to handle incomplete information and uncertainty. Uncertainty is a common feature of financial engineering problems. The ESs' technology can provide estimations and conclusions in cases where all the necessary information is not available.
- The ESs' estimations are consistent. Unlike human, an ES consistently examines and analyzes all the available information and data in detail, without overlooking facts of possible solutions.
- Through the use of ESs the transfer of knowledge is achieved. The ESs can be used by non-experts to solve complex decision problems, using the knowledge of the experts in the problem domain under consideration. Therefore, through the continuous use of an ES, a non-expert can learn the procedure, the heuristics and the problem solving methodology, in general, that an expert would use to solve a specific problem.

Although ESs can be very useful, providing expert advice as a human expert would, and explaining their reasoning and conclusions, they have some limitations and problems:

- One of the major bottlenecks with the ES development process is the elicitation of the expert's knowledge of the problem (Barr and Feigenbaum, 1982). The human reasoning is often too complicated to be adequately represented in an ES. The complete representation of the domain knowledge may require numerous production rules. Therefore, the time needed to draw conclusions increases considerably and the flexibility of the ES to changes in the decision environment deteriorates.

- Beyond the problems encountered in the knowledge acquisition and representation process, it should also be noted that the knowledge depends on the expert. Therefore, a different human expert could provide different knowledge, new heuristics and new solutions strategies.
- An ES represents shallow knowledge. The advantage of using shallow knowledge is that the ES will behave in a similar way to an expert. The basic disadvantage is that shallow knowledge concerns special purpose methods, heuristics and solution procedures, suitable only in specific and narrowly defined problem domains. Thus, although ESs achieve high performance in few narrow tasks they are helpless elsewhere.
- Users of ESs have natural cognitive limits. Humans, often, see what they are prepared to see, ignoring other important information. The fact that the ES has always the control of the inference process often causes a misunderstanding of its role and its aim. Thus, ESs are sometimes considered as a tool which replaces the decision maker in making decisions rather than as a tool in supporting the decision making process.

Chapter 4

KNOWLEDGE-BASED DECISION SUPPORT SYSTEMS

1. CONNECTIVES BETWEEN DSSs AND ESs TECHNOLOGIES

In the international literature, over the last decade, several studies have been conducted trying to investigate possible connections and relationships among the DSSs and ESs frameworks. Turban and Watkins (1986) identified the differences among the two approaches on four aspects:

1. As far as the goals of DSSs and Ess are concerned, the former focus on providing support to decision makers, while the later focus on providing specific conclusions.
2. As far as the problem domain is concerned, DSSs have a broad applicability to several fields involving complex decision situations, while ESs are restricted on more specific and well-defined problems (closed-world assumption; cf. Turban and Watkins, 1986; Edwards, 1992).
3. Although the database, a key component of the DSSs framework, includes data and facts, the knowledge base of an ES includes both the facts and the procedures used to address a specific decision problem.
4. Finally with regard to the flexibility, DSSs are more flexible with respect to changes in the decision environment and the judgement of

the decision maker, while ESs' closed-world assumption makes them less flexible.

In a similar study Ford (1985) examined the similarities and differences between DSSs and ESs from the objectives and intent points of view (similarly to the study of Turban and Watkins, 1986), the operational point of view, the user point of view as well as the development methodology point of view. According to the author, as far as the objectives and intentions are concerned, although the fundamental goal of DSSs and ESs is basically the same (the improvement of the quality of decisions), their underlying philosophies and objectives differ. Concerning the operational point of view, DSSs allow the user to confront a decision problem in a personalized manner, providing the ability to manipulate data and models in different ways. On the other hand, ESs provide little flexibility in the way the decision problem is analyzed. As far as the users are concerned, Ford argues that DSSs are primarily applied in the business or organizational fields, while ESs are typically associated with scientific research. The users of DSSs are actively involved in the development of the system, while the users of ESs do not participate in the development process. Finally, according to the development methodology, both DSSs and ESs are designed through an iterative or prototyping approach.

Doukidis (1988) carried out a survey on 67 ESs to investigate whether they employ DSS concepts. The survey was based on a questionnaire model composed of a list of key concepts of DSSs, such as their role, their design features, their components and the phases of the decision they support. The results of this survey show that three fundamental issues of DSSs are employed in ESs: semi-structured task, support, and effectiveness. The main differences concern the boundary of the problem space and the way that the problem is solved. Henderson (1987) investigated the existence of synergy between the DSSs and the ESs research. He concluded that in many respects, the similarities between these areas appear to dominate the differences.

Similar studies regarding the similarities and differences of DSSs and ESs have been conducted by Edwards, 1992; Hederson, 1987; Connell and Powell, 1990; Klein and Methlie, 1995. All these studies indicate that although both fields of DSSs and ESs have evolved separately, they have several common features and most important of all they share the same goal: to support the decision making process either by providing the means to perform quantitative analysis or by providing conclusions and evaluations. Thus, it becomes apparent that their integration could provide new significant potentials to decision makers including financial engineers.

2. KNOWLEDGE-BASED DECISION SUPPORT SYSTEMS

According to the brief description of DSSs and ESs in the previous chapters, it is clear that actually DSSs are commonly used to perform a quantitative analysis of the decision problem under consideration (in this case the term quantitative is used to describe the mathematical formulation of the problem), while ESs are mainly oriented towards employing a qualitative form of reasoning in addressing decision problems. However, decisions related to financial engineering problems are usually too complex and ill-structured, so that their modeling requires both a qualitative approach to understand the problem under consideration, its characteristics and basic features and a mathematical formulation to describe the problem and obtain "optimal" or generally "satisfying" solutions.

To address this twofold nature of financial engineering decisions and in the light of the ongoing research in both DSSs and ESs, financial and operational researchers as well as computer scientists have exploited the combination of DSSs and ESs in the framework of an integrated computerized system. The term "knowledge-based decision support system" (KBDSS) has been consecrated and is being used to describe this new type of system which integrates the database and model base management capabilities of DSSs with the symbolic reasoning and inference/explanation capabilities of the ESs' technology. The subsequent subsections describe the details of this integration and its expected benefits.

2.1 Integrating DSSs with ESs

The integration of DSSs with ESs technology can be achieved in two ways: either by incorporating several ESs in the different modules of a DSS (data base, model base, user interface) or by considering an ES and a DSS as two distinct but complementary parts of an integrated KBDSS.

- *Associating ESs to all structural components of a DSS*

In this form of the DSSs-ESs integration, the DSS is the key component in the KBDSS framework, while the role of the ESs is rather supportive (Figure 4.1). The ESs are not used to provide recommendations, estimations or conclusions on the actual problem that is addressed. Instead, the ESs interact with all modules of the DSS helping the decision maker (financial/credit analyst, investor, portfolio manager, etc.) to use effectively and appropriately the database and model base management capabilities, while furthermore the ESs facilitate the development of user friendly interfaces.

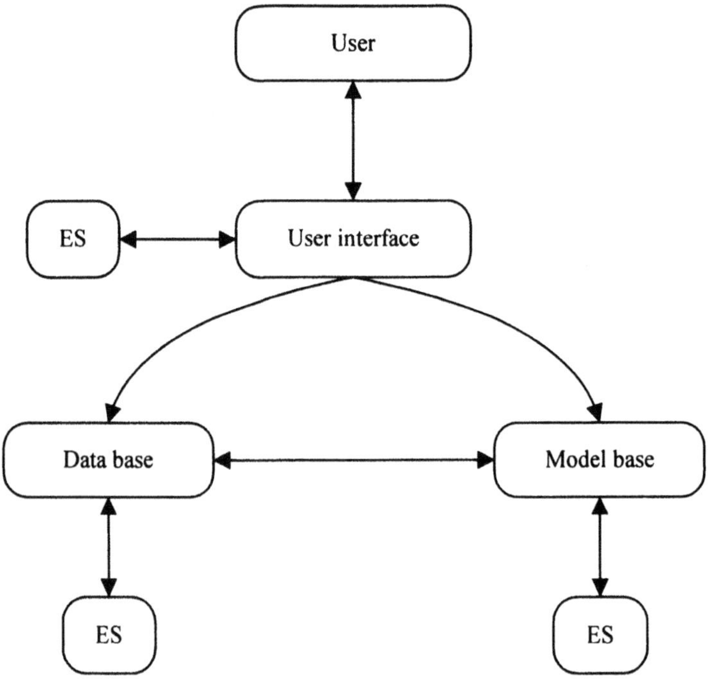

Figure 4.1. Integration of DSSs and ESs as separate parts in the KBDSS framework

More specifically, associating an ES to the database of a DSS enables the improvement of the database management including:

- advanced query capabilities that facilitate the easy search, classification and maintenance of data;
- guidance during data input and database construction;
- data mining capabilities to identify the underlying patterns and features of the data considered;
- consistency and integrity checking capabilities based on the knowledge of the problem domain to identify inconsistencies and related problems to the information that the user inserts in the database.

In addition to the support that an ES can provide in database management, the integration of an ES with the database of a DSS enables the continuous flow of information and data to the ES, thus automating the reasoning operations performed by the ES and reducing the time that is required by the ES to draw conclusions.

Since in the DSSs framework the whole analysis of the problems under consideration is performed through the model base, users often require significant support over the exploitation of the decision analysis tools implemented in the system. Associating an ES to the model base of the DSS can provide such support. From a financial engineering perspective this is a functionality of significant interest. The complexity of the financial engineering problems and the diversity that is evident in their nature, necessitate the careful structuring of the solution process as well as the appropriate selection of the tools that should be used to obtain solutions. An ES implementing domain knowledge can facilitate the problem-structuring phase. On the other hand an ES implementing knowledge on the management science/decision analysis tools that are employed in the DSS's model base, can be used to specify the tools that are appropriate for addressing the considered problem on the basis of the structuring phase, the nature and the patterns of the data that are involved. The same ES can be used to guide the analyst in applying properly the selected analysis tools, to specify the technical parameters that are involved, to explain their results in terms that are easily understandable by the user and to manage the sensitivity analysis process. Some additional functionalities that an ES can provide to the model base capabilities of a DSS include:

- guidance in designing experiments and conducting simulations for more effective model building and validation;

- support in generating and analyzing scenarios to address the uncertain or stochastic factors that are involved;

Finally, associating an ES to the user interface of a DSS can advance significantly the communication form between the system and the end user. This is achieved mainly through the use of natural language processing techniques, which facilitate the use of the system by users who do not process the necessary background on the methodological tools implemented in the model base or who do not have the experience in using computerized systems and databases. In addition to the development of natural language processing user interfaces, ESs can provide advanced visual interactive modeling capabilities. In this case they facilitate the improvement of the user's understanding of the system throughout all the phases of its use, including data entry, model structuring, development and validation.

- *Integrating ESs and DSSs as separate but complementary components*

In contrast to the aforementioned approach of the ESs-DSSs integration within the KBDSSs framework, in this second approach the structure of the KBDSS in considered as the combination of two major modules (Figure 4.2): the ES module and the DSS module. These parts are both used separately to support the financial modeling process, taking advantage of the specific characteristics and capabilities that each one can provide.

In this case, the purpose of the ES is not to facilitate the use of all parts of the system (database, model base, user interface), but rather to perform specific tasks that can involve either overall or partial conclusions and estimations on the considered problem or specific analysis which is integrated with the results of the DSS component.

In the latter case the integration of the ES's results with the ones obtained by the DSS can be performed by transferring the ES's output to the DSS module for further analysis and vice versa. For instance, consider a KBDSS developed for portfolio selection and management. To provide the required support to the portfolio manager/investor, the system should facilitate three major tasks:

1. the analysis of all available securities,
2. the construction of a portfolio of selected securities,

3. the trading of the constructed portfolio.

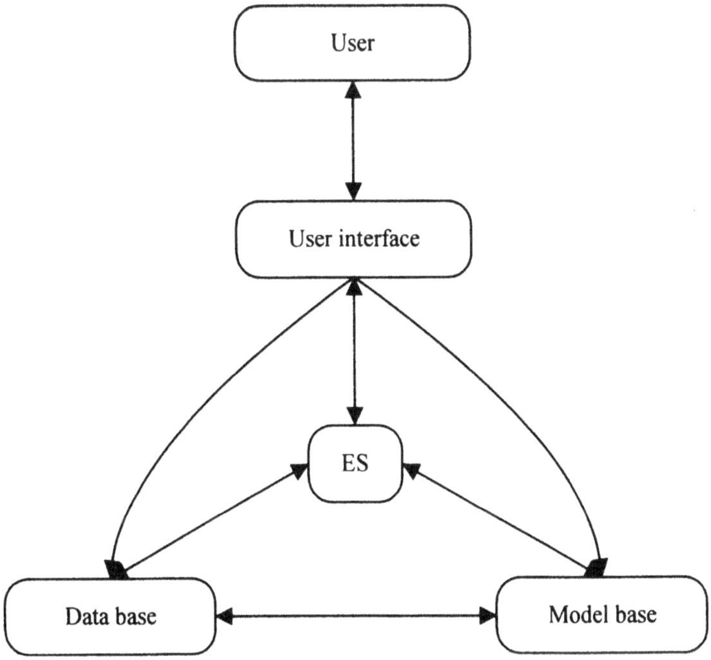

Figure 4.2. Integration of DSSs and ESs as complementary parts in the KBDSS framework

The analysis of the available securities can be accomplished through a variety of approaches in order to aggregate all factors that are related to the expected performance of the securities. Such approaches include among others multivariate statistical techniques, econometric analysis methodologies as well as multicriteria decision aid. Despite the relative advantages that such analytical methods can provide, they often require expertise by the user with regard to their technical features. If the user does not own the required expertise and theoretical background, an ES incorporating the knowledge of experts on the considered forms of securities can provide the support needed to identify the securities that constitute the most suitable investment opportunities for the portfolio manager/investor taking into account his/her investment policy. The second stage of the process, i.e. the construction of a portfolio of securities selected in the previous stage, cannot be addressed through an inference procedure based on symbolic reasoning. Instead, analytical tools should be used to construct the portfolio that best meets the portfolio manager's/investor's objectives. Several forms of optimization techniques are suitable to address this issue, using either single-objective formulations (e.g., maximization of expected return) or multiobjective ones. Thus, in portfolio construction stage the process flow moves from the ES part to the model base of the DSS module in order to formulate and solve the appropriate optimization problem. The final stage of the process, the trading phase, is actually related to the way that the portfolio manager/investor should manage the constructed portfolio. At this stage the portfolio manager/investor requires real-time support in deciding when and how the constructed portfolio should be updated through buy and sell decisions. Once again, an ES with knowledge of expert traders can facilitate the identification of buying and selling signals. Thus, the output of the DSS module (i.e., the constructed portfolio) is used as input to the ES part. The process flow continues on in the same way, beginning always from the identification of possible investment opportunities through security analysis, the construction of a portfolio and the trading process.

In this example the ES is used to provide recommendations and overall conclusions which are integrated with the results of the DSS module. However, clearly if the portfolio manager/investor is an expert on security analysis and trading, then the ES part in the aforementioned example would be of no use to him/her. Only the DSS part would be relevant to the decision making process in order to construct the most appropriate portfolio. Of course this is also true in other areas of financial engineering as well. Nevertheless, this does not mean that integration of the ESs' technology with a financial engineering DSS should not be considered. Indeed, an ES could be introduced as a complementary part of the DSS module, and therefore used as an integral part of the decision analysis process. In that respect, the ES could either carry out specific tasks to complement the analysis performed by the DSS. Such tasks may include providing support and guidance with regard to sensitivity analysis, model validation and testing, where the outputs of the DSS are used as inputs to the ES module, or generating alternatives and scenarios, where the output of the ES is used as input to the DSS for further analysis.

2.2 Benefits of integrating DSSs and ESs in the KBDSS framework and new potentials

The above discussion of the integration of ESs with DSSs has already highlighted the way through which each of these two technologies can contribute within the KBDSSs framework to improve the decision making process. Turban and Watkins (1986) have also discussed the benefits of this integration and identified them from the database management, model base management, user interface development perspective as presented in Table 4.1.

Table 4.1. Contribution of DSSs and ESs in the KBDSSs framework (Source: Turban and Watkins, 1986)

	Ess' contribution	**DSSs' contribution**
Database management	• Improvement of the development, operation and management of databases • Reduction of the time needed to access large databases and use data mining procedures • Enable the symbolic representation of data	• Provide database management capabilities
Model base management	• Improve the management of decision analysis models and techniques • Support the selection of the appropriate models • Improve the sensitivity analysis process • Provide support and guidance in conducting experimental designs and simulations • Enable the development of scenarios and alternative solutions • Support the proper structuring of the problem • Facilitate the trial and error process	• Provide an initial problem structuring • Enable the use of decision analysis models and techniques • Provide model development and computational capabilities
User interface	• Provide guidance and tutorial capabilities	• Facilitate the appropriate presentation of the results

Table 4.1. Contribution of DSSs and ESs in the KBDSSs framework (Source: Turban and Watkins, 1986) (continued)

	ESs' contribution	DSSs' contribution
Overall system capabilities	• Provide conclusions and estimations • Provide explanations on the obtained results	• Support the gathering and analysis of the appropriate information • Facilitate the learning process, through the appropriate examination and analysis of the data • Provide support to decision makers that meets their preferences and decision policy

As far as the database and database management (DBMS) are concerned, DSSs provide database capabilities to ESs. On the other hand ESs can provide support in the construction of the database and improve its operation especially in the case of large databases using useful data mining techniques.

Concerning the model base and the model base management system (MBMS), DSSs provide an initial problem structuring through standard models and computations as well as data to models and storage of models developed by the decision makers in the model base. The use of ESs improves the model base management by supporting the generation of alternatives, the selection of the appropriate models according to the available data as well as the structuring of the problem analysis process. Furthermore, ESs contribute to the interpretation of the results of the models, provide guidance to decision makers through the basic assumptions underlying the application of these models and finally, they support the sensitivity analysis and trial-error processes.

The contribution of DSSs in the design of user-friendly interfaces focuses mainly on the incorporation of the appropriate presentation means that match the requirements of the decision maker. On the other hand, ESs provide explanations concerning the use of the system, communication with the decision maker using natural language, interactivity throughout the problem solving process and tutoring capabilities.

Finally, concerning the overall system capabilities, DSSs help the decision maker to get experience in data collection as well as in the implementation of several sophisticated decision models. They also incorporate the preferences and decision policy of the decision maker in the decision making process. ESs using the knowledge and experience of experts can provide intelligent advice along with explanations concerning their estimations and conclusions.

On the basis of these contributions of DSSs and ESs in the development of integrated KBDSSs, one could distinguish the new possibilities, perspectives and contribution of KBDSSs development and implementation, in the improvement of the decision making process, especially in the field of financial modeling, in the following three main aspects:

- *Understanding the operation and the results of the system*

Incorporating a knowledge base in a DSS can help the decision makers understand the results of the mathematical models. The knowledge base provides the necessary explanations concerning the reasoning process of the system, its basic assumptions and its operation. Thus, the methodology used by the system can be clearly presented to the decision makers, helping them to learn the decision analysis process of the problem under consideration. At the same time the interpretation of the results is achieved, avoiding their misunderstanding and misinterpretation. The quantitative results are transformed into qualitative explanations, which are easiest to understand and are often of greater significance to the decision makers.

Specifically, in the field of financial management, the significance of the decisions taken necessitates their full justification. For instance, in the credit granting problem, the credit analyst should be able to argue upon the rejection of a loan application to the applicant, while on the other hand he/she should be able to justify the granting or rejection of a credit to the top managers of the bank or the credit institution. Although a mathematical model could be used to derive a credit granting decision, the credit analyst can hardly use the score of a credit application obtained through a credit scoring system to justify the acceptance/rejection of the application either to the applicant or to his/her senior officers. The justification must be based upon the special characteristics of the applicant (weaknesses or strengths on each evaluation criterion) and the way that these characteristics affect the final decision. A knowledge base incorporating the expertise of credit granting experts as well as knowledge on the mathematical models that are used, can provide a qualitative interpretation of the quantitative results and support the credit analyst in implementing the final decision.

- *Improving the objectiveness and the completeness of the results*

The combination of the ES's results with those derived from mathematical models and analytical techniques, increases the objectiveness of the final results. The subjective results of the ES (which depend on the expert's knowledge) are not the final estimations of the system. The decision maker except for the expert's knowledge, represented in the ES's results, is also provided with the results derived from mathematical models from the fields of multicriteria analysis, multivariate statistical analysis and mathematical programming. The results of this combination correspond not only to the expert's opinion, but also to the preferences and the policy of the decision maker.

For instance, consider the portfolio selection problem, where the objective of the investor is initially to identify the stocks, bonds or mutual funds which constitute the best investment opportunities; then taking into consideration his/her risk aversion policy as well as the available amount of money that he/she is willing to invest, the objective is to determine the "optimal" or more generally the "most satisfying" portfolio. An ES incorporating the knowledge of expert portfolio managers can be used to examine the current economic and stock exchange condition as well as the financial and stock market behavior of the stocks, bonds and mutual funds and provide an evaluation of the available investment opportunities. However, an ES is difficult to encompass an analysis of all the special characteristics, behavior and preferences of an investor. On the other hand, a sophisticated mathematical model can consider these key factors in portfolio selection and can be used to determine the efficient set of portfolios (considering the alternatives which have been identified in the previous stage as the most appropriate investment opportunities). Finally in can select, from this set, the portfolio that meets the preferences of the investor and the constraints that he/she poses.

- *Structuring the proper decision analysis*

The usefulness and the suitability of the decision analysis techniques often vary, depending on the available data of the examined decision problem. According to the existing data, the use of a certain analysis or a mathematical model may be unnecessary or even inappropriate, and consequently the decision maker could be led to incorrect estimations and conclusions. The knowledge concerning the problem domain represented in a knowledge base can be used to face such problems, recommending the decision analysis process and the appropriate analytical models, which correspond to the available data. Thus, the structuring of the decision analysis process is achieved, ensuring the effectiveness, the applicability, and the validity of the decision analysis models and techniques.

A common problem of this type, which is often overlooked in real world financial applications, involves the application of multivariate statistical methods that are based on specific statistical assumptions. For instance, applying linear discriminant analysis to predict business failure when qualitative variables should be considered violates the assumption that the variables follow a multivariate normal distribution. In this case the logit or probit analysis would be more appropriate to use. Similarly, when the equal variance-covariance matrix assumption is violated, the quadratic discriminant analysis, instead of the linear discriminant analysis, should be applied. Using a knowledge base and according to the specific nature of the data considered in financial decision problems such as business failure, recommendations can be provided on the methods and models which should be used to reach a decision. Furthermore, the ES can be used as a data mining tool to analyze the characteristics of the alternatives which are considered (firms, investment projects, countries, loan applications, etc.), to determine their specific features, and even to identify possible outliers which are common in finance (as much as 10% of financial data may consist of outliers; Duarte Silve and Stam, 1994) and should be studied in more detail by the analyst.

3. ALTERNATIVE ARTIFICIAL INTELLIGENCE TECHNIQUES FOR INTELLIGENT DECISION SUPPORT

The ESs' development and implementation issues have long been the focal point of the research interest within the artificial intelligence community. Nevertheless, over the last decades researchers have proposed several alternative approaches towards the development of systems that can behave "intelligently" in a way similar to human reasoning. Among these approaches neural networks, rough sets, fuzzy sets, genetic algorithms, and case-based reasoning can be considered as the most popular artificial intelligence approaches with several applications in financial engineering and business in general. In contrast to the traditional ESs' framework these alternative approaches provide a more analytic form of decision support rather than just a symbolic representation and exploitation of experts' knowledge. These methods have already attracted the interest of financial engineers. This is evident by the five international conferences conducted since 1995 on the applications of computational intelligence in financial engineering organized by the International Association of Financial Engineers (IAFE), in cooperation with IEEE.

3.1 Neural networks

Neural networks have been introduced by artificial intelligence researchers as an approach to emulate the way that the human brain reacts to specific inputs to produce an output. The structure of the human brain consists of numerous neurons, each of which constitutes an elementary processing unit. All neurons are linked to each other through a highly complex network structure. Each neuron collects information from the environment, processes it and produces an output signal that is transmitted to the other neurons for further processing. The ultimate result of this processing procedure is a decision regarding the action(s) that should be taken on the basis of the initial inputs.

This biological process is exactly the underlying basis of neural networks. Neural networks (also known as artificial neural networks) are networks whose nodes involve parallel processing units (i.e., the neurons) organized into layers. A typical structure of a neural network involves an input layer including one node for each input to the network, an output layer consisting of several nodes whose number depends upon the outcome of the network and some intermediate layers (hidden layers). The links between the nodes of the network can be defined so that either all nodes are linked to each other (fully connected neural network) or only nodes of successive layers are connected. Figure 4.3 presents an example of the structure of a fully connected neural network model with one hidden layer. Generally, there are no rules to determine the neural network's architecture, especially with regard to the number of hidden layers and the number of nodes in these layers. This is accomplished through trial and error processes on the basis of the problem being studied.

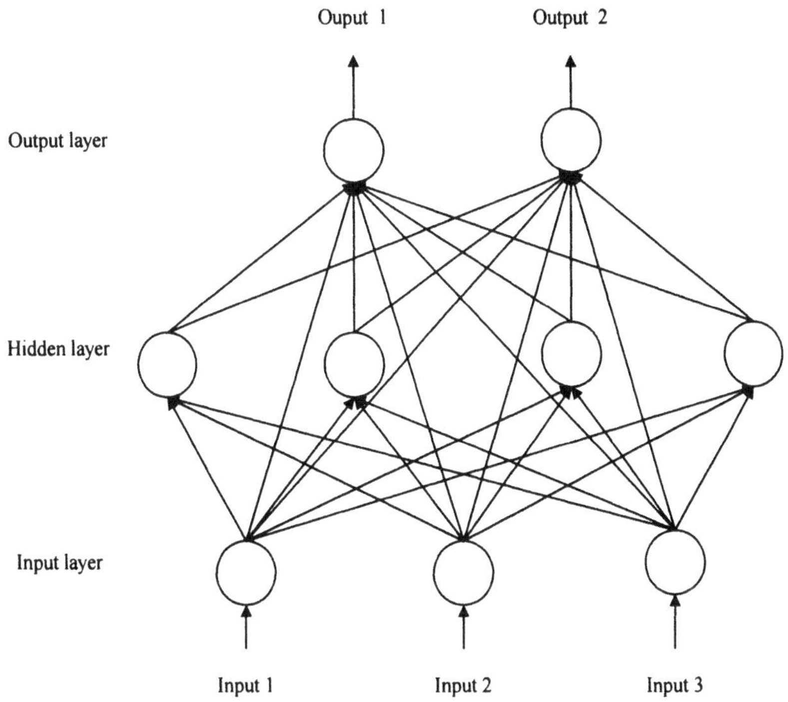

Figure 4.3. Neural networks' structure

With each arc linking two nodes, a weight representing the strength of the connection is associated. On the basis of these weights each node calculates a weighted sum of its inputs, transforms it to an output and passes this output to all other nodes to which it is connected. For a fully connected neural network, the input in_{ir} to a node i on the layer r is calculated as follows:

$$in_{ir} = \sum_{j=0}^{i-1} \sum_{k=1}^{n_j - 1} w_{ik}^{j} o_{kr} + \phi_{ir}$$

where:

n_j is the number of nodes at layer j,

w_{ik}^{j} is the weight associated with the connection between the node i at layer r and node k at layer j,

o_{kr} is the output of node k at layer r,

ϕ_{ir} is an error term (node bias) used similarly to regression analysis.

The output of each neuron can be determined through any form of function. However, the transformation function most commonly used is the logistic function:

$$o_{ir} = \frac{1}{1+e^{-\frac{in_{ir}}{T}}}$$

where the T is a constant representing the steepness of the logistic function.

During the development of a neural network model, the most significant stage involves the training (learning) of the network. In this stage the weights of all the connections of the network must be specified, so that the network can provide the desired outcome. Generally, there are two broad paradigms of learning:

- *Supervised learning*: The supervised learning process is quite similar to regression analysis. The neural network is presented with a set of representative examples (training set) of the problem that it should address for which the outcome is known. The neural network must adjust its weights so as to minimize the differences between its results and the pre-specified outcomes. The learning process is stopped when the results of the network are sufficiently close to the observed ones.
- *Unsupervised learning*: In contrast to supervised learning in unsupervised learning the outcome to which the neural network should result is not pre-specified. Instead, the neural network itself must identify the patterns that are evident in the data being analyzed, and adjust its neurons appropriately (self-organizing). This approach is similar to clustering.

The parallel processing functionality of neural networks, their ability to approximate highly non-linear situations as well as their generalizing ability has made them one of the most popular artificial intelligence techniques among both academic researchers and practitioners. Numerous applications of neural networks on financial engineering have been reported in the international literature regarding bond rating, stock price prediction, business failure risk evaluation, fraud detection, commodities trading, financial forecasting, etc. (Trippi and Turban, 1996).

Despite this popularity neural networks have also been criticized for their computational burden during the learning phase, and mainly for their black-box form of operation, which does not enable the users to argue upon the results of the network and the significance of the decision parameters (evaluation criteria) involved.

3.2 Rough sets

The rough set theory was introduced by Pawlak (1982) as a tool to describe dependencies between attributes, to evaluate the significance of attributes and to deal with inconsistent data. As an approach to handle imperfect data (uncertainty and vagueness), it complements other theories that deal with data uncertainty, such as probability theory, evidence theory, fuzzy set theory, etc. Generally, the rough set approach is a very useful tool in the study of classification problems, regarding the assignment of a set of objects (firms, bonds, stocks, etc.) to pre-specified classes. Recently however, there have been several advances in this field to allow the application of the rough set theory to choice and ranking problems as well.

The rough set philosophy is founded on the assumption that with every object some information (data, knowledge) is associated. This information involves two types of attributes, condition and decision attributes. Condition attributes are those used to describe the characteristics of the objects. For instance the set of condition attributes describing a firm can be its size, its financial characteristics (profitability, solvency, liquidity ratios), its organization, its market position, etc. The decision attributes define a partition of the objects into classes according to the condition attributes. For instance, in the case of bankruptcy prediction a decision attribute would involve the viability of the firms, thus defining a partition of the considered firms into two or more classes (e.g., bankrupt and non-bankrupted firms).

On the basis of these two types of attributes an information table is formed such as the one presented in Table 4.2. The rows of the information table represent the objects and its columns represent the condition and decision attributes. In the example of Table 4.2, the decision attribute d defines a dichotomic classification of the set of objects: d = A means acceptance, d = R means rejection. The classification $Y = \{Y_A, Y_R\}$ is composed of two decision classes: $Y_A = \{x_1, x_4, x_6, x_7, x_{10}\}$ and $Y_R = \{x_2, x_3, x_5, x_8, x_9\}$, corresponding to the objects accepted and rejected by the decision maker, respectively. The set of condition attributes is denoted by $A=\{a_1, a_2, a_3, a_4\}$.

Table 4.2. Example of an information table

Objects	Condition attributes				Decision attribute
	a_1	a_2	a_3	a_4	d
x_1	1	2	1	3	A
x_2	1	1	1	1	R
x_3	2	1	1	2	R
x_4	3	3	1	1	A
x_5	3	2	1	1	R
x_6	3	3	1	3	A
x_7	1	3	0	2	A
x_8	2	1	0	3	R
x_9	1	1	1	1	R
X_{10}	3	2	1	1	A

Objects characterized by the same information are considered to be indiscernible. This indiscernibility relation constitutes the main mathematical basis of the rough set theory. Any set of all indiscernible objects is called an elementary set and forms a basic granule of knowledge about the universe. In the example of Table 4.2, there are eight A-elementary sets: the couples of indiscernible objects $\{x_2, x_9\}$, $\{x_5, x_{10}\}$ and six remaining discernible objects.

Any set of objects being a union of some elementary sets is referred to as crisp (precise) otherwise the set is rough (imprecise, vague). Consequently, each rough set has a boundary-line consisting of cases (objects) which cannot be classified with certainty as members of the set or of its complement. Therefore, a pair of crisp sets, called the lower and the upper approximation can represent a rough set. The lower approximation consists of all objects that certainly belong to the set and the upper approximation contains objects that possibly belong to the set. The difference between the upper and the lower approximation defines the doubtful region, which includes all objects that cannot be certainly classified into the set. The lower and the upper approximations as well as the doubtful region of the decision classes Y_A and Y_R in the example of Table 4.2, are the following:

Lower approximation of Y_A: $\underline{P}Y_A = \{x_1, x_4, x_6, x_7\}$,

Upper approximation of Y_A: $\overline{P}Y_A = \{x_1, x_4, x_5, x_6, x_7, x_{10}\}$,

Doubtful region of Y_A: $\mathrm{BN}(Y_A) = \{x_5, x_{10}\}$,

Lower approximation of Y_R: $\underline{P}Y_R = \{x_2, x_3, x_8, x_9\}$,

Upper approximation of Y_R: $\overline{P}Y_R = \{x_2, x_3, x_5, x_8, x_9, x_{10}\}$,

Doubtful region of Y_R: $BN(Y_R) = \{x_5, x_{10}\}$.

On the basis of the lower and upper approximations of a rough set, the accuracy of approximating the rough set can be calculated as the ratio of the cardinality of its lower approximation to the cardinality of its upper approximation. In the example used, the accuracy of approximating the sets A and R is equal in both cases to 0.67 (4/6). The overall quality of classification, defined as the ratio of the sum of the cardinalities of all lower approximations to the total number of objects is 0.8 (8/10).

On the basis of these approximations, the first major capability that the rough set theory provides is to reduce the available information, so as to retain only what is absolutely necessary for the description and classification of the objects being studied. This is achieved by discovering subsets of the attributes' set that describes the considered objects, which can provide the same quality of classification as the whole attributes' set. Such subsets of attributes are called reducts. Generally, the reducts are more than one. In such a case the intersection of all reducts is called the core. The core is the collection of the most relevant attributes, which cannot be excluded from the analysis without reducing the quality of the obtained description (classification). In the example used, there are two reducts. The first consists of the condition attributes a_1 and a_2, while the second one consists of the condition attributes a_2 and a_4. Thus, the core includes only the condition attribute a_2.

The decision maker can examine all obtained reducts and proceed to the further analysis of the considered problem according to the reduct that best describes reality. The subsequent steps of the analysis involve the development of a set of rules for the classification of the objects into the classes where they actually belong. The rules developed through the rough set approach have the following form:

IF *conjunction of elementary conditions*

THEN *disjunction of elementary decisions*

The developed rules can be consistent if they include only one decision in their conclusion part, or approximate if their conclusion involves a disjunction of elementary decisions. Approximate rules are consequences of an approximate description of decision classes in terms of blocks of objects (granules) indiscernible by condition attributes. Such a situation indicates that using the available knowledge, one is unable to decide whether some objects belong to a given decision class or not.

Each rule is associated with a strength, that represents the number of objects satisfying the condition part of the rule and belonging to the class that the conclusion of the rule suggests (for approximate rules, the strength is calculated for each class separately). The higher the strength of the rules, the more general the rule is considered to be (its condition part is shorter and less specialized).

The development of the rule set within the rough set theory can be performed in a variety of ways, using an inductive learning process. The existing induction algorithms use one of the following strategies:

- generation of a minimal set of rules covering all objects,
- generation of an exhaustive set of rules consisting of all possible rules,
- generation of a set of strong decision rules, even partly discriminant, covering relatively many objects.

In the example of Table 4.2, two sets of minimal decision rules can be developed on the basis of the two reducts mentioned above. These rules are the following (the numbers in brackets indicate the strength of the rules):

1. Rules corresponding to the reduct $\{a_1, a_2\}$:
   rule No. 1: **if** $a_2 = 3$ **then** $d = \text{A}$ [3],
   rule No. 2: **if** $a_1 = 1$ **and** $a_2 = 2$ **then** d = A [1],
   rule No. 3: **if** $a_2 = 1$ **then** $d = \text{R}$ [4],
   rule No. 4: **if** $a_1 = 3$ **and** $a_2 = 2$ **then** $d = \text{R}$ **or** $d = \text{R}$ [1 / 1].

2. Rules corresponding to the reduct $\{a_2, a_4\}$:
   rule No. 1: **if** $a_2 = 3$ **then** $d = \text{A}$ [3],
   rule No. 2: **if** $a_2 = 2$ **and** $a_4 = 3$ **then** $d = \text{A}$ [1],
   rule No. 3: **if** $a_2 = 1$ **then** $d = \text{R}$ [4],
   rule No. 4: **if** $a_2 = 2$ **and** $a_4 = 2$ **then** $d = \text{A}$ **or** $d = \text{R}$ [1 / 1].

In both sets of rules there are three exact decision rules (rules 1-3) and one approximate decision rule (rule 4).

Once the rules are developed, the final stage of the rough set analysis involves the exploitation of the developed rules for recommendations regarding the classification of any new object being considered. The classification of a new object is achieved by matching its description to one of the rules developed. This matching process may lead to one of four situations (cf. Slowinski and Stefanowski, 1994):

(a) the new object matches one exact rule,

(b) the new object matches more than one exact rule indicating, however, the same decision class,

(c) the new object matches one approximate rule or several rules that indicate different decision classes,

(d) the new object does not match any of the rules.

In cases (a) and (b), the recommendation is univocal. In case of ambiguous matching (c), the user is informed about the total strength of all matching rules with respect to suggested decision classes. In case the new object does not match any of the developed rules, then the decision maker can identify a set of the rules that best match the description of the new object. Slowinski (1993) proposed a distance measure based on a valued closeness relation, to identify such "best matching" rules. The development of the value closeness relation implements the common notions used in the MCDA framework such as indifference, strict difference and veto thresholds on particular attributes, used in concordance and discordance tests, similar to the outranking relations approach of MCDA. The goals of these tests are to:

(i) identify attributes, which are considered to be in concordance with the affirmation "*object x is close to rule y*", and assess the relative importance of this group,

(ii) identify attributes, which are in discordance with the above affirmation, as well as attributes whose discordance is strong enough to reduce the credibility of the closeness.

The applications of the rough set theory to financial engineering include business failure prediction (Slowinski and Zopounidis, 1995; Dimitras et al., 1999), prediction of corporate mergers and acquisitions (Dimitras et al., 1997) as well as stock price prediction (Jog et al., 1999). Furthermore, it should be noted that the rough set theory has evolved rapidly over the last years and significant extensions have been made towards the rough set approach in addressing choice and ranking problems (Greco et al., 1999).

3.3 Fuzzy sets

In many cases decision making does not involve crisp (precise) evaluations but vague and fuzzy ones, in which case all evaluations (global or partial) are associated with a degree of truth. Some very simple, yet typical examples, involve the common use of terms like "almost", "often", "mostly", etc. that decision makers often use in describing and evaluating alternatives. Such verbal statements are clearly imprecise and their use implies that fuzziness is involved in the decision making process. The fuzzy set theory, first introduced by Zadeh (1965), is a tool that can be used to formalize the decision making process in problems where fuzziness is involved.

The core concept of the fuzzy set theory, the fuzzy set, is defined as any set of objects that does not have crisp boundaries. In the case of a crisp set A, for any object x the proposition "x belongs to A" is either true or false. On the other hand, in the case of a fuzzy set this proposition is not necessarily true or false only. Since the set has no crisp boundaries the above form of proposition can be partly true. In the fuzzy set theory the degree of truth of such verbal statements is measured through the definition of a membership function. The membership degree that an object belongs to a fuzzy set calculated through the membership function ranges between 0 and 1. The higher the membership degree is, the higher is the truth of the aforementioned proposition. In addition to the calculation of the membership degree for an object to belong to a fuzzy set, the membership degree for the object to belong to the complement (negation) of the fuzzy set is also calculated. Figure 4.4 presents an example membership function to evaluate the truth of the proposition "firm x according to its quick ratio is healthy".

In order to perform a global evaluation of an object so as to conclude on whether it belongs to a fuzzy set or not, it is necessary to evaluate its membership degree over all of its characteristics (evaluation criteria). The aggregation of all partial membership degrees can be achieved through several operators, which enable to calculate the membership degree for the intersection and union of fuzzy sets. The most common and simple intersection operator is the min, while the most common union operator is the max. Similarly to fuzzy sets, fuzzy numbers can also be defined and formulated.

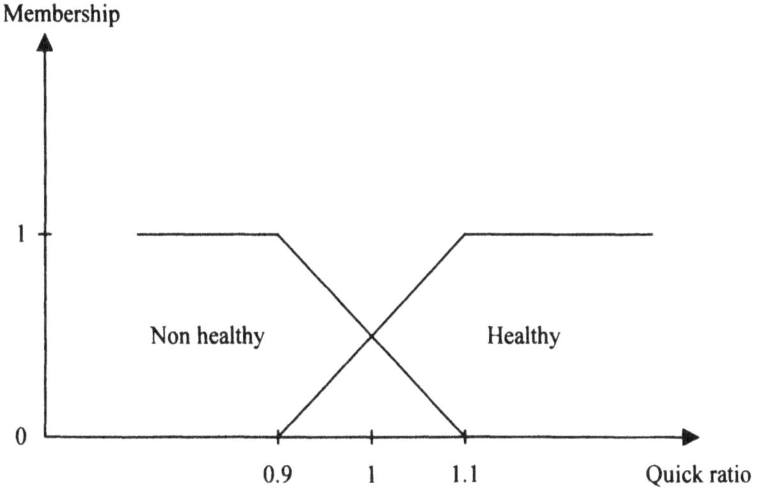

Figure 4.4. An example of membership function

Despite the fact that fuzzy set theory has raised some debate on the soundness of its theoretical foundations and its relationship to the traditional probability theory, its applications to several fields including finance are numerous. With regard to financial engineering it provides an alternative approach to model and handle the imprecision and uncertainty that is often involved both with respect to the decision makers' preferences and the decision variables (evaluation criteria). Furthermore, fuzzy set theory has contributed significantly through its integration with other artificial intelligence approaches including ESs (development of fuzzy rule-based Ess; Langholz et al., 1996) and neural networks (neurofuzzy systems; Von Altrock, 1996) as well as with conventional operations techniques (e.g., fuzzy mathematical programming; Zimmermann, 1978).

3.4 Case-based reasoning

During problem solving humans often try to match the current problem conditions to a similar situation that they have encountered in the past. Once such a match is found, they adapt the solution process that they have used in the previous situation to the current one and proceed with the solution based on their past experience. This procedure constitutes the underlying basis of case-based reasoning (Slade, 1991). In that respect, the major difference between case-based reasoning and other artificial intelligence approaches relies on the fact that instead of constructing analytical models describing the relationship between the decision making factors (evaluation criteria, attributes) and the decisions that should be taken, case-based reasoning exploits specific knowledge derived from previous experiences that are similar to the current problem conditions.

The general process of the case-based reasoning approach is described in Figure 4.5. The first stage of the process involves the description of the features of the current problem situation. On the basis of these features, the second stage involves the search of the case base in order to identify (retrieve) a case that best matches the current problem. This is probably the most critical step of the process for the success of a case-based reasoning system. This matching-retrieving process often requires the consideration of specific knowledge on the considered problem domain, in order to identify cases that are similar to the current one with respect to the most important features. Common similarity measures such as the Euclidean distance are often employed to estimate the closeness of past cases to the current one. In the case base, all cases are indexed in order to facilitate their organization and labeling so that they can be retrieved efficiently and accurately. The indexing/organization of the cases can be performed through a variety of ways, using for instance specific knowledge on the problem domain (knowledge-guided indexing), inductive methods (inductive indexing), or other techniques that can facilitate the classification/clustering of the cases (e.g., nearest-neighbor indexing). Once the retrieving process is completed, the features of the identified case are modified to best fit the current problem situation. This is the adaptation stage, which is of special interest when the outcome of the decision is a quantitative one (e.g., forecasting the price of a stock), in which case the perfect matching between the past case and the present one is rare. On the other hand, if the decision involves a qualitative outcome (e.g., a classification), adaptation is not necessary. This is due to the fact that the present case can be easily matched to a past one, even if their descriptions are not exactly the same. The next stage involves the testing/evaluation of the solution developed on the basis of the retrieved case. If the solution is found satisfactory, then the procedure stops and the new case is inserted in the case base, otherwise there must be either a re-adaptation of the selected case or a new search to retrieve a new past case.

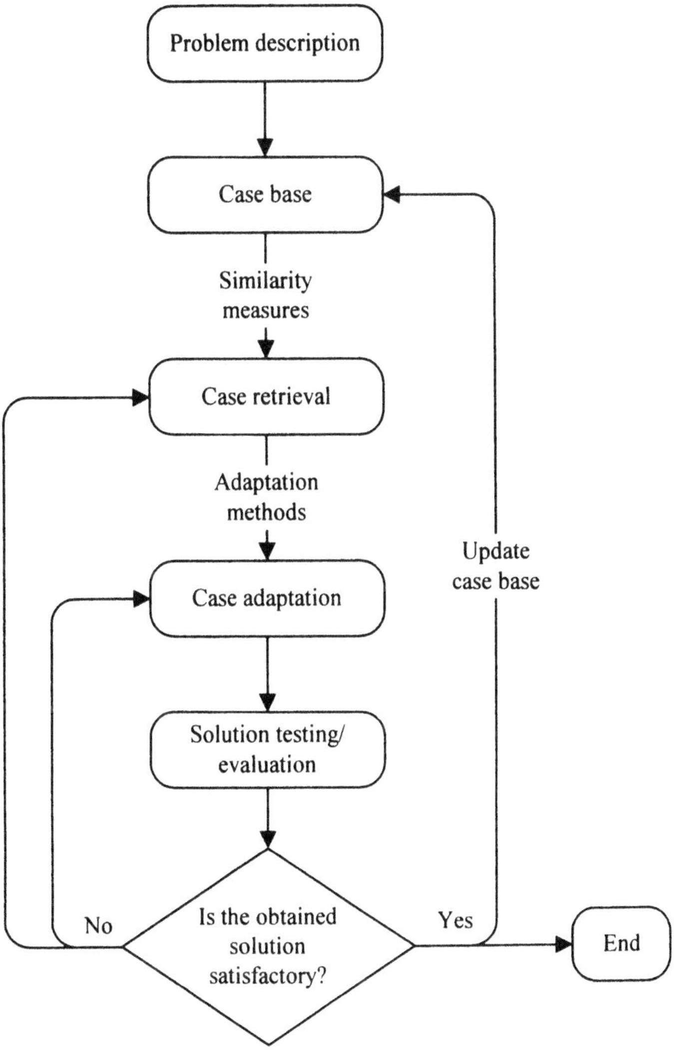

Figure 4.5. The case-based reasoning process

Compared to the traditional rule-based framework of ESs, case-based reasoning is particularly useful in problems domains which lack a casual structure, they are highly complex, or they require a great amount of specific knowledge and experiences that cannot be captured in detail through a comprehensive set of rules. In such cases past decision situations can provide guidance and support in addressing a present decision problem. This appealing feature of the case-based reasoning approach has led to several financial applications over the last decade, including bond rating (Shin and Han, 1999), bankruptcy prediction (Bryant, 1997) and interest rate prediction (Kim and Noh, 1997).

3.5 Genetic algorithms

Genetic algorithms, first introduced by Holland (1975), are powerful stochastic search techniques used for optimization purposes over large and complex solution spaces. The underlying philosophy and operation of genetic algorithms is based on the biological evolution process, which involves three key operations: natural selection (survival of the fittest), reproduction and mutation.

The general process of genetic algorithms is presented in Figure 4.6. Initially, a population of individuals –called chromosomes in the genetic algorithms' terminology– each representing a possible solution to the considered problem, is created at random. All chromosomes are represented as strings consisting of binary, integer or even real numbers. Each of the selected chromosomes is then evaluated using a fitness function to measure its performance on the specified goal. On the basis of the fitness of the initially selected population, a new one is generated. The generation of a new population process involves three steps:

1. Initially, two parent chromosomes are randomly selected according to their fitness (the better the fitness, the higher the chance to be selected).
2. Then, a crossover operation takes place to form a new offspring (children) from the selected chromosomes. The crossover is accomplished by swapping specific segments of the parent chromosomes' strings. The crossovers are performed with some probability that determines how often a crossover will be performed. If the crossover probability is 100%, then any new offspring is developed through a crossover operation. On the other hand, if the crossover probability is 0%, then the whole new generation consists of exact copies of chromosomes from the old population. Generally, the crossover operation is performed in order to increase the number of best chromosomes in the population, thus forming new improved generations.

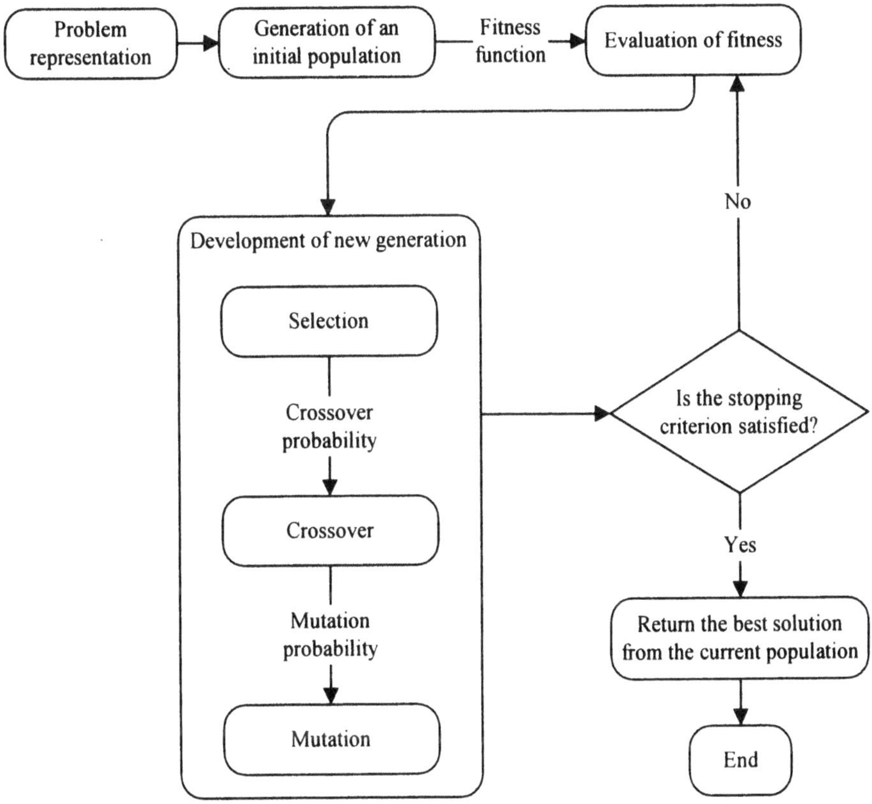

Figure 4.6. The process flow of a genetic algorithm

3. After the crossover process is completed, a mutation phase takes place. The mutation involves the selection, at random, of a chromosome and the random change of its string representation. This process is necessary in order to prevent falling into a local optimum for the considered problem. Similarly to crossover, mutation is also performed with some probability. If the mutation probability is 0%, then the chromosome obtained after crossover remains unchanged. On the other hand, if the mutation probability is 100%, then the whole chromosome is completely changed (actually it is inverted), in which case the search procedure can degenerate to a random search process.

The final step of the genetic algorithms' process involves the checking on whether the conditions for stopping the search are satisfied and in which case the procedure stops. The best solution (in terms of fitness) in the current population is returned as the optimal solution to the considered problem. If the stopping conditions are not fulfilled, then the procedure proceeds with evaluating the fitness of the members of the new population and developing a new generation through the selection-crossover-mutation process.

The capability of genetic algorithms to search effectively large solution spaces for optimization purposes makes them a significant new tool with numerous potential applications, including financial engineering problems. The discussion in Chapter 1 illustrated that several financial engineering problems, including portfolio construction, financial planning, working capital management, etc., are studied from an optimization perspective, either a single-objective or multi-objective one. Often the optimization formulations that are developed are highly complex and the solution spaces are considerably large due to the increasing number of available financial instruments and alternative solutions. Thus, the use of conventional solution approaches is inappropriate to tackle such problems. Among the existing new optimization tools, genetic algorithms constitute a promising approach to address effectively financial optimization problems.

4. KBDSSs IN FINANCIAL ENGINEERING

Recently, several KBDSSs have been proposed in the modeling of financial decision problems: The ISPMS (Intelligent Stock Portfolio Management System) system (Lee et al., 1989), the PMIDSS (Portfolio Management Intelligent Decision Support System) system (Lee and Stohr, 1985) and the StockAdvisor system (Liu and Lee, 1997) for portfolio selection and management; the HYPER-SAVINGS system (Lee and Nam, 1997) and the CASH MANAGER system (McBride et al., 1989) for financial planning; the LASS (Lending Analysis Support System) system (Duchessi and Belardo, 1987) and the MARBLE system (Shaw and Gentry, 1988) for credit granting problems; the KABAL (Kabal is the Norwegian word for patience) system (Hartvigsen, 1990) for financial analysis and the systems proposed by Hashemi et al. (1998) and Shin and Han (1999) for predicting the ownership status of banks and corporate bond rating, respectively. The subsequent subsections present the main features and functionalities of these systems in order to illustrate how the KBDSSs' framework contributes to the solution of financial engineering problems.

4.1 Portfolio selection, management and trading

4.1.1 The ISPMS system

Lee et al. (1989) developed an intelligent portfolio management system called ISPMS (Intelligent Stock Portfolio Management System), which integrates the quantitative optimization models with the capabilities of an ES. The system uses the quadratic programming model proposed by Markowitz (1952) to provide normative decisions and an ES to analyze the preferences of the decision maker and to exploit the experts' knowledge on portfolio selection and management. Therefore, the final recommendations of the system are not just based on the subjective knowledge of an expert, but they also take into account the preferences and the investment policy of the portfolio manager/investor. Furthermore, the ES helps the portfolio manager/investor to formulate his/her preferences as constraints in the quadratic programming model. Thus, the role of the ES is not to replace the decision maker, but to support him instead. The architecture of the proposed system is presented in Figure 4.7.

The key components of the IPMS system are the following:

(i) Two independent external relational databases. The first database provides the information about individual stocks (stock prices, industrial sector, beta values, firms' ratios, past years' financial results, etc.). The second database concerns historical instances of investment decisions, which may be updated to reflect new investments.

(ii) The knowledge base of the system is constructed based on both the historical database (through machine learning techniques; Quinlan, 1983) and the advice of an expert in stock investment (through the knowledge acquisition system).

(iii) The preference revelation system is used to capture the personal preferences of the investor. These preferences may involve the desired investment amount and/or the percentage of a specific stock (or a group of stocks) in the constructed portfolio, which are not included in the expert knowledge. The possible conflicts between the preferences of the investor and the expert knowledge are resolved either by a priori revelation and/or by interactive revelation. In the a priori revelation a parameter is defined for the preference base or for every separate preference rule to determine if the conflicting expert knowledge should be overridden or not. According to the interactive revelation, the investor's preference is revealed whenever he disagrees with the expert's opinion.

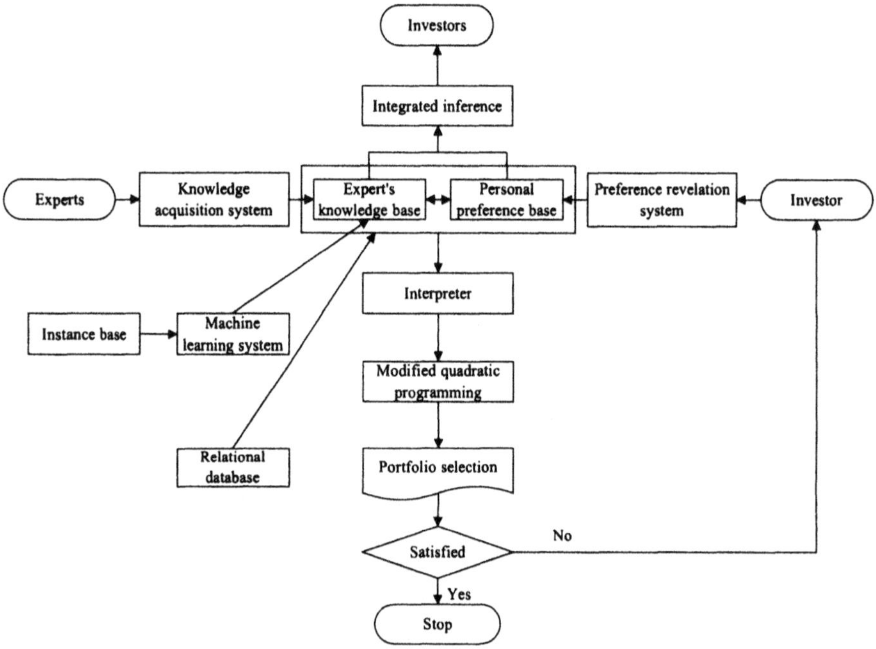

Figure 4.7. Structure of the ISPMS system (Source: Lee et al., 1989)

(iv) Using an interpreter the qualitative factors in the knowledge and preference base are associated with the quadratic programming model, by interpreting them as decision variables or additional constraints. For example, consider the rule:

IF	Company = C_1
OR	Company = C_2
THEN	AMOUNT $\leq$ 100.000
AND	PERCENTAGE = 0.1

From this rule, the following two constraints are derived:

$$M \cdot (x_1 + x_2) \leq 100.000$$
$$x_1 + x_2 = 0.1$$

where M is the total invested amount, and x_1 and x_2 are the portions of the total invested amount which are invested in companies C_1 and C_2 respectively.

The integration of expert knowledge, personal preference, quadratic programming and machine learning, constitutes the major advantage of the ISPMS system. This integrated architecture and concept of the ISPMS system could also be applied in the selection of bonds, personnel, and other complex decision making problems. Furthermore, it is worth noting that the development of the ISPMS system was achieved with the cooperation of a leading investment company in Korea.

4.1.2 The PMIDSS system

Lee and Stohr (1985) developed a prototype intelligent decision support system (PMIDSS) for portfolio management decision making. The prototype uses a mixed knowledge representation scheme: production rules, directed networks and frames to achieve greater flexibility and efficiency. In PMIDSS, domain knowledge is divided into four different layers: general economy and stock market, industries, companies and selected stocks. The knowledge (expertise) in each layer is used to forecast the stock market, to match the current economic situation to prototypical ones in the system and finally to select the most promising stocks (Table 4.3).

Table 4.3. Problem solving steps and knowledge representation schemes in the PMIDSS system (Source: Lee and Stohr, 1985)

Domain	Problem Solving Phase	Knowledge Representation Scheme
Investment-Timing	Forecast stock market and match current situation with prototypes	Question nets Networks Frames Production rules
Stock Selection	Select stocks from a candidate set	Question nets Network of frames Production rules

The system, initially, determines general trends in the economy and stock market and analyzes the observed data to forecast future movements in the stock market. This step uses question nets (a net with nodes representing questions to the decision maker and arcs representing the answers of the decision maker) for observation and a directed network representation, called expectation derivation net, for analysis. In the second step, a collection of frames is used to select scenarios fitting the economic conditions. During the third step, a set of production rules uses the output of the expectation derivation net and the frames to determine if the situation is favorable for common stock investment. Once the problem context has been determined, the system using question nets formulates investor's objectives (step four). In the fifth step, a directed network of frames is used to select a set of promising stocks. Finally, with a set of promising stocks selected, a management science model (mean-variance analysis) is used to determine an optimal portfolio of stocks.

From the above brief description of the PMIDSS system, it is clear that the development of this system focused mainly on the organization and representation of knowledge. Its main goal is the structure of the appropriate decision making process in portfolio selection and management problems. A future step would be the practical implementation of this representation scheme in real world problems.

4.1.3 The StockAdvisor system

In contrast to the previous two KBDSSs which were oriented towards the stock selection and portfolio construction problems, the StockAdvisor system developed by Liu and Lee (1997) is oriented towards stock trading. The system's main functionality is to perform a technical analysis of the stocks and to provide appropriate buy/sell recommendations to the portfolio manager/investor. Rather than developing a stand-alone system, the StockAdviror has been designed and developed as a supplement (add-in) to Microsoft's Excel taking advantage of the database and graphical illustration capabilities that this well-known spreadsheet software can provide. Figure 4.8 presents the structure of the system.

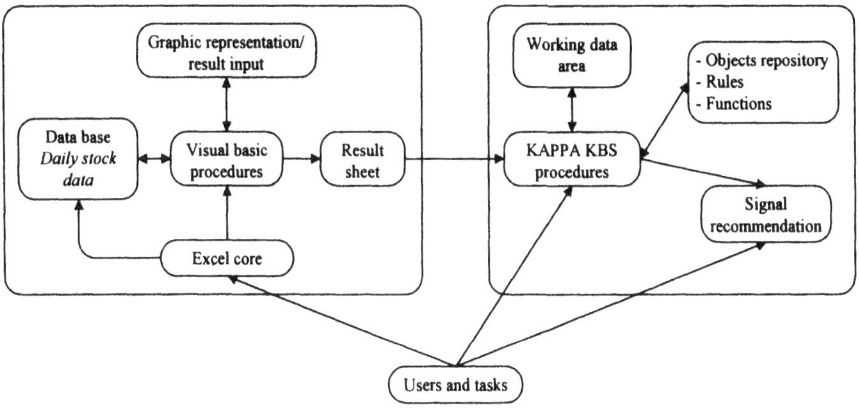

Figure 4.8. Structure of the StockAdvisor system (Source: Liu and Lee, 1997)

The recommendations of the system are based on three classes of technical analysis indicators, including momentum indicators (stochastic, relative strength index, money flow), moving averages (simple and exponential moving average) and trendlines (support and resistance lines). Each of these three major classes includes a series of indicators, all represented in the system through a hierarchical frame-based representation form. The production rules incorporated in the knowledge base of the system were derived according to the technical analysis theory on the selected indicators. The analysis performed by the system is based on daily stock market data of the stocks including their closing price, their highest and lowest intra-day price as well as the daily volume of transactions. On the basis of these data, the system constructs several technical analysis charts which except for a data representation means, they are also used to elicit qualitative information from the user with regard to the technical analysis charts. The ultimate result of the system involves buy/sell recommendations, which are associated with a degree of certainty measured through a four-point qualitative scale (low, moderate, high and very high). The conducted analysis involves short-term, long-term and mid-term periods. Finally, the system enables the user to incorporate in the analysis his/her risk-aversion policy through the definition of appropriate weights of the three major classes of technical analysis indicators that are considered. The performance of the system has been tested by the authors to the Hong Kong stock exchange with encouraging results in terms of the return of the stock trading strategies formulated through system.

4.2 Financial planning

4.2.1 The HYPER-SAVINGS system

The HYPER-SAVINGS system developed by Lee and Nam (1997) is a KBDSS for constructing savings portfolios consisting of multiple investment products that banks provide. The construction of the portfolios is based on the solution of an integer programming problem. The objective of the integer programming formulation is to maximize the cash value at the end of the planning horizon. The output of the solution process involves the amount of investment for each product per day along the planning horizon (i.e., the deposits and withdrawals from the considered savings accounts) as well as the type and day of computing interests. Binary 0-1 variables are introduced in the integer programming formulation to represent some logical relationships, such as the fact that if the balance of a product, which has mutually exclusive products, is not zero then the balance of the mutually exclusive products should be zero.

Similarly to the ISPMS system that has been described above for portfolio selection and management, the HYPER-SAVINGS system also uses a knowledge-based approach to facilitate the formulation of the integer programming problem to be solved. Using a frame-based approach the system represents the investor characteristics, the savings products characteristics, the characteristics of the institutions that issue the considered products as well as the characteristics of the investment schedule such as the initial amount of capital, the planning horizon, the cash flow schedule, etc. The system transforms all this information into the integer programming formulation to determine the savings portfolio of the investor as well as the savings schedule that he/she must follow. Overall the architecture of the system is presented in Figure 4.9.

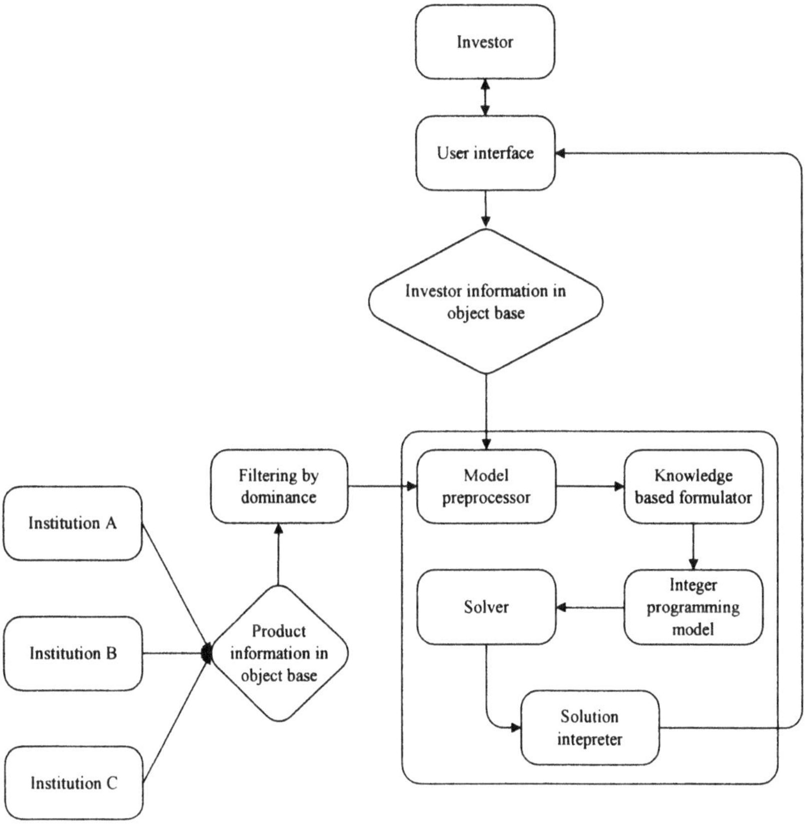

Figure 4.9. Structure of the HYPER-SAVINGS system (Source: Lee and Nam, 1997)

4.2.2 The CASH MANAGER system

The CASH MANAGER (McBride et al., 1989) system employs a similar approach to the HYPER-SAVINGS system. The objective of the CASH MANAGER system is to provide support in making decisions involving cash management problems. The system addresses the cash management problem using a network-based approach. The nodes of the network represent the points in time where decisions are taken, while the arcs linking the nodes represent the cash flows from one time period to another. The exploitation of the constructed network in order to maximize the cash available at the end of the considered time period is achieved through linear programming techniques.

The system incorporates two knowledge bases. The first one involves the financial instruments, which are available as investment alternatives. The instruments are defined and represented using a frame-based approach. The second knowledge base is responsible for structuring the problem in a network form and for managing the solution process. The main task performed by this knowledge base is to perform feasibility tests on the problem that is formulated in order to ensure that an acceptable solution can be found. Initially feasibility checks are performed during the definition of the available investment instruments to avoid possible inconsistencies. In a second stage a series of feasibility checks is performed on the constructed network. If infeasibility is detected the user is informed and feedback is provided regarding the limitations of the considered investment instruments. An additional functionality of this knowledge base is to facilitate the sensitivity analysis process in order to consider the possible uncertainty encountered in the inflows and outflows during the investment period.

4.3 Credit granting

4.3.1 The LASS system

The LASS system (Lending Analysis Support System) was developed by Duchessi and Belardo (1987) for commercial loan analysis problems. The aim of the system is to structure the commercial loan analysis process, proposing the proper models that should be used and the analyses that the decision maker should take, according to the available data. Additionally, the system takes into account the applicability of several analytical models and techniques. Thus, the system provides guidance throughout the decision process interpreting the derived results and proposing the appropriate further steps that the decision maker should take.

The structuring of the analysis process is carried out through the knowledge base of the system. This knowledge base includes knowledge concerning the problem domain (i.e. the commercial loan analysis) and the available data, the structuring of an analysis in this problem domain and the financial modeling techniques that constitute the solution procedures. These three parts of the knowledge base are structured in a hierarchy from the most abstract concepts to the most specific concepts. The most abstract concepts define the problem domain and are related to several categories of loan analyses, such as commercial loan analysis, real estate loan analysis, personal loan analysis, etc. The more specific concepts provide the means to focus on specific areas of the loan analysis, such as capacity, collateral, and capital. Each of these are further defined by more detailed structural elements. For example, capital analysis involves the analysis of the financial structure, profitability analysis and assets analysis.

The knowledge is represented in the knowledge base of the system through the combination of a semantic network with production rules. The semantic network provides a graphical representation of several concepts and objects related to the loan analysis as well as the relations among them (Figure 4.10). The nodes of the network represent different concepts, while the links represent the relation of the concepts. For example, a relationship called "a-kind-of" (AKO) is used to represent knowledge such as "commercial loan analysis is a kind of loan analysis". Combining a set of link types such as "a-component-of" (ACO), "determines" (D) and "modeled-by" (MB), it is possible to represent more complicated knowledge, such as "profitability analysis is a component of capital analysis and it is modeled by return on investment and return on equity".

The use of the semantic network is combined with the use of production rules. The production rules provide the means for moving across the several parts of the network, according to the available data and problem conditions. An example of a production rule of the LASS system is the following:

IF	earnings are stable
AND	revenue is increasing
THEN	calculate a trend for gross margin and examine market conditions.

Through a powerful user interface it is possible to move from the knowledge base to the model base which includes several analysis techniques. Through the user interface it is also possible to transfer the results derived from the analytical decision models back in the knowledge base. The results are evaluated through the knowledge base and thus, new analyses may be proposed (the interpretation of the obtained results is achieved). More specifically, the LASS system performs the analysis of commercial loans in the following four phases:

1. Initially, the system attempts to collect information about the problem and the available data for subsequent analyses.

2. Next, the system begins to construct the analysis process according to the relationships represented in its knowledge base.
3. During the third phase, the actual analysis is performed for the loan officer, either automatically by the system or suggesting available models.
4. Finally, during the fourth phase of the process, the system activates other analysis according to the results of the most recent analysis and the logical problem structuring provided by the results.

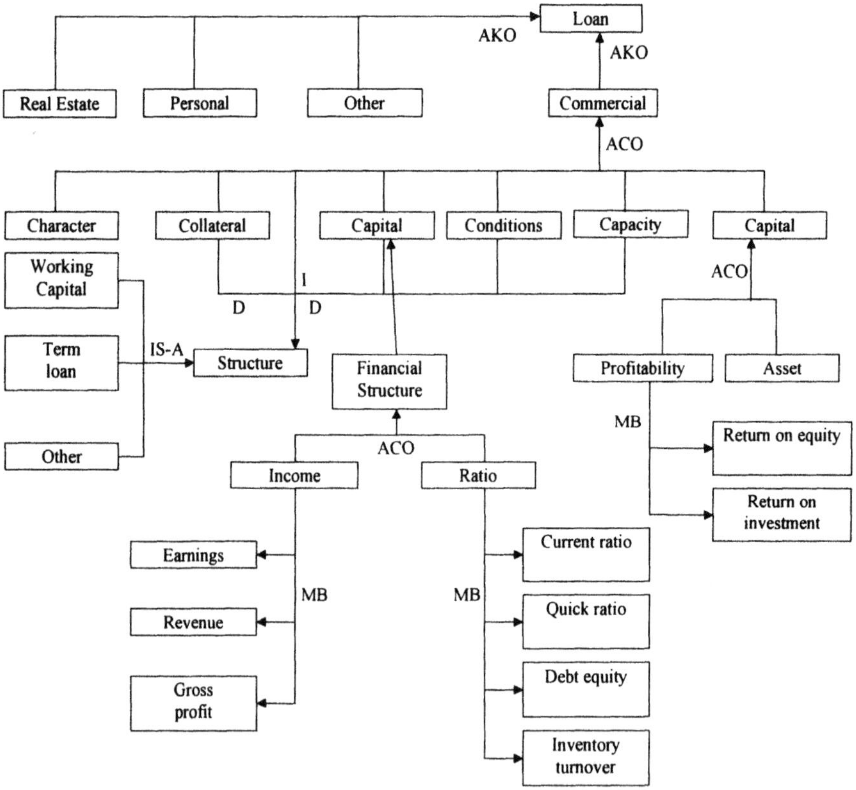

Figure 4.10. Partial network representation of the LASS system (Source: Duchessi and Belardo, 1987)

The LASS system has been developed in a prototype form (it has not been commercially used yet) concerning only commercial loan analysis problems. Therefore, more rules could be included in its knowledge base to evaluate all kinds of loan applications and new more sophisticated models should be added in its model base to perform a complete loan analysis.

4.3.2 The MARBLE system

Similarly to the previous two systems described above, the MARBLE system (Managing and Recommending Business Loan Evaluation; Shaw and Gentry, 1988) is also developed for the study of credit granting problems. The special feature of the system is its ability to induce knowledge from decision instances using inductive learning techniques. An additional special feature of the system is its ability to handle incomplete information using a probabilistic approach that associates a certainty factor to each production rule of the knowledge base of the system. Figure 4.11 presents the structure of the system.

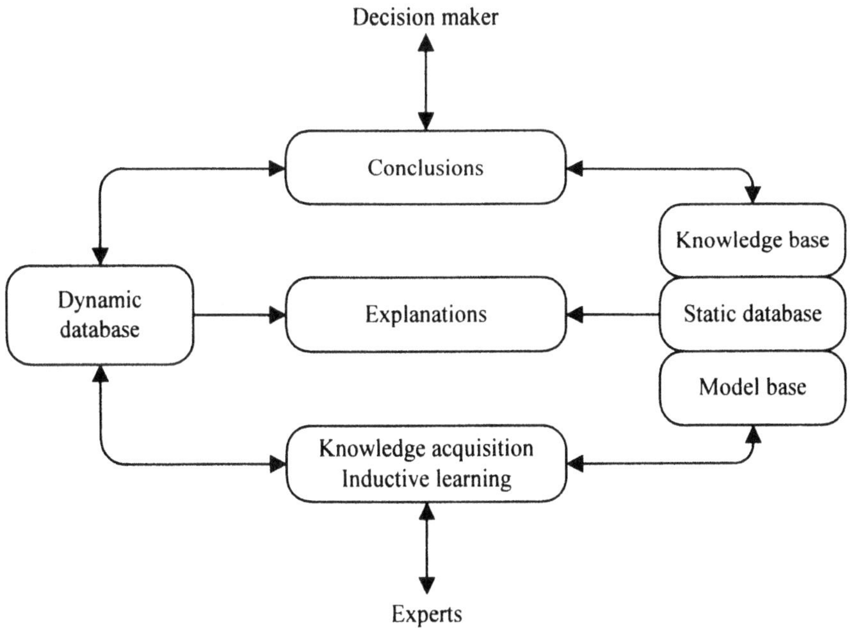

Figure 4.11. Structure of the MARBLE system (Source: Shaw and Gentry, 1988)

The system includes two distinct databases, the static database and the dynamic database. The static database includes historical information and data on the firms that apply for credit, while the dynamic database is used to store temporarily the conclusions and the estimations drawn by the system. The knowledge base of the system includes production rules that are used to derive decisions on the acceptance or rejection of a credit application. The rules are organized into homogenous sets, each one of which is used to evaluate different aspects of the firms that seek financing. For instance there are rules related to the profitability of the firms, their solvency, the collateral that they provide, etc. The model base includes several decision analysis tools including mathematical programming and regression analysis.

The system begins the analysis by asking the credit analyst to provide information for the firm under consideration. The analyst does not have to provide complete information. In case of incomplete information on the characteristics of a firm, the result of the evaluation process will have a probabilistic form involving the level of certainty of the derived conclusion. The ultimate outcome of the system involves the classification of each firm into three classes according to its level of credit risk: (i) the low-risk class, (ii) the class of intermediate risk and (iii) the high-risk class. The decisions taken through the system can be used to update and modify the knowledge of the system through the inductive learning techniques.

4.3.3 The KABAL system

Hartvigsen (1990) presented the KABAL knowledge-based system (Kabal is the Norwegian word for patience) for financial analysis in the trade and industry portfolio in Norwegian saving banks (the system was developed with the cooperation of a Norwegian bank which uses it for the evaluation of firms' performance). The KABAL system includes analysis of the financial statements, guarantees, market, and company management and organization. Figure 4.12 gives an overview of the structure of the KABAL system, its different modules and their relationships.

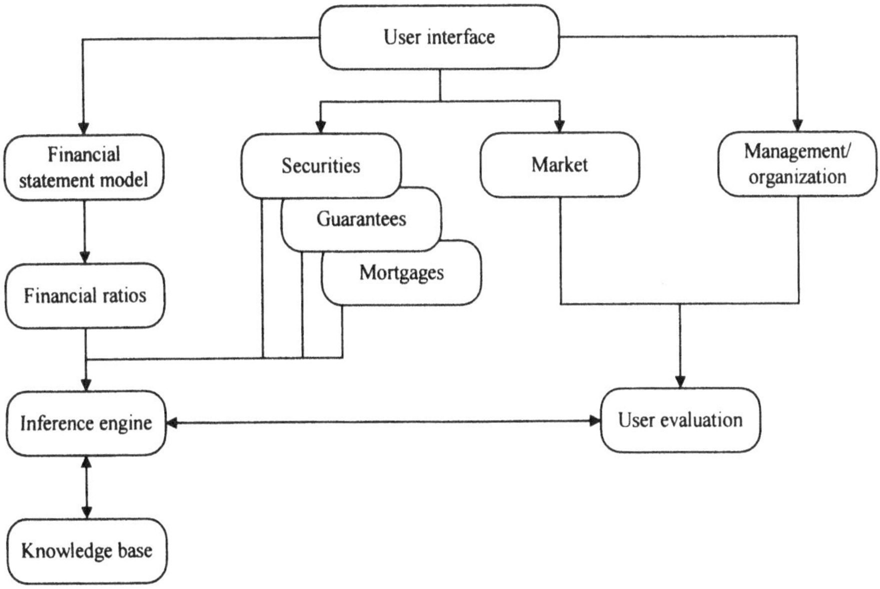

Figure 4.12. Structure of the KABAL system (Source: Hartvigsen, 1990)

The "heart" of the KABAL system is its knowledge base. It contains knowledge concerning the analysis of financial statements. This analysis is accomplished through the examination of their profitability, solidity, liquidity and financial structure. Each one of these four categories is further divided in more specific sub-categories, which are evaluated across one or more financial ratios.

Table 4.4 presents an example of the analysis that the KABAL system performs, concerning the profitability of a firm.

The system during the analysis examines not only the financial data of the companies but also some external factors of the companies, such as inflation, the rate of interest on deposits, the bank overdraft, the average risk and the average gross income of the branch where the firm belongs.

In the development of the KABAL system, the protocol analysis was used as the main acquisition technique to acquire the knowledge from the expert financial analysts of a Norwegian bank. The protocol analysis is recursive and concurrent. In the recursive protocol sessions the financial analyst is asked to look at previous cases of loan control, while in the concurrent protocol sessions the analyst is asked to analyze a complex case expressing his actions until his final decision.

Table 4.4. The results of a profitability analysis by the KABAL system (Source: Hartvigsen, 1990)

Profitability

The company's profitability, i.e. the operational performance of the company, is set to be relatively bad.

	1980	1981	1982
Return on investment	27.78	22.49	15.58
Return on equity	15.72	10.15	5.52
Gross income	46.15	46.67	47.14

- The reasons for the reduction of the return on investment are that the
  - Operation costs increase by 5%
  - Costs of goods sold increase by 3%
  - Wage bill increases by 6%
  - Other operating costs increase by 9%
  - Depreciation increases by 20%
  - Total current assets increase by 51%
  - Inventory semi and finished products increase by 62%
  - Accounts receivable increase by 40%
- The reasons for the reduction of the return on equity are that the
  - Total operating costs increase by 5%
  - Total financial costs increase by 43%
  - Average equity costs increase by 8%
- The reasons for the growth of the gross income are that the
  - Interest charges increase by 4%

The basic characteristic of the KABAL system is the combination of both quantitative and qualitative criteria (market, management, organization, etc.) in the analysis of corporate performance. The system provides several tools for handling qualitative information such as questionnaires and checklists. The knowledge base of the system evaluates the financial status of the firms, while the evaluation of the qualitative information concerning the operation of the firm is made by the decision maker with the assistance of questionnaires and checklists. A possible future direction in the development of the KABAL system could be the incorporation of another knowledge base to analyze the non-financial elements. Furthermore, the system does not distinguish the companies according to their business sectors. The business sector which a firm belongs to affects the assessment of its performance and therefore should be examined during the evaluation process.

4.4 Mergers and acquisitions

Hashemi et al. (1998) developed a hybrid intelligent system to predict the ownership status of banks. The system performs an analysis of the financial characteristics of the banks based on a financial ratio analysis involving liquidity, leverage and profitability ratios. Additionally some other aspects of the banks' operation are also considered such as their credit risk exposure, their efficiency and productivity as well as the structure of their loan portfolios. On the basis of this information the banks are classified into four groups according to their holding structure:

(i) banks not owned by another company,

(ii) single banks owned by another company,

(iii) pairs of banks held by another company and

(iv) three or more banks held by another company.

Using this four-group classification approach the system enables the user to relate the characteristics of the banks to their ownership status. It enables the development of models to predict bank mergers and acquisitions and identify potential target banks for merger or acquisition.

The development of the bank merger/acquisition prediction models through the system is accomplished through the use of artificial intelligent techniques and more specifically through the integration of the rough sets with neural networks. In the proposed intelligent system, the rough set theory is used to reduce the available data into the most significant ones that can contribute to the classification of the banks into the four considered classes. In contrast to the traditional rough set theory, data reduction in the system is performed in two dimensions, including the condition attributes (i.e., the characteristics of the banks) which is the common approach used within the rough set theory framework as well as the objects (i.e., banks) considered during the model development stage (training sample). Thus, all redundant conditions (banks or characteristics) that do not contribute to the classification performance of the system during model development are ignored. The outcome of this rough set analysis is used as a training set to a neural network, used to develop the model for the prediction of bank holding structures.

The performance of the system has been examined on a sample of 256 U.S. banks described over 28 variables regarding all the aforementioned aspects of their performance and operation. The evaluation of the performance of the system has been conducted in two stages in order to identify whether the combination of rough sets with neural networks could provide synergetic results or not. In that respect, initially the system has been applied without considering the data reduction process through the rough set approach. The configuration of the constructed neural network consisted of one hidden layer of 8 nodes, an input layer of 28 nodes and an output layer of 4 nodes. This neural network classified correctly all banks included in the training sample, while its performance in a testing sample reached the classification accuracy of 83.3%. In a second stage the rough set approach has been used to achieve the reduction of the available information. Among the initially considered 28 characteristics of the banks 18 were found significant and thus retained in the analysis, while 12 banks were found non significant to contribute in the classification performance of the system and they were, therefore, discarded. The new neural network constructed had the same configuration with the initial one, but with one node less in its hidden layer. The performance of the neural network model in the training set was once again 100%, while its performance in the testing set was significantly improved compared to the neural network developed in the previous stage from 83.3% to 95.8%. In the same case study a multiple discriminant analysis was also performed for comparative purposes. In the initial sample, were no data reduction was considered, discriminant analysis resulted to a classification accuracy of 25% (in the testing sample), while after data reduction the accuracy increased to 45.8%. In both cases the superiority of the developed hybrid intelligent system is apparent.

Slowinski et al. (1997) have also used successfully the rough set approach in predicting corporate acquisitions. The comparison that they have conducted with discriminant analysis has also shown the superiority of the rough set theory over conventional statistical classification approaches.

4.5 Bond rating

Similarly to the above system for predicting bank holding structures, Shin and Han (1999) also proposed an hybrid intelligent system for corporate bond rating. The main methodological feature of the system is the combination of a case-based reasoning approach with genetic algorithms (Figure 4.13).

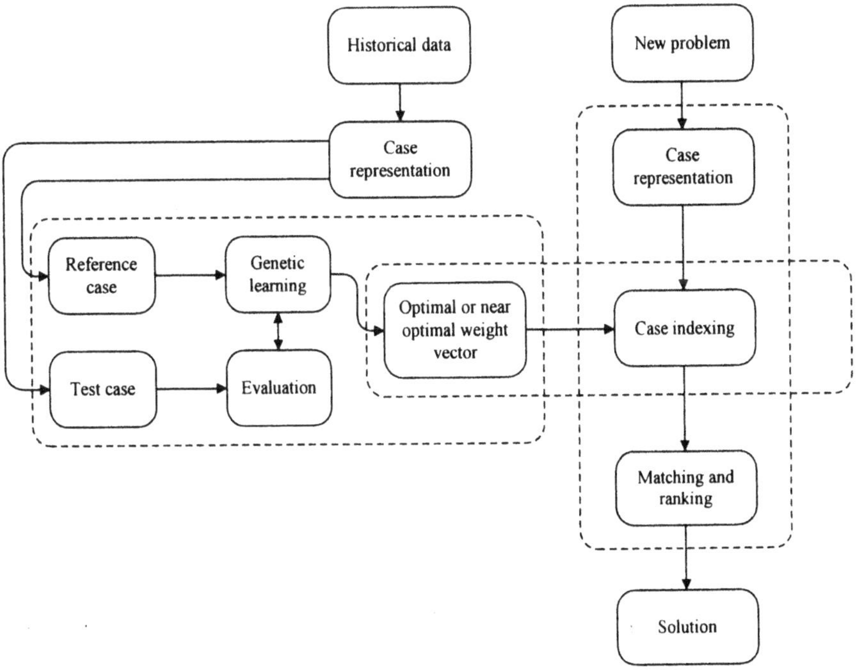

Figure 4.13. Structure of the case-based reasoning/genetic algorithms system for corporate bond rating (Source: Shin and Han, 1999)

The aim of the system is to evaluate the bonds issued by corporate entities and classify them into credit level classes on the basis of the financial characteristics of the firms and their type. The classification of the bonds is achieved through a case-based reasoning approach. The case indexing and retrieving processes which are necessary during the application of case-based reasoning are facilitated through genetic algorithms used to determine the significance of the attributes considered in the bond rating process. The analysis conducted by the system proceeds through three phases.

1. In the first phase a genetic optimization problem is formulated to determine an optimal or near optimal weight vector for the considered bond rating evaluation criteria, using the case base, which consists of corporate bonds already classified into one of the four predefined classes.
2. During the second stage a validation of the derived weight vector is performed. The weight vector is applied for case retrieval in order to evaluate and classify a set of validation cases (bonds) for which their rating is known. If the validation test does not provide a satisfactory result (classification accuracy), then the genetic optimization problem is reformulated with new solution parameters to determine an alternative weight vector.
3. If the validation tests are successful, the process proceeds to the third and final phase, where the user can ask for the rating and classification of any new corporate bond. In this stage the system retrieves cases that match the description of the current bond, from the case base. This is done using the weight vector determined through the genetic optimization problem.

The performance of the system was evaluated on a sample of 3886 corporate bonds issued by Korean companies. The sample was split into three subsets: 80% for estimating the optimal weight vector through the genetic optimization approach, 10% for evaluating the optimal weight vector (validation tests) and 10% for testing purposes. The results of the hybrid case-based reasoning/genetic algorithms approach were compared to multiple discriminant analysis, the ID3 rule induction algorithm (Quinlan, 1986) as well as several alternative approaches to introduce weights into the case-based reasoning framework, including experts' opinion, Pearson's coefficients, regression analysis, F tests, and naïve equal criterion weighting. With respect to all comparison the proposed hybrid approach provided considerably better results, classifying correctly 75.5% of the corporate bonds of the testing sample, while the results of the other considered approaches ranged from 56% (case-based reasoning in combination with F tests) to 63.5% (case-based reasoning in combination with Pearson's coefficients).

Chapter 5

INTELLIGENT MULTICRITERIA DSSs

1. BRIEF HISTORY ON MULTICRITERIA DECISION SUPPORT

The discussion of the basic MCDA concepts and approaches in chapter 2 demonstrated that the decision maker and his/her preferences constitute the focal point of interest within the MCDA methodological framework. This special characteristic of MCDA is in accordance with the decision making process in complex and ill-structured problem domains. In such cases, since there is no apparent straightforward, algorithmic solution process, the way that the problem will be tackled depends on the decision makers' perception and policy. Consequently a comprehensive model that describes reality cannot be developed. Instead, it is possible to develop a model that corresponds to the decision maker's perception of the problem at hand, his/her requirements, preferences and judgement.

The development of such a model within the MCDA framework is achieved through an iterative and interactive process, until the decision maker's preferences are consistently represented in the model. Such an iterative and interactive process can be time-consuming and consequently highly impractical, especially in case of large problem domains involving many alternative solutions as well as in cases where real-time support is required. Financial engineering is such a field requiring the analysis and consideration of a plethora of alternatives and scenarios over limited time.

This difficulty has been acknowledged even from the early stages of MCDA research. The pioneer MCDA researchers soon realized that one of the key issues regarding the implementation of MCDA in practice, should not only be the advances on the theoretical aspects regarding the founding disciplines of MCDA and its methodological developments, but also the design and development of computerized systems incorporating the MCDA theory into their structure. The existing DSSs framework provided the necessary means to implement this goal. Associating database capabilities to an advanced user interface facilitating the interactive and iterative nature of the MCDA methodologies was clearly a significant research direction towards the further development and success of MCDA. Thus, gradually a new form of DSS has been established, incorporating in its model base MCDA methodologies. The term "multicriteria decision support system" (MCDSS) has been consolidated to describe this special category of DSSs.

The first MCDSSs to be developed in the 1970s were mainly oriented towards the study of multiobjective mathematical programming problems (Dyer, 1973; Wallenius and Zionts, 1976). These early pioneer systems, mainly due to the limited capabilities of computer technology during that period, were primarily developed for academic purposes, they were implemented in mainframe computers, with no documentation available, while they had no visual representation capabilities (Korhonen et al., 1992). After the appearance of these first systems, MCDSSs became one of the major areas of DSSs research and significant progress has been made both on the theoretical and the practical/implementation viewpoints. The survey of Eom et al. (1993) confirms this remark. The authors conducted a comprehensive study on 259 articles related to DSSs applications over the period 1971-1989 to identify the various sub-fields of DSSs research, the major contributing disciplines and the subsets of functional management that influenced DSSs' development. The results of a factor analysis showed that MCDA was the third important factor that has influenced DSSs research and development, just after the founding disciplines of DSSs and the group DSSs research. MCDSSs was the sixth most significant factor.

The special issue on MCDSSs published in the Journal of Information Science and Technology (Siskos and Zopounidis, 1993) presents some of the advances made in this field over the last decade and several applications in portfolio selection and management, environmental management, regional development and group decision support.

Today, after almost thirty years of ongoing research and advances in MCDA, DSSs, and computer science, there are several MCDSSs developed academically or even for commercial use. Table 5.1 reports some of the most representative MCDSSs that have been developed, categorized according to the MCDA approach that they employ.

Table 5.1. Some representative example well-known MCDSSs

MCDA approach employed	MCDSSs
Multiobjective/goal programming	STRANGE (Teghem et al., 1986) VIG (Korhonen, 1987) VIDMA (Korhonen, 1988) ADELAIS (Siskos and Despotis, 1989) DIDAS (Lewandowski et al., 1989) TRIMAP (Climaco and Antunes, 1989) ADBASE (Steuer, 1992) AIM (Lofti et al., 1992) TOMMIX (Antunes et al., 1992)
Multiattribute utility theory	EXPERT CHOICE (Selly and Forman, 1986) VISA (Belton and Vickers, 1989) MACBETH (Bana e Costa and Vansnick, 1994)
Outranking relations	PRIAM (Levine and Pomerol, 1986) ELECTRE TRI (Yu, 1992) ELECCALC (Kiss et al., 1994) PROMCALC/GAIA (Brans and Mareschal, 1994)
Preference disaggregation analysis	PREFCALC (Jacquet-Lagrèze, 1990) MINORA (Siskos et al., 1993) MIIDAS (Siskos et al., 1999) FINCLAS (Zopounidis and Doumpos, 1998a) PREFDIS (Zopounidis and Doumpos, 2000)

2. MCDSSs FUNCTIONALITY AND MAIN FEATURES

The general characteristics and basic tasks that a MCDSS performs do not differ from those of traditional DSSs, including database management (storage, retrieval, query, etc.) and model base management (model development, update, etc.). However, the specific functionalities and operations that MCDSSs perform should be viewed with respect to the MCDA context that constitutes their underlying methodological tool and major distinguishing characteristic from other forms of DSSs. The major issue in all MCDA methodologies is to identify the criteria aggregation model that best fits the decision problem at hand, allow the decision maker to define the economic or technical parameters of the model in an interactive and iterative way and ultimately evaluate the considered alternatives on the basis of the constructed model to select the most appropriate, to rank or classify them. Throughout this analysis process the identification and development of the aggregation model is the most critical step. Thus, the tasks performed by a MCDSS are mainly oriented towards criteria and preference modeling as well as the management of the aggregation process, including among others (Pomerol, 1993):

- Interactive addition, deletion or modification of criteria.
- Assessment and management of weights.
- Visual interactive modeling to facilitate problem structuring and analysis.
- Interactive definition of parameters of the aggregation process, facilitated by visual representations.
- Sensitivity analysis regarding the significance of the evaluation criteria and their impact on the outcome of the aggregation process.
- Selection of the form of the criteria aggregation model.

Some of these points, including visual representations and sensitivity analysis, are also common features in other forms of DSSs. Nevertheless, their implementation with the MCDSSs framework usually serves different purposes than the ones used in the traditional DSSs' context. For instance, while sensitivity analysis in the DSSs' context is usually conducted in order to identify how the changes in the decision environment can affect the decision taken, within the MCDSSs context sensitivity analysis is mainly focused on determining how changes in the significance level assigned to the evaluation criteria can affect the outcome of the aggregation process. Some common issues addressed through sensitivity analysis in the MCDSSs framework include the change of the evaluation of the alternatives (choice, ranking, sorting/classification) according to the weights of the criteria, the determination of appropriate ranges in the weights of the criteria so that the evaluation of the alternatives is retained unchanged, as well as the identification of the weighting scheme leading to a specific evaluation result. On the other hand, the visual representations used within the MCDSSs context are not only used for presenting results and reports; they also serve as a significant tool that facilitates the interactivity of the system, in order to elicit information by the decision maker regarding his/her preferences, in order to define appropriately the parameters of the criteria aggregation model and proceed appropriately with the interactive solution process.

With regard to the aggregation model functionalities, most MCDSSs support one or at most two types of decision problems (i.e., choice, ranking, sorting/classification). This depends on the MCDA methodologies that each system employs. For instance, MCDSSs implementing multiobjective/goal programming techniques support only choice problems. Such systems typical employ a specific process to solve the considered multiobjective/goal programming problem, rather than an arsenal of solution methodologies. There are two main reasons that justify this "limitation". Firstly, multiobjective/goal programming techniques are often quite complex while the parameters they incorporate differ. Consequently, incorporating more than one multiobjective/goal programming technique into the same MCDSS would increase significantly the complexity of the system and consequently the effort required by the decision maker in order to use it effectively. Secondly, all methods would actually yield the same result, since they all search the solution that best meets the decision makers' preferences. Therefore, assuming that the form of interaction between the system and the decision maker can result to the successful elicitation of the decision maker's preferences, there should be no divergence on the obtained solution, regardless of the solution technique that is employed. The only difference among the existing multiobjective/goal programming techniques involves their efficiency regarding their ability to converge as fast as possible to the final solution.

MCDSSs employing multiattribute utility theory, outranking relations, or preference disaggregation analysis techniques, accommodate choice, ranking as well as classification problems. Some of them can address both choice and ranking problems since several MCDA methods originally developed to address choice problems have variants that are appropriate for ranking problems as well. For instance the PROMETHEE I develops an outranking relation and exploits it to addresses choice problems, while PROMETHEE II employs the developed outranking relation in a different way to solve ranking problems. To our knowledge there is no MCDSSs that can support all three types of "problematiques", despite the fact that some of them enable the decision maker to select different form of aggregation models, which however are based on the same theoretical stream of MCDA.

The determination of the parameters of the criteria aggregation models (model development) is a process that involves the direct interrogation of the decision maker. This interrogation can be performed in two distinct levels.

1. At the first level, the decision maker is the only one responsible for the specification of the parameters of the aggregation model. The MCDSS employs an interactive dialog to facilitate the specification of the parameters by the decision maker, using terms which are as less technical as possible. Often, throughout the interrogation process the MCDSS performs consistency checks on the responses of the decision maker. This form of interrogation is commonly employed in MCDSSs incorporating multiobjective/goal programming techniques, outranking relations or MAUT approaches.
2. At the second level, initially the MCDSS performs an automatic parameter estimation procedure. The results regarding the estimated parameters and the evaluation of the considered alternatives according to the selected aggregation model are presented to the decision maker. At this point the interrogation with the decision maker takes place. The decision maker is asked to evaluate the obtained results considering his/her preferences and make any necessary adjustments either to the parameters' estimates obtained through the MCDSS, or to the structure of the model by removing criteria from the analysis, adding new ones, etc. Such an approach is typically employed by MCDSSs based on the preference disaggregation approach.

In contrast to this aggregation model specification and criteria/preference modeling orientation of MCDSSs, for most of them the alternatives are less important. Of course, several forms of graphical representations are employed to represent the alternatives in the criteria space, thus facilitating the comparison either between each other, or to some reference profiles (e.g., ideal points), but typically alternatives are assumed to be already known and pre-specified by the decision maker. Thus, the scope of MCDSSs is commonly restricted to the evaluation of the existing alternatives rather than their construction. This is only achieved, at least partially, in MCDSSs that employ multiobjective/goal programming techniques. Such systems enable the decision maker to search the solution space (infinite feasible solutions) in order to identify a non apparent solution that meets the imposed constraints. However, even in this case the systems do not design new alternatives, but instead they search for an existing, yet not easy identifiable one.

3. THE CONTRIBUTION OF ARTIFICIAL INTELLIGENCE

MCDSSs address a series of issues throughout the decision making process to include preference modeling, criteria modeling, decision model development and specification, sensitivity analysis, etc. This very broad decision analysis context has the potentials and often the requirement for additional improvements over its elementary aspects, involving methodological issues as well as the decision maker's role and form of participation in the conducted analysis. The wide range of tools developed within the framework of artificial intelligence and the diversity in the decision modeling potentials has attracted the interest of MCDA researchers towards their integration in the existing MCDSSs context. Generally, the contribution of this new approach can be distinguished with respect to the following three aspects:

1. The interaction between the user and the system.
2. The operation of the methodological tools employed in the MCDSS.
3. The special features of the problem domain.

The subsequent subsections discuss in more details the new potentials that artificial intelligence techniques provide with respect to each of these three aspects.

3.1 The interaction between the user and the system

Despite the significant functionalities that MCDSSs provide to decision makers in addressing real-world problems through a comprehensive and realistic approach, they are often too "technical" to be used by decision makers that do not have the required background on the methodological tools employed in MCDSSs. Of course, the advances made towards the development of graphical user interfaces and the resulting extensive use of visual interactive modeling techniques in most of the modern MCDSSs have contributed in addressing this issue. However, still more support is required.

The artificial intelligence technology provides the means to incorporate the required additional supportive functionalities to the existing MCDSSs' framework. ESs are the basic tools used for this purpose. The integration of ESs with the MCDSSs framework can be achieved on the basis of the principles described in the previous chapter regarding the integration of ESs with DSSs. Since the aim of the ESs is to help the decision maker in using the MCDSS effectively, the first form of integration between ESs and DSSs is adopted (i.e., the association of an ES to each structural component of the DSS, in this case to each structural component of the MCDSS). The tasks that the ESs can perform in this form of integration include:

- Guidance during data entry in order to ensure that the available information on the considered problem is used appropriately as input to the MCDA methods.
- Explanations on the parameters of the MCDA methods that are employed in the model base of the MCDSS.
- Elicitation of preferential information by the decision maker, using natural language terms and appropriate representation of the acquired information so that it can be used by the MCDA methods.
- Consistency checks to detect inconsistencies in any preferential information specified by the decision maker.
- Support on the selection of the MCDA methods and the form of the aggregation model that should be used to address the considered problem.
- Appropriate presentation and explanation of the results in natural language to facilitate the decision maker's understanding of the outcomes of the MCDSS.

Of course, all these tasks do not improve directly the performance of the MCDSS, in terms of the quality of the results that it provides. However, there is an indirect improvement through the increase of the decision maker's understanding of the functionalities of the system and the guidance provided towards its appropriate use.

3.2 The operation of the methodological tools employed in the MCDSS

Except for the integration of artificial intelligence techniques within the MCDSSs framework to facilitate the decision maker in using the systems, another major line of MCDA research is to exploit the tools provided by artificial intelligence towards the development of an advanced decision analysis, modeling and solution framework. Some of the existing issues on this research direction involve the implementation of innovative solution techniques in multiobjective/goal programming formulations, the management of uncertainty and fuzziness within the MCDA framework as well as the implementation of innovative approaches in eliciting preferential information from the decision makers and representing it.

To all these issues neural networks, fuzzy sets, rough sets as well as genetic algorithms have provided significant contributions.

- *Neural networks*

The estimation of a utility function representing the decision maker's preferences is often a crucial process within the MCDA problem solving context. The direct estimation process employed in multiattribute utility theory, involving the direct interrogation of the decision maker, is often a cumbersome process that can be time consuming. Neural networks provide the means to overcome this problem in order to estimate the utility function that underlies the decision making policy of the decision maker. The non-linear behavior of neural networks enables the accurate estimation of even highly non-linear utility functions, taking at the same time into consideration all properties of the traditional multiattribute utility theory such as monotonicity, concavity and convexity. Malakooti and Zhou (1994) were among the first to employ this approach in solving ranking problems, while Sun et al. (1996) employed the neural network paradigm in representing the decision maker's preferences during the solution of multiobjective programming problems.

- *Rough sets*

In contrast to other machine learning approaches, the rough set theory has evolved rapidly over the past two decades not only as a tool for rule induction but also as an approach to handle the vagueness encountered in decision making and to describe dependencies among the considered attributes (factors). The former two issues (i.e., handling vagueness and describing dependencies) are of major concern within the MCDA framework. The traditional MCDA approaches often assume that the decision maker implicitly uses a well-structured preference system that leads to decision making. However, decision makers often perform vague evaluations which are quite difficult to model through the traditional MCDA approaches. The rough set theory provides the means to identify vagueness in the decision makers' preferential system and to model this vagueness through a rule-based approach. Furthermore, the rough set can be used as a data analysis tool in order to identify the redundant information in a data set, thus reducing it to consider only the most significant attributes. Finally, over the last years there has been significant research over the construction and exploitation of outranking relations using the rule-based approach employed in the rough set theory (Greco et al., 1998). This enables the application of the rough set theory not only to the study of classification problems but to ranking and choice problems as well.

- *Fuzzy sets*

Similarly to rough sets, the fuzzy set theory has also been extensively used within the MCDA framework, to enable the analysis of fuzziness encountered in decision making. Fuzziness involves several aspects of the decision making process, including among others:

- the fuzzy preferences of the decision makers,
- the fuzzy features of the alternatives with respect to evaluation criteria,
- the fuzzy nature of the decision that should be reached (for instance, deciding on the performance of a firm requires the definition of healthy firms, non-healthy firms, and intermediate firms, among which the boundaries are often not crisp, but fuzzy),
- the fuzziness in the state of the decision environment.

The fuzzy set theory provides an excellent tool to address and model these issues and therefore it is not surprising that MCDA researchers have exploited the potentials of the fuzzy set theory in several ways, including the development and solution of fuzzy multiobjective programming formulations (Lootsma, 1997) and mainly the development and exploitation of fuzzy outranking relations for preference modeling (Roy, 1977).

3.3 The special features of the problem domain

The previous two forms of integration between artificial intelligence techniques and MCDSSs are mainly concerned with the improvement of the general operation of the MCDSSs and their communication with the decision maker as well as with the enchantment of their modeling and solution methodologies.

Nevertheless, decision makers often require some additional form of support that is concerned with the special features of the considered problem domain. For instance, in a financial engineering MCDSS, the potential intelligent support should not only be restricted to the operation of the system and the features of its modeling tools. It could also be extended to accommodate specific financial engineering knowledge. In this way the financial engineer who is the ultimate user of the MCDSS would be benefited from the knowledge of expert financial engineers with respect to the problem that he/she faces.

Incorporating this form of intelligent support enables the MCDSS to conduct an integrated analysis of the problem taking advantage of the preferential information provided by the decision maker as well as of the experts' knowledge. Thus, the ESs technology becomes once again the main tool to introduce some elementary form of intelligence in the MCDSSs' framework. The integration of the two approaches in this case can be performed in two ways:

1. either the ES performs a preliminary investigation and analysis of the problem based on the experts' knowledge, which is refined and extended in a later stage by the MCDA tools of the MCDSS, or
2. the MCDA analysis is initially invoked and the results are introduced into the ES for recommendations and conclusions using

both experts' knowledge as well as knowledge on the MCDA tools employed.

This is actually the ES output-DSS input (and vice versa) form of integration of ESs and DSSs as two separate but complementary modules of a KBDSS, already discussed in Chapter 5.

4. APPLICATIONS OF INTELLIGENT MCDSSs TO FINANCIAL ENGINEERING

The functionalities of intelligent MCDSSs described above, provide a new framework in the study of financial engineering problems, combining the advantageous features of the MCDA approach, with the information processing and decision analysis framework of the DSSs' technology, and the advanced knowledge representation/management, inference procedures, and modeling tools provided by the artificial intelligence field. The subsequent subsections illustrate the way that this new framework can be applied in the context of financial engineering problems, through the presentation of some representative intelligent MCDSSs developed for credit granting (the CGX and CREDEX systems), the assessment of corporate performance and viability (the FINEVA system) and investments appraisal (the INVEX system).

4.1 Credit granting

4.1.1 The CGX system

The CGX system (Srinivasan and Ruparel, 1990) is a multicriteria intelligent decision support system for credit granting problems. The credit granting decision process is modeled through the multicriteria method Analytic Hierarchy Process-AHP (Saaty, 1980), as a 3-level hierarchical problem of the form presented in Figure 5.1.

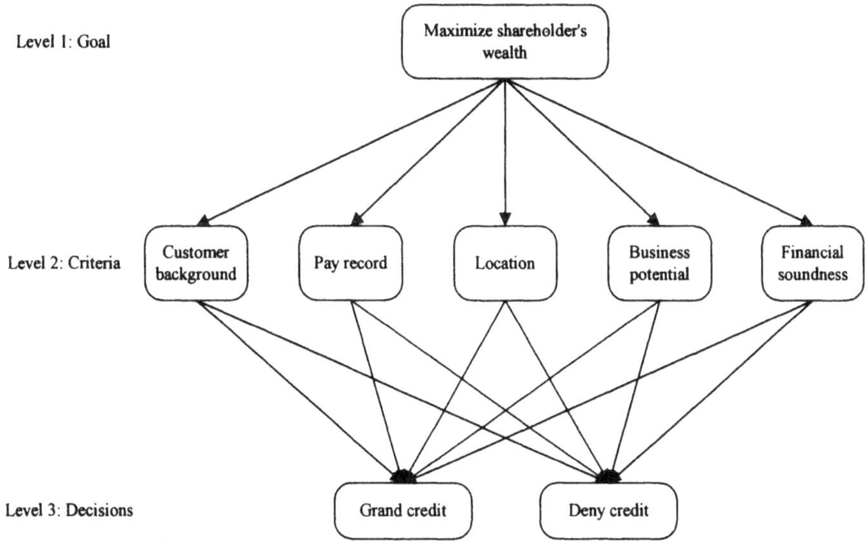

Figure 5.1. Modeling of the credit granting process using the multicriteria method AHP (Source: Srinivasan and Ruparel, 1990)

The first level of the process includes the goal of the credit-granting problem, which should be in accordance with the overall goal of the financial operation of the lending institution, that is the maximization of shareholders' wealth. The second level of the hierarchy includes the evaluation criteria on which the investigation of each credit application will be based. The evaluation criteria are organized into five categories involving the customer's background, pay record, location, business potential and financial soundness. Each of these categories consists of several evaluation criteria that appear into the lower levels of the hierarchy (they are not presented in Figure 5.1 for simplicity reasons). It is important to note that the evaluation criteria include both financial ratios (dept capacity ratios, profitability ratios, liquidity ratios, etc.) as well as qualitative criteria (customer background, pay record, geographical location, business potential, etc.). Finally, the third level of the hierarchy includes the alternative decisions that could be taken, that is the granting or the denying of the credit application. Integrating the local weights of the final level with the appropriate global weights from the criterion level yields a final set of weights for granting and denying credit, representing the probabilities of payment and default respectively. The weights for granting and denying credit are, then, integrated with the expected cash flows associated with the two outcomes, to determine the amount of loan to grant.

The input to the AHP method involves relative comparison data, which are specified in a pairwise way for all pairs of elements in each level with respect to each of the elements in the preceding level of the hierarchy. The first level does not require any comparisons, since it contains only one element (maximization of shareholders' wealth). In the second level, the credit analyst has to compare all five elements (criteria categories) in a pairwise fashion with respect to the element of the first level (the maximization of shareholders' wealth). The comparisons involve the relative significance of each criteria group with respect to the maximization of the shareholders' wealth; for instance how much more important is the financial soundness of the applicant than his/her pay record in the view of the maximization of the shareholders' wealth. The 9-point scale of the AHP method (Saaty, 1980) is employed during these comparisons. In the third level, the two elements (granting and denying the credit) should be compared with respect to all the elements from the criteria level (level 2). This is a rather complicated and time-consuming task to be carried out by the credit analyst, because each criterion includes a number of sub-criteria and thus, the number of comparisons is too large.

To overcome this problem, the system incorporates an ES to support the decision maker in comparing the two decisions of the final level with respect to the elements of the criteria level. The rules included in the knowledge base of the ES evaluate the customers (credit applicants) along with the evaluation criteria and conclude on a result regarding the performance of the customer on each of the five criteria groups. The necessary information concerning each evaluation criterion (customer background, pay record, location, business potential, financial soundness and the sub-criteria), is included in a relational database, with valuable information concerning industry standards. For each criteria group there is a specific set of rules that is used. For instance, the following rules are used to evaluate the customers' background, its profitability, liquidity, debt management and overall financial health (Srinivasan and Ruparel, 1990):

If customer has not filed for bankruptcy within the last 4 years
And customer has been in business for more than 5 years
And customer has had business relationship with us (the credit institution) for more than 3 years
And customer's management quality is perceived to be excellent
Then customer's background is considered excellent.

If sales trend is improving
And customer's net profit margin is greater than 5%
And customer's net profit margin trend is improving
And customer's gross margin is greater than 12%
And customer's gross margin trend is improving
Then customer's profitability is excellent.

If sales trend is improving
And customer's current ratio is greater than 1.5
And customer's current ratio trend is increasing
And customer's quick ratio is greater than 0.8
And customer's quick ratio trend is increasing
Then customer's liquidity is excellent.

If sales trend is improving
And customer's debt to net worth ratio is less than 0.3
And customer's debt to net worth ratio trend is decreasing
And customer's short-term debt to total debt is less than 0.4
And customer's short-term debt to total debt trend is decreasing
And customer's interest coverage is greater than 4
Then customer's debt exposure is excellent.

If customer's profitability is excellent
And customer's liquidity is excellent
And customer's debt exposure is excellent
Then customer's financial health is excellent.

An intensity value according to the 9-point scale of AHP is associated to the result of each rule. In the above example the result "excellent" on the customer's financial health is associated with an intensity value of 9 (the maximum possible value). This intensity value indicates that granting the credit is of absolute importance compared to denying it (i.e., granting the credit is absolutely preferred to denying it) taking into account the excellent customer's financial health. The intensity values estimated through the ES, for all pairs of elements in each level of the hierarchy, are integrated through the AHP method in order to derive an overall result on the basis of the maximization of the shareholders' wealth. The combination of the ES's estimations with the multicriteria method AHP leads to a set of weights for denying and granting the credit, which represent the possibilities of payment and default. These weights are integrated with the expected cash-flows associated with the granting and denying of the credit to compute the net present value (NPV). If the NPV is positive, then the credit is granted, otherwise the credit is denied. The system also provides recommendations concerning the maximum amount of credit that should be granted.

Therefore, in this case the ES is used to draw partial conclusions, which are aggregated through the AHP method to draw to the final estimations of the system. In this way the combination of the personal preferences of the credit manager with the expert's knowledge is achieved. Furthermore, the combination of the ES with the AHP method guides the analysis process, preventing the possible inconsistencies in the pairwise comparisons that are necessary as input of the AHP method.

4.1.2 The CREDEX system

The CREDEX system (CREDit EXpert; Pinson, 1989; 1992), demonstrates the feasibility of a multi-expert approach driven by a meta-model, in the assessment of credit risk associated with credit granting decisions. The system using quantitative data (economic and financial) as well as qualitative data (social) concerning the examined company and its business sector as well as the credit institution's lending policy, provides a diagnosis of the firm's functions (commercial, financial, managerial, industrial) in terms of weaknesses and strengths. The system integrates simple heuristics (surface knowledge), used by experts when judging the acceptance or the rejection of a loan application. This is done with a deeper understanding of the information aggregation process (deep knowledge), based on multi-attribute models. Figure 5.2 presents the architecture of the CREDEX system.

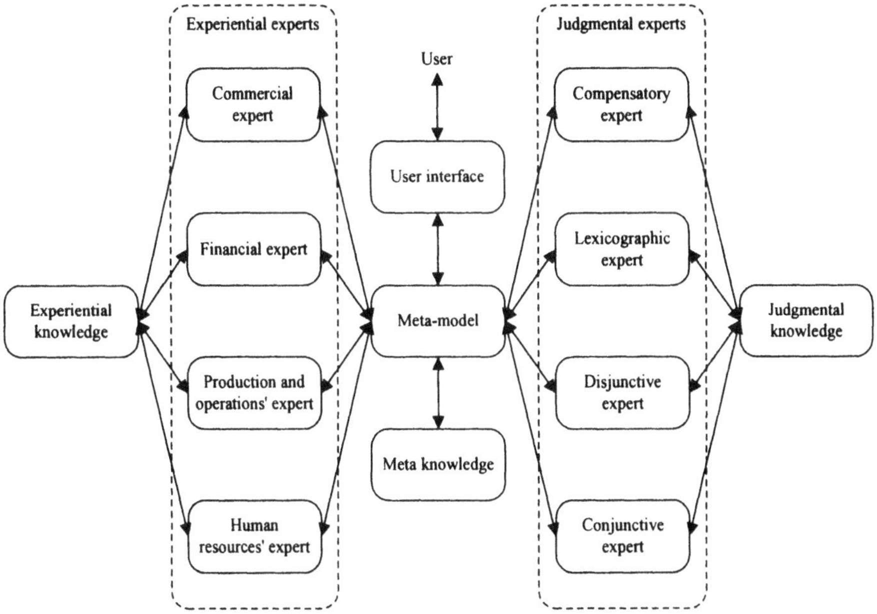

Figure 5.2. Architecture of the CREDEX system (Source: Pinson, 1992)

In CREDEX, the level of risk associated with each loan application is determined through a multi-attribute aggregation process. Each firm applying for a loan is evaluated along with four major aspects of its operation:

(i) The commercial aspect regarding the type of firm's activities, the evolution of its business sector, its customers, etc.

(ii) The financial aspect regarding the financial characteristics of the firm (debt structure, profitability, cash-flow) and its financial soundness.

(iii) The production and operations aspects involving the production systems that the firm employs along with its research and development level.

(iv) The management aspect (human resources) involving the quality of the management team and the holding structure of the firm (i.e., structure of its shareholders' capital).

Each of these aspects is associated with a weight representing its importance to the overall evaluation of the firms' credit risk. These weights are defined either interactively by the credit analyst or calculated by the system according to the banking policy, the sector of activity and the goal of the assessment. Furthermore, each of the aforementioned aspects involves the examination of several elementary characteristics of the firms, associated with weights representing their importance in assessing the quality of the corresponding aspect.

The evaluation of the firms to the lower level of this hierarchical structuring, involving the evaluation of the elementary characteristics of the firms, is performed using the experiential knowledge of expert analysts on the general aspects of the firms' operation. This experiential knowledge is represented into four knowledge bases. The same knowledge bases (experiential experts) can also be used to define the weights required for the aggregation process. The aggregation process is performed using judgmental knowledge on several forms of aggregation models including the compensatory model, the lexicographic model, the disjunctive model and the conjunctive model. The whole evaluation process is supervised at a higher level by a meta-expert, which decides on the experiential and judgmental experts that should be employed. A semantic network representation is used to structure and represent the evaluation procedure in the meta-expert module.

The CREDEX system demonstrates how the combination of a MCDSS integrating the ESs' technology with simple multiattribute evaluation models could help the decision makers in structuring the credit granting problem taking into account the knowledge of an expert credit analyst and the preferences of the decision maker as well. The ES is used to support the decision makers in determining the importance of each characteristic of a firm and in performing elementary evaluations which are aggregated at a higher level through simple multi-attribute models in order to derive an overall evaluation of the credit risk of the firms. Furthermore, the use of a meta-expert for controlling the analysis process provides the capability of structuring the decision process according to the available data and the operating assumptions of the system. Thus, the possible misinterpretation of the derived results is prevented.

4.2 Corporate performance and viability

4.2.1 The FINEVA system

The FINEVA system (FINancial EVAluation; Zopounidis et al., 1996a;b) is a multicriteria knowledge-based decision support system for the assessment of corporate performance and viability. The system was developed to run on IBM PC compatible computers using the operating system MS WINDOWS 3.1 or higher. The software has been written using Microsoft's Visual Basic 3.0 Professional Edition, while the ES part of the system has been developed using the ES shell M4 (Cimflex Teknowledge, 1991). Figure 5.3 illustrates the structure of the FINEVA system and its basic components.

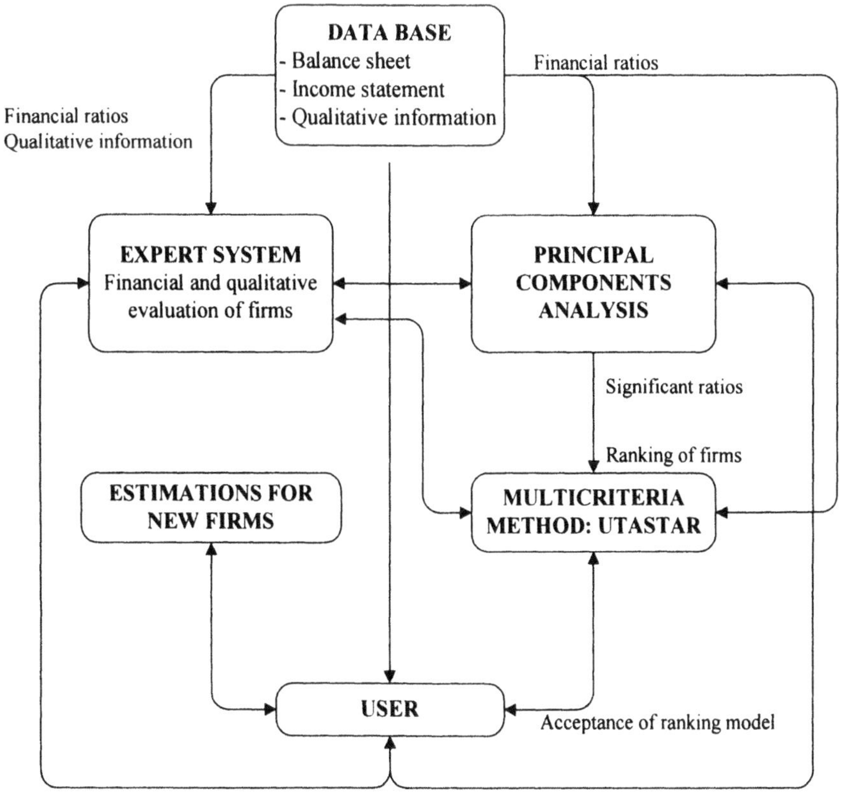

Figure 5.3. Structure of the FINEVA system (Source: Zopounidis et al., 1996a)

The basic characteristic of the FINEVA system is the combination of an ES with a multivariate statistical method (principal components analysis) and the multicriteria method UTASTAR (Siskos and Yannacopoulos, 1985) to estimate the corporate performance and the viability of firms.

The ES part represents the methodology used by experts in the field of financial analysis and it is used to provide a first evaluation of firms based on their financial characteristics (financial ratios) and qualitative information with regard to their internal operation and their relation to the market (e.g., quality of management, market trend, market niche/position, organization, technical facilities, etc.). This information is inserted in the database of the system for a five-year period. According to the results of the ES the firms are classified into four groups: (i) the firms that are in a very satisfactory position, (ii) the satisfactory firms, (iii) the medium firms, and (iv) the non-satisfactory ones. Principal components analysis can be used by the decision maker to identify the most significant financial ratios and to describe the financial behavior of the firms.

The UTASTAR multicriteria method ranks the firms from the most healthy to the most risky ones, thus indicating the competitive level between the firms. It also provides the relative importance of each criterion in the firms' ranking. In the case of corporate assessment, once the decision maker has expressed (sometimes, with the help of the ES's results) his judgement in the form of a ranking of the firms, the system, using of the UTASTAR ordinal regression method, estimates an additive utility function that is as consistent as possible with the decision maker's ranking. If a satisfactory level of consistency is achieved the additive utility model developed through the UTASTAR method can be stored, so that it is available for the evaluation of any new firm that is inserted in the system.

The estimation of the additive utility function is performed similarly to the procedure used in the UTADIS methods (cf. Appendix to Chapter 2). The form of the linear programming formulation that is employed in the case of the UTASTAR method is the following:

$$\text{Minimize } F=\sum_{a\in A}\left\{\sigma^{+}(a)+\sigma^{-}(a)\right\}$$

s.t.

$$u[g(\alpha)]-u[g(\beta)]+\sigma^{+}(\alpha)-\sigma^{-}(\alpha)-\sigma^{+}(\beta)+\sigma^{-}(\beta)\geq\delta \text{ if } \alpha \text{ is preferred to } \beta$$

$$u[g(\alpha)]-u[g(\beta)]+\sigma^{+}(\alpha)-\sigma^{-}(\alpha)-\sigma^{+}(\beta)+\sigma^{-}(\beta)=0 \text{ if } \alpha \text{ is indifferent to } \beta$$

$$\sum_{i=1}^{m}\sum_{j=1}^{a_i-1} w_{ij} = 1$$

$$w_{ij} \geq 0, \sigma^+(\alpha) \geq 0, \sigma^-(a) \geq 0, u_i \; \forall a \in A, \forall i, j$$

where A is the set of reference alternatives used to develop the additive utility model, $u[g(\alpha)]$ is the global utility of an alternative $a \in A$, σ^+ and σ^- are two error functions (over-estimation and under-estimation error, respectively), δ is a threshold used to ensure the strict preference of an alternative a over an alternative β, a_i is the number of subintervals $[g_i^j, g_i^{j+1}]$ into which the range of values of criterion g_i is divided, and w_{ij} is the difference $u_i(g_i^{j+1}) - u_i(g_i^j)$ of the marginal utilities between two successive values g_i^j and g_i^{j+1} of criterion g_i. Similarly to the UTADIS methods, in a second stage the UTASTAR method proceeds in a post-optimality analysis in order to identify other optimal or near optimal solutions, which could better represent the preferences of the decision maker. A detailed description of the UTASTAR method can be found in Siskos and Yannacopoulos (1985).

The results of the ES could help the decision maker define the preordering of the firms which is required by the UTASTAR method. This feature of the ES part is particularly useful if the decision maker does not have a clear view and knowledge of the considered firms. In such a case the ES part can provide the decision maker with the opinion of an expert credit analyst about the viability and the performance of the examined firms, which can be integrated with the personal preferences of the decision maker to have the final estimation of the firms, through the UTASTAR method.

Furthermore, in addition to the ranking of the firms, the UTASTAR method can also be used to classify the firms into three groups according to their performance and viability (Zopounidis, 1987; 1995). To achieve this trichotomic classification, the decision maker must define two fictitious firms (reference profiles) with their multicriteria evaluations in order to discriminate the set of firms. These reference profiles are easy to be determined on the basis of the past experience of the decision maker and of the repetitive character of financial decisions related to the assessment of corporate performance and viability. Thus, for a given firm (a), there are three possibilities:

$$u[g(a)] \geq u_1 \Rightarrow a \in C_1 \text{ (low-risk, healthy firm)}$$

$$u_2 \leq u[g(a)] < u_1 \Rightarrow a \in C_2 \text{ (uncertain, firm to be studied further)}$$

$$u[g(a)] < u_2 \Rightarrow a \in C_3 \text{ (high-risk, bankrupt firm)}$$

where $u[g(a)]$ is the global utility of the firm (a), u_1 and u_2 are the global utilities of the two reference profiles called utility thresholds, all calculated by the UTASTAR method. The utility threshold u_1 distinguishes the firms among those which can be characterized as dynamic (low-risk) from those which need further study (uncertain). The utility threshold u_2 distinguishes the firms among those which need further study (uncertain) from those which can be characterized as failured (high-risk).

The estimation model (ranking or classification model) derived by the UTASTAR multicriteria method, is used as basic knowledge in the ES part (as a production rule based on the ranking or segmentation model) for the evaluation of new firms which are inserted in the data base of the system (Zopounidis et al., 1996b).

The FINEVA system has been applied in the assessment of business failure risk (Zopounidis et al., 1996b), the evaluation of corporate performance and viability of Greek transportation firms (Doumpos et al., 1997). Other applications of the UTASTAR method have been conducted in venture capital investments (Siskos and Zopounidis, 1987), country risk evaluation (Cosset et al., 1992), corporate financing (Siskos et al., 1994; Zopounidis et al., 1992) and business failure (Zopounidis, 1987).

4.3 Investment analysis

4.3.1 The INVEX system

The INVEX system (Vranes et al., 1996) is a multicriteria KBDSS developed to support the evaluation process of investment projects. The special feature of the system is the combination of five different techniques that provide the means to perform an integrated evaluation of the investment projects: (i) heuristic rules, (ii) expert system, (iii) fuzzy set theory, (iv) utility-based risk aversion model and (v) PROMETHEE II multicriteria method. Figure 5.4 presents the structure of the system.

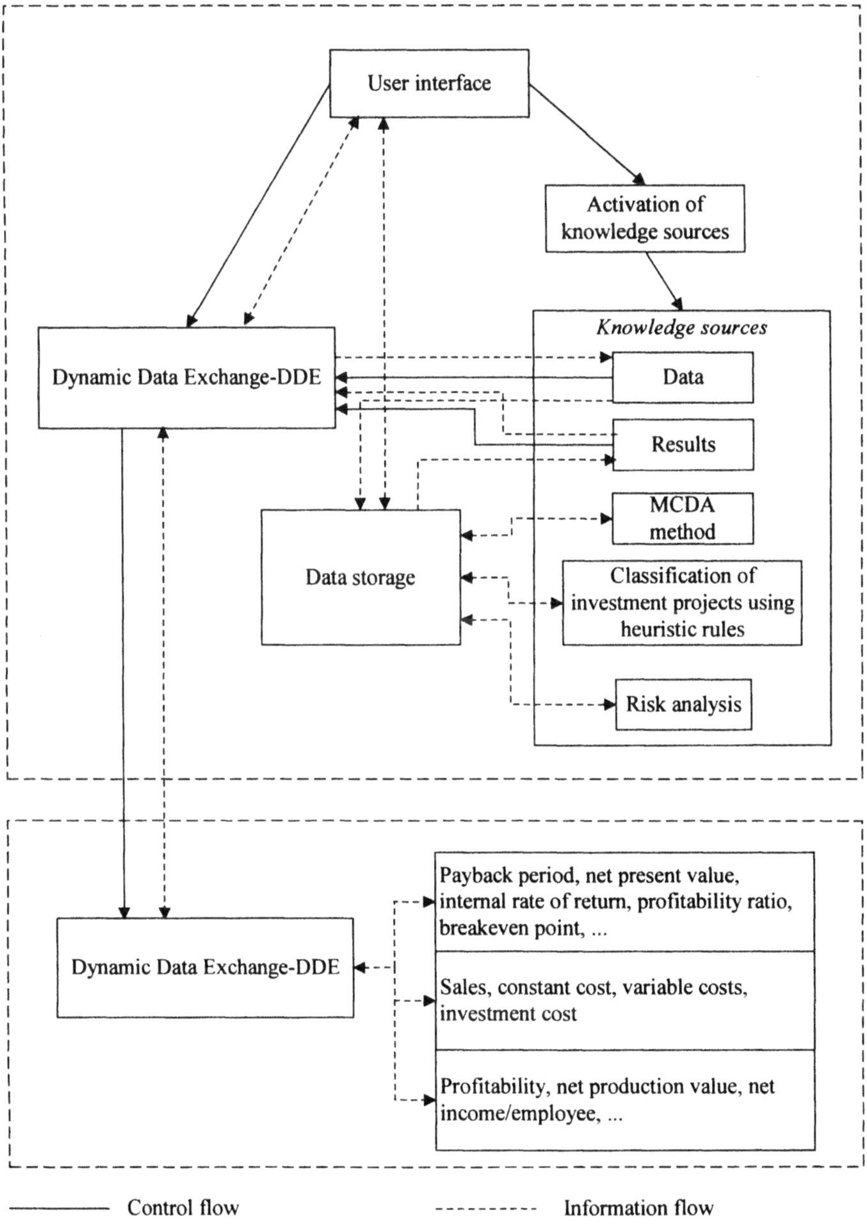

Figure 5.4. Structure of the INVEX system (Source: Vranes et al., 1996)

In the first phase of the evaluation process, the system employs simple heuristic rules along with fuzzy set theory to classify the considered investment projects into five groups, ranging from the very good projects to the very bad projects. At this stage, the analysis is based on commonly used investment appraisal criteria such as the net present value and the internal rate of return. Each of the five groups is defined as a fuzzy set and membership functions are introduced to estimate the membership degree of the investments to belong into the five groups according to their net present value and internal rate of return. This heuristic analysis based on these two commonly used investment appraisal criteria is performed for preprocessing purposes in order to identify and exclude from any further consideration all investment projects that fall in the very bad group.

In a second stage, a sensitivity analysis is performed for projects classified as good, average or bad, in order to examine how the changes in the business environment can affect their evaluation (for instance to identify under which conditions a good project could become bad or very bad). The conducted sensitivity analysis involves several parameters including the delay of the exploitation of the investment, the increase in the exploitation costs, the decrease in sales revenues, etc. On the basis of the sensitivity analysis results, the set of alternative investment projects can be further reduced to a more compact set.

The third step of the analysis involves the consideration of all uncertain factors in estimating the risk of the investment projects. Monte Carlo simulations are conducted to estimate the net present value's probability distribution, while a utility function approach representing the risk aversion policy of the investment analyst is employed to determine the expected utility of the projects. Furthermore, the simulations conducted in this stage of the process are used to estimate several statistical parameters regarding the possible outcome of the investments including among others the mean, the standard deviation and the coefficient of variation of their net present value and their return.

After all the aforementioned analyses, the appraisal of the investment projects is performed using the PROMETHEE II MCDA method (Brans and Vincke, 1985). The evaluation criteria considered in this stage include all the well-known investment appraisal measures, the statistical measures estimated through the simulation process conducted in the previous stage of the analysis as well as several financial ratios related to the investment projects and their impact on the operation of the firm. The aggregation of all this information that is performed through the PROMETHEE II multicriteria method provides a ranking of the considered investment projects from the best to the worst ones, thus facilitating the selection process. However, PROMETHEE II requires the definition of several parameters including the weights of the evaluation criteria as well as the strict preference and indifference thresholds. Asking the decision makers to define these parameters is often a cumbersome procedure. To overcome this problem the system incorporates an ES that facilitates the definition of the required parameters through an interactive procedure that takes into consideration the preferences and the investment policy of the decision maker.

Thus, similarly to the CGX system, the ES component in the INVEX system is a supportive module for the operation of the MCDA methodology that is employed. This minimizes the cognitive effort required by the decision maker to determine the parameters of the method.

Chapter 6

INTELLIGENT MCDSSs IN FINANCIAL ENGINEERING PRACTICE

1. IS THERE ANY NEED FOR INTELLIGENT MULTICRITERIA DECISION SUPPORT?

The whole presentation in the previous chapters of this book has adopted a rather theoretical view of the forms of systems that constitute the basis of intelligent MCDSSs development, including DSSs, ESs and KBDSSs. This was necessary in order to introduce gradually the underlying concepts implemented in the intelligent MCDSSs framework and to illustrate their main functionalities and major benefits. However, one could easily pose the question on if and how this new framework has been adopted in the financial engineering practice of financial institutions, organizations and firms.

The up to now experience reveals that intelligent MCDSSs are still mainly limited to an academic research perspective. One could argue that this is due to the fact that the effectiveness of the methodological tools employed in such systems (i.e., MCDA methodologies) has not reached the level of alternative approaches commonly used by financial engineering practitioners. However, this is hardly the case. The results obtained from several applications of MCDA within the financial engineering field and financial management in general have shown that MCDA methodologies are indeed capable of providing better support to financial engineers, both in terms of the realism of the approach employed to study financial engineering problems and the quality of their results. Some of these results were reported in Chapter 1

Another possible explanation that one could provide is that actually financial engineers do not need such support systems in their daily practice, since their experience and knowledge is enough. This argument is also easily refuted. In the international literature one can find numerous reports on financial institutions, organizations and firms that employ some form of computerized support systems, DSSs, ESs or KBDSSs, in their financial engineering practice (Leinweber, 1988; Klein and Methlie, 1995; Mulvey et al., 1997; Shao et al., 1997). Some typical examples include the US Security and Exchange Commission (SEC), American Express, Arthur Andersen & Co., Price Waterhouse, Crédit Lyonnais, Lehman Brothers, Barclays Bank, the Midland Group, Banque de France, Lockheed Corporation and the Ionian Bank of Greece, just to name a few. Actually the complex nature of the problems encountered within the financial engineering field, along with the large volume of available information, make impossible to tackle such problems on an empirical basis. This will obviously result to trivial solutions, which are out of the scope of financial engineering and, of course, they could hardly meet the requirements of the existing financial and business environments

These examples clearly demonstrate that financial engineers need the tools provided by information technology not only for simple information processing tasks but also as decision support tools. In that respect, intelligent MCDSSs, a tool entirely devoted to support decision makers rather than replace them, has significant potentials in the financial engineering field.

However, the MCDA research community, which is the one mainly involved with the design and development of such systems, has recently (mostly over the last decade) realized and exploited the potential benefits of the integration of artificial intelligence tools with the MCDA approach. The significant undergoing research is focused both on the theoretical aspects of this integration as well as on its implementation issues. As this integration gradually consolidates its position, more intelligent MCDSSs are expected to be developed for financial engineering applications.

The exceptional features of such integrated intelligent systems, including advanced problem structuring and preference modeling, incorporating both financial engineering knowledge and MCDA expertise, advanced solution development and parameter estimation procedures, interactive sensitivity and robustness analysis guided by the knowledge of MCDA/decision analysis experts, can provide the most comprehensive form of real-time support to financial engineers, without any expense on realism, scientific soundness, or user-friendliness.

2. THE ROAD AHEAD

The rapid transformation of the global financial and business environment, along with the new technological developments and innovations pose additional challenges to the designers and developers of computerized support systems, including intelligent MCDSSs. Since the advances on the theoretical aspects of the MCDA approach will continue with more rapid steps in the subsequent years due to the consolidation of MCDA as an integral part of the operations research/management science community, the focus regarding the development of intelligent MCDSSs for financial engineering should be placed on meeting the new requirements of financial engineers imposed by the changing environment within which they practice.

The exploitation of the Internet could turn out to be one of the most significant areas. The potentials of such a research direction are significant for financial engineering in several aspects. Firstly, for information search and retrieval. Expect for its commercial aspect, Internet constitutes a valuable source of financial information, since there is an increasing number of organizations and firms providing on-line, real-time financial data on the Internet. Incorporating in the intelligent MCDSSs framework the capability to retrieve, process and exploit this information, constitutes a crucial aspect towards providing real-time support. Furthermore, the apparent establishing trend to perform financial transactions through the Internet indicates the significance of integrating the Internet technology in the intelligent MCDSSs framework, not only for information retrieval purposes but also for supporting financial decisions regarding the new financial instruments and processes, which are based on the Internet technology.

An additional aspect/implication of this new research direction is providing support to geographically dispersed collaborative tasks and group decision support. With respect to the top management level this can be a crucial point, bearing in mind that strategic financial decisions are taken not by individuals, but rather by the group of the top management team, often working on geographically dispersed locations. Group decision making has already evolved significantly within the MCDA research community, and the incorporation of the theoretical advances in the intelligent MCDSSs framework could provide a new form of support to financial engineers.

Finally, the designers and developers of intelligent MCDSSs have to keep pace with the rapid advances made within the financial engineering field and the development of new financial instruments and processes. This is done to provide up-to-date support in financial engineering decisions and meet the challenges that such innovations pose.

REFERENCES

Altman, E.I., Avery, R., Eisenbeis, R. and Stinkey, J. (1981), *Application of Classification Techniques in Business, Banking and Finance*, Contemporary Studies in Economic and Financial Analysis, vol. 3, JAI Press, Greenwich.

Anastassiou, Th. and Zopounidis, C. (1997), "Country risk assessment: A multicriteria analysis approach", *The Journal of Euro-Asian Management* 3/1, 51-73.

Andenmatten, A. (1995), *Evaluation du Risque de Défaillance des Emetteurs d'Obligations: Une Approche par l'Aide Multicritère à la Décision*, Presses Polytechniques et Universitaires Romandes, Lausanne.

Antunes, C.H., Alves, M.J., Silva, A.L. and Climaco, J. (1992), "An integrated MOLP method base package-A guided tour of TOMMIX", *Computers and Operations Research* 1/4, 609-625.

Ashford, R.W., Berry, R.H. and Dyson, R.G. (1988), "Operational research and financial management", *European Journal of Operational Research* 36, 143-152.

Bana e Costa, C.A. and Vansnick, J.C. (1994), "MACBETH-An interactive path towards the construction of cardinal value functions", *International Transactions on Operations Research* 1, 489-500.

Barr, A. and Feigenbaum, E. (1982), *The Handbook of Artificial Intelligence*, Vol. II, Pittman Books Ltd., London.

Baumol, W.J. (1959), *Economic Theory and Operations Analysis*, Prentice-Hall, Englewood Cliffs, N.J.

Belton, V. and Vickers, S.P. (1989), "V.I.S.A.-VIM for MCDA", in: A.G. Lockett and G. Islei (eds.), *Improving Decision Making in Organizations*, Springer-Verlag, Berlin, 319-334.

Ben-David, A. and Sterling, L. (1986), "A prototype expert system for credit evaluation", in: L.F. Pau (ed.), *Artificial Intelligence in Economics and Management*, Elsevier Science Publisher, North-Holland, 121-128.

Bergeron, M., Martel, J.M. and Twarabimenye, P. (1996), "The evaluation of corporate loan applications based on the MCDA", *Journal of Euro-Asian Management* 2/2, 16-46.

Bhaskar, K. (1979), "A multiple objective approach to capital budgeting", *Accounting and Business Research*, Winter, 25-46.

Bhaskar, K. and McNamee, P. (1983), "Multiple objectives in accounting and finance", *Journal of Business Finance and Accounting* 10/4, 595-621.

Black, F. and Scholes, M. (1973), "The pricing of options and corporate liabilities", *Journal of Political Economy* 81, 659-674.

Borch, O.J. and Hartvigsen, G. (1991), "Knowledge-based systems for strategic market planning in small firms", *Decision Support Systems* 7, 145-157.

Bouwman, M.J. (1983), "Human diagnostic reasoning by computer: An illustration from financial analysis", *Management Science* 29/6, 653-672.

Brans, J.P. and Vincke, Ph. (1985), "A preference ranking organization method", *Management Science* 31/6, 647-656.

Brans, J.P. and Mareschal, B. (1994), "The PROMCALC & GAIA decision support system for multicriteria decision aid", *Decision Support Systems* 12, 297-310.

Bryant, S.M. (1997), "A case-based reasoning approach to bankruptcy prediction modeling", *International Journal of Intelligent Systems in Accounting Finance and Management* 6, 195-214.

Butera, G., Frascari, E. and Iacono, G. (1990), "Parmenide: An expert system for assessing the credit of industrial clients", International Journal of Expert Systems 3/1, 73-85.

Charnes, A. and Cooper, W.W. (1961), *Management Models and Industrial Applications of Linear Programming*, Wiley, New York.

Cimflex Teknowledge (1991). *M4: User's Guide.* Palo Alto, CA.

Clei, J. (1994), "La méthodologie d'analyse de la Coface", *Banque Stratégie* 109, Octobre, 5-6.

Climaco, J. and Antunes, C.H. (1989), "Implementation of a user friendly software package- A guided tour of TRIMAP", *Mathematical and Computer Modelling* 12/10-11, 1299-1309.

Colasse, B. (1993), *Gestion Financière de l'Entreprise*, Presses Universitaires de France, Paris.

Colson, G. and de Bruyn, Ch. (1989), "An integrated multiobjective portfolio management system", *Mathematical and Computer Modelling* 12/10-11, 1359-1381.

Connell, N.A.D. and Powell, P.L. (1990), "A comparison of potential applications of expert systems and decision support systems", *Journal of the Operational Research Society* 41/5,431-439.

Cook, W.D. and Kress, M. (1991), "A multiple criteria decision model with ordinal preference data", *European Journal of Operational Research* 54, 191-198.

Cook, W.D. and Hebner, K.J. (1993), "A multicriteria approach to country risk evaluation: With an example employing Japanese data", *International Review of Economics and Finance* 2/4, 327-438.

Cosset, J.C., Siskos, Y. and Zopounidis, C. (1995), "Evaluating country risk: A decision support approach", *Global Finance Journal* 3/1, 79-95.

Courtis, J.K. (1978), "Modelling a financial ratios categoric framework", *Journal of Business Finance & Accounting* 5/4, 371-387.

Cronan, T.P., Glorfeld, L.W. and Perry, L.G. (1991), "Production system development for expert systems using a recursive partitioning induction approach: An application to mortgage, commercial and consumer lending", *Decision Sciences* 22, 812-845.

Cyert, R.M. and March, J.G. (1963), *A Behavioral Theory of the Firm*, Prentice-Hall, Englewood Cliffs, N.J.

Dahl, H., Meeraus, A. and Zenios, S.A. (1993a), "Some financial optimization models: I Risk management", in: S.A. Zenios, *Financial Optimization*, Cambridge University Press, Cambridge, 3-36.

Dahl, H., Meeraus, A. and Zenios, S.A. (1993b), "Some financial optimization models: II Financial engineering", in: S.A. Zenios, *Financial Optimization*, Cambridge University Press, Cambridge, 37-71.

Danila, N. (1980), "Méthodologie d'aide à la décision dans le cas d'investissements fort dépendants", Thèse de Doctorat de 3e Cycle, UER Sciences des Organisations, Université de Paris-Dauphine.

Despotis, D.K., Yannacopoulos, D. and Zopounidis, C. (1990), "A review of the UTA multicriteria method and some improvements", *Foundations of Computing and Decision Sciences* 15/2, 63-76.

Diakoulaki, D., Mavrotas, G. and Papagyannakis, L. (1992), "A multicriteria approach for evaluating the performance of industrial firms", *OMEGA: International Journal of Management Science* 20/4, 467-474.

Dimitras, A.I., Slowinski, R., Susmaga, R. and Zopounidis, C. (1999), "Business failure prediction using rough sets", *European Journal of Operational Research* 114, 263-280.

Dimitras, A.I., Zanakis, S.H. and Zopounidis, C. (1996), "A survey of business failures with an emphasis on prediction methods and industrial applications", *European Journal of Operational Research* 90, 487-513.

Dimitras, A.I., Zopounidis, C. and Hurson, Ch. (1995), "A multicriteria decision aid method for the assessment of business failure risk", *Foundations of Computing and Decision Sciences* 20/2, 99-112.

Dirks, S. Kingston, J.K.C. and Haggith, M. (1995), "Development of a KBS for personal financial planning guided by pragmatic KADS", *Expert Systems with Applications* 9/2, 91-101.

Doukidis, G.I. (1988), "Decision support system concepts in expert systems: An empirical study", *Decision Support Systems* 4, 345-354.

Doumpos, M. and Zopounidis, C. (1998), "The use of the preference disaggregation analysis in the assessment of financial risks", *Fuzzy Economic Review* 3/1, 39-57.

Doumpos, M., C. Zopounidis and S. Hecker (1997), "Multicriteria evaluation of transportation firms in Greece", in: M. Papageorgiou and A. Pouliezos (eds.), *Transportation Systems, Vol. I*, Pergamon, Oxford, 169-174.

Doumpos, M., Zopounidis, C. and Anastassiou, Th. (1998), "Assessing country risk using multicriteria analysis", in: C. Zopounidis (ed.), *Operational Tools in the Management of Financial Risks*, Kluwer Academic Publishers, Dordrecht, 309-326.

Duarte Silve, A.P. and Stam, A. (1994), "Second order mathematical programming formulations for discriminant analysis", *European Journal of Operational Research*, 72, 4-22.

Duchessi, P. and Belardo, S. (1987), "Lending analysis support system (LASS): An application of a knowledge-based system to support commercial loan analysis", *IEEE Transactions on Systems, Man, and Cybernetics* 17/4, 608-616.

Dyer, J. (1973), "A time-sharing computer program for the solution of the multiple criteria problem", *Management Science* 19, 1379-1383.

Edwards, J.S. (1992), "Expert systems in management and administration-Are they really different from decision support systems?", *European Journal of Operational Research* 61, 114-121.

Ekeland, I. (1993), "Finance: Un nouveau domaine des mathématiques appliquées", *Revue Française de Gestion*, Novembre-Décembre, 44-48.

Elliot, R.K. and Kielich, J.A. (1985), "Expert systems for accountants", *Journal of Accountancy*, September, 126-134.

Elmer, P.J. and Borowski, D.M. (1988), "An expert system approach to financial analysis: The case of S&L bankruptcy", *Financial Management* 17, 66-76.

Elton, E.J. and Gruber, M.J. (1995), *Modern Portfolio Theory and Investment Analysis* (5th edition), John Wiley and Sons, New York.

Eom, H.B. and Lee, S.M. (1990), "Decision support systems applications research: A bibliography (1971-1988)", *European Journal of Operational Research* 46, 333-342.

Eom, H.B., Lee, S.M., Snyder, Ch.A. and Ford, F.N. (1987-88), "A multiple criteria decision support system for global financial planning", *Journal of Management Information Systems* 4/3, 94-113.

Eom, S.B., Lee, S.M. and Ayaz, A. (1993), "Expert systems applications development research in business: A selected bibliography (1975-1989)", *European Journal of Operational Research* 68, 278-290.

Eom, S.B., Lee, S.M. and Kim, J.K. (1993), "The intellectual structure of decision support systems (1971-1989)", *Decision Support Systems* 10, 19-35.

Er, M.C. (1988), "Decision support systems: A summary, problems, and future trends", *Decision Support Systems* 4, 355-363.

Evrard, Y. and Zisswiller, R. (1982), "Une analyse des décisions d'investissement fondée sur les modèles de choix multi-attributs", *Finance* 3/1, 51-68.

Finnerty, J.D. (1988), "Financial engineering in corporate finance: An overview", *Financial Management* 17, 14-33.

Fishburn, P.C. (1965), "Independence in utility theory with whole product sets", *Operations Research* 13, 28-45.

Ford, N.F. (1985), "Decision support systems and expert systems: A comparison", *Information and Management* 8, 21-26.

Gastineau, G. (1992), *Dictionary of Financial Risk Management*, Probus, Chicago.

Gerrity, T.P. Jr. (1971), "Design of man-machine decision systems: An application to portfolio management", *Sloan Management Review* 12, 59-75.

Goedhart, M.H., and Spronk, J. (1995), "Financial planning with fractional goals", *European Journal of Operational Research* 82, 111-124.

Grablowsky, B.J. and Talley, W.K. (1981), "Probit and discriminant factors for classifying credit applicants: A comparison", *Journal of Economics and Business* 33, 254-261.

Greco, S., Matarazzo, B. and Slowinski, R. (1998), "A new rough set approach to evaluation of bankruptcy risk", in: C. Zopounidis (ed.), *Operational Tools in the Management of Financial Risks*, Kluwer Academic Publishers, Dordrecht, p. 121-136.

Greco, S., Matarazo, B. and Slowinski, R. (1999), "Rough approximation of a preference relation by dominance relations", *European Journal Of Operational Research* 117, 63-83.

Hansen, J.V. and Messier, W.F. Jr. (1986), "A knowledge-based expert system for auditing advanced computer systems", *European Journal of Operational Research* 26, 371-379.

Hartvigsen, G. (1990), "KABAL: A knowledge-based system for financial analysis in banking", *Expert Systems For Information Management* 3/3, 213-231.

Hashemi, R.R., Le Blanc, L.A., Rucks, C.T. and Rajaratnam, A. (1998), "A hybrid intelligent system for predicting bank holding structures", *European Journal of Operational Research* 109, 390-402.

Hayen, R.L. (1982), "Applying decision support systems to small business financial planning", *Journal of Small Business Management*, July, 35-46.

Hayes-Roth, F., Waterman, D.A. and Lenat, D. (1983), *Building Expert Systems*, Addison-Wesley, Reading MA.

Henderson, J.C. (1987), "Finding synergy between decision support systems and expert systems research", *Decision Sciences* 18, 333-349.

Hertz, D.B. (1964), "Risk analysis in capital investment", *Harvard Business Review* 42, 95-106.

Heuer, S., Koch, U. and Cryer, C. (1988), "INVEST: An expert system for financial investments", *IEEE Expert*, Summer, 60-68.

Hillier, F.S. (1963), "The derivation of probabilistic information for the evaluation of risky investments", *Management Science* 9, April, 443-457.

Ho, P.C. and Paulson, A.S. (1980), "Portfolio selection via factor analysis", *The Journal of Portfolio Management*, Spring, 27-30.

Holland, J.H. (1975), *Adaptation in Natural and Artificial Systems*, Ann Arbor, The University of Michigan Press, MI.

Holland, J.H., Holyoak, K.J., Nisbett, R.E. and Thagard, R.R. (1986), *Induction: Processes of Inference, Learning and Discovery*, The MIT Press, Cambridge, MA.

Hui, T.K. and Kwan, E. (1994), "International portfolio diversification: A factor analysis approach", *Omega* 22/3, 263-267.

Hurson, Ch. and Zopounidis, C. (1995), "On the use of multi-criteria decision aid methods to portfolio selection", *Journal of Euro-Asian Management* 1/2, 69-94.

Hurson, Ch. and Zopounidis, C. (1997), *Gestion de Portefeuille et Analyse Multicritère*, Economica, Paris.

Jablonsky, J. (1993), "Multicriteria evaluation of clients in financial houses", *Central European Journal of Operations Research and Economics* 3/2, 257-264.

Jacquet-Lagrèze, E. (1995), "An application of the UTA discriminant model for the evaluation of R&D projects", in: P.M. Pardalos, Y. Siskos and C. Zopounidis (eds.), *Advances in Multicriteria Analysis*, Kluwer Academic Publishers, Dordrecht, 203-211.

Jacquet-Lagrèze, E. and Siskos, J. (1983), *Méthodes de Décision Multicritère*, Editions Hommes et Techniques, Paris.

Jacquet-Lagrèze, E. and Siskos, Y. (1982), "Assessing a set of additive utility functions for multicriteria decision making: The UTA method", *European Journal of Operational Research* 10, 151-164.

Jacquet-Lagrèze, E. (1990), "Interactive assessment of preferences using holistic judgments: The PREFCALC system", in: C.A. Bana e Costa (ed.), *Readings in Multiple Criteria Decision Making*, Springer-Verlag, Berlin, 335-350.

Jacquillat, B. (1972), "Les modèles d'évaluation et de sélection des valeurs mobilières: Panorama des recherches américaines", *Analyse Financière* 11, 4e trim., 68-88.

Jenkins, J. (1973), "Computer based financial planning", *Omega* 1/5, 539-550.

Jog, V., Michalowski, W., Slowinski, R. and Susmaga, R. (1999), "The Rough Sets Analysis and the Neural Networks Classifier: A Hybrid Approach to Predicting Stocks' Performance", in: D.K. Despotis and C. Zopounidis (eds.), *Integrating Technology & Human Decisions: Bridging into the 21st Century*, Vol. II, Proceedings of the 5th International Meeting of the Decision Sciences Institute, New Technologies Editions, Athens, 1386-1388.

Kastner, J., Apte, C., Giesmer, J., Hong, S.J., Karnaugh, M., Mays, E. and Tozawa, Y. (1986), "A knowledge-based consultant for financial marketing", *The AI Magazine* 7, 71-79.

Keeney, R.L. and Raiffa, H. (1993), *Decisions with Multiple Objectives: Preferences and Value Trade-offs*, Cambridge University Press, Cambridge.

Khorramshahgol, R. and Okoruwa, A.A. (1994), "A goal programming approach to investment decisions: A case study of fund allocation among different shopping malls", *European Journal of Operational Research* 73, 17-22.

Khoury, N.T. and Martel, J.M. (1993), "Nouvelles orientations dans l'étude des marchés financiers: Asymétrie d'information et analyse multicritère", *L'Actualité Economique, Revue d'Analyse Economique* 69/1, 5-7.

Khoury, N.T., Martel, J.M. and Veilleux, M. (1993), "Méthode multicritère de sélection de portefeuilles indiciels internationaux", *L'Actualité Economique, Revue d'Analyse Economique* 69/1, 171-190.

Kim, B-O. and Lee, S.M. (1995), "A bond rating expert system for industrial companies", *Expert Systems with Applications* 9/1, 63-70.

Kim, S.H. and Noh, H.J. (1997), "Predictability of interest rates using data mining tools: A comparative analysis of Korea and US", Working Paper, KAIST.

Kiss, L.N., Martel, J.M. and Nadeau, R. (1994), "ELECCALC-An interactive software for modelling the decision maker's preferences", *Decision Support Systems* 12, 311-326.

Kivijärvi, H., and Tuominen, M. (1992), "A decision support system for semistructured strategic decisions: A multi-tool method for evaluating intangible investments", *Revue des Systèmes de Décision* 1, 353-376.

Klein, M. and Methlie, L.B. (1995), *Expert Systems: A Decision Support Approach with Applications in Management and Finance*, Addison-Wesley, Wokingham.

Koopmans, T.C. (1951), *Activity Analysis of Production and Allocation*, John Wiley and Sons, New York.

Korhonen, P. (1987), "VIG-A visual interactive support system for multiple criteria decision making", *Belgian Journal of Operations Research, Statistics and Computer Science* 27, 3-15.

Korhonen, P. (1988), "A visual reference direction approach to solving discrete multiple criteria problems", *European Journal of Operational Research* 34, 152-159.

Korhonen, P., Moskowitz, H. and Wallenius, J. (1992), "Multiple criteria decision support-A review", *European Journal of Operational Research* 63, 361-375.

Lagarde, J. (1983). *Initiation à l'analyse des données*, Bordas, Dunod, Paris.

Lam, K.F. and Choo, E.U. (1995), "Goal programming in preference decomposition", *Journal of the Operational Research Society* 46, 205-213.

Lane, S. (1972), "Submarginal credit risk classification", *Journal of Financial and Qualitative Analysis* 7, 1379-1386.

Langen, D. (1989), "An (interactive) decision support system for bank asset liability management", *Decision Support Systems* 5, 389-401.

Langholz, G., Kandel, A., Schneider, M. and Chew, G. (1996), *Fuzzy Expert System Tools*, John Wiley and Sons, New York.

Lee, Ch.F. (1985), *Financial Analysis and Planning: Theory and Application*, Addison-Wesley, Reading, Massachusetts.

Lee, H., Kwak, W. and Han, I. (1995), "Developing a business performance evaluation system: An analytic hierarchical model", *The Engineering Economist* 30/4, 343-357.

Lee, J.B. and Stohr, E.A. (1985), "Representing knowledge for portfolio management decision making", Working Paper 101, Center for Research on Information Systems, New York University.

Lee, J.K. and Nam, S.Z. (1997), "An object-oriented optimal savings system: HYPER-SAVINGS", *International Journal of Intelligent Systems in Accounting Finance and Management* 6, 303-320.

Lee, J.K., Kim, H.S. and Chu, S.C. (1989), "Intelligent stock portfolio management system", *Expert Systems* 6/2, 74-85.

Lee, K.H. and Jo, G.S. (1999), "Expert system for predicting stock market timing using a candlestick chart", *Expert Systems with Applications* 16, 357-364.

Lee, S.M. and Chesser, D.L. (1980), "Goal programming for portfolio selection", *The Journal of Portfolio Management*, Spring 22-26.

Leinweber, D. (1998), "Knowledge-based system for financial applications", *IEEE Expert*, Fall, 18-31.

Leung, H.M., Chuah, K.B. and Rao Tummala, V.M. (1998), "A knowledge-based system for identifying potential project risks", *Omega* 26/5, 623-638.

Levine, P. and Pomerol, J.Ch. (1986), "PRIAM, an interactive program for chosing among multiple attribute alternatives", *European Journal of Operational Research* 25, 272-280.

Lévine, P. and Pomerol, J.C. (1989), "Knowledge representation by schemata in financial expert systems", *Theory and Decision* 27, 147-161.

Lewandowski, A., Kreglewski T., Rogowski, T. and Wierzbicki, A. (1989), "Decision support systems of DIDAS family (Dynamic Interactive Decision Analysis & Support)", in: A. Lewandowski and A. Wierzbicki (eds.), *Aspiration Based Decision Support Systems*, Springer-Verlag, Berlin, 21-27.

Lin, W.T. (1978), "Multiple objective budgeting models: A simulation", *The Accounting Review* LIII/1, 61-76.

Liu, N.K. and Lee, K.K. (1997), "An intelligent business advisor system for stock investment", *Expert Systems* 14/4, 129-139.

Lofti, V., Stewart, T.J. and Zionts, S. (1992), "An aspiration-level interactive model for multiple criteria decision making", *Computers and Operations Research* 19, 677-681.

Lootsma, F.A. (1997), *Fuzzy Logic for Planning and Decision Making*, Kluwer Academic Publishers, Dordrecht.

Malakooti, B. and Zhou Y.Q. (1994), "Feedforward artificial neural networks for solving discrete multiple criteria decision making problems", *Management Science* 40/11, 1542-1561.

Mareschal, B. and Brans, J.P. (1991), "BANKADVISER: An industrial evaluation system", *European Journal of Operational Research* 54, 318-324.

Mareschal, B. and Brans, J.P. (1993), "BANKADVISER: Un système interactif multicritère pour l'évaluation financière des entreprises à l'aide des méthodes PROMETHEE", *L'Actualité Economique, Revue d'Analyse Economique* 69/1, 191-205.

Mareschal, B. and Mertens, D. (1990), "Evaluation financière par la méthode multicritère GAIA: Application au secteur bancaire belge", *Revue de la Banque* 6, 317-329.

Mareschal, B. and Mertens, D. (1992), "BANKS: A multicriteria, PROMETHEE-based, decision support system for the evaluation of the international banking sector", *Revue des Systèmes de Décision* 1/2-3, 175-189.

Mareschal, B. and Mertens, D. (1993), "Evaluation multicritère par la méthode multicritère GAIA: Application au secteur de l'assurance en Belgique", *L'Actualité Economique, Revue d'Analyse Economique* 69/1, 206-228.

Markowitz, H. (1952), "Portfolio selection", *The Journal of Finance* 7/1, 77-91.

Markowitz, H. (1959), *Portfolio Selection: Efficient Diversification of Investments*, Wiley, New York.

Marshall, J.F. and Dorigan, M.P. (1996), "Financial engineering: Information technology and its place in the new finance", *Technology in Society* 18/2, 185-201.

Martel, J.M., Khoury, N.T. and Bergeron, M. (1988), "An application of a multicriteria approach to portfolio comparisons", *Journal of the Operational Research Society* 39/7, 617-628.

Martel, J.M., Khoury, N.T. and M'Zali, B. (1991), "Comparaison performance-taille des fonds mutuels par une analyse multicritère", *L'Actualité Economique, Revue d'Analyse Economique* 67/3, 306-324.

Mays, E., Apte, C., Giesmer, J. and Kastner, J. (1987), "Organizing knowledge in a complex financial domain", *IEEE Expert*.

McBride, R.D., O'Leary, D.E. and Widmeyer, G.R. (1989), "A knowledge-based system for cash management with management science expertise", *Annals of Operations Research* 21, 301-316.

Merton, R.C. (1995), "Influence of mathematical models in finance on practice: Past, present and future", in: S.D. Howison, F.P. Kelly and P. Wilmott (eds.), *Mathematical Models in Finance*, Chapman & Hall, London, 1-13.

Messier, W.F. and Hansen, J.V. (1988), "Inducing rules for expert system development: An example using default and bankruptcy data", *Management Science* 34/12, 1403-1415.

Methlie, L.B. (1987), "On knowledge-based decision support systems for financial diagnostics", in: C.W. Holsapple and A.B. Whinston (eds.), *Decision Support Systems: Theory and Application*, Springer-Verlag, Berlin, 335-371.

Michaelsen, R.H. (1984), "An expert system for tax planning", *Expert Systems* 1, 149-167.

Michalopoulos, M. and Zopounidis, C. (1993), "An expert system for the assessment of bankruptcy risk", in: B. Papathanassiou and K. Paparrizos (eds.), *Proceedings of 2nd Balkan Conference on Operational Research*, 151-163.

Michalopoulos, M., Zopounidis, C. and Doumpos, M. (2000), "L'évaluation des succursales d'une banque à l'aide d'une méthode multicritère de segmentation", *Revue FINECO, Finance, Economie, Comptabilité* (in press).

Michalski, R.S. (1983), "A theory and methodology of inductive learning", in: R.S. Michalski, J.G. Carbonell and T.M. Mitchell (eds.), *Machine Learning: An Artificial Intelligence Approach*, Tioga Publishing Company, Palo Alto, CA.

Minsky, M. (1975), "A framework for representing knowledge", in: P. Winston (ed.), *The Psychology of Computer Vision*, McGraw-Hill, New York.

Mondt, K. and Despontin, M. (1986), "Evaluation of country risk using multicriteria analysis", *Technical Report*, Vrije Universiteiet Brussel, September.

Mui, G. and McCarthy, W.E. (1987), "FSA: Applying AI techniques to the familiarization phase of financial decision making", *IEEE Expert*, 33-41.

Mulvey, J.M., Rosenbaum, D.P. and Shetty, B. (1997), "Strategic financial risk management and operations research", *European Journal of Operational Research* 97, 1-16.

Muzyka, D., Birley, S. and Leleux, B. (1996), "Trade-offs in the investment decisions of European venture capitalists", *Journal of Business Venturing* 11, 273-287.

Myers, S.C. and Pogue, G.A. (1974), "A programming approach to corporate financial management", *The Journal of Finance* 29, 579-599.

Myers, S.C. (1988), "Notes on an expert system for capital budgeting", *Financial Management* 17, 23-31.

Nikbakht, N. and Tafti, M.H.A. (1989), "Application of expert systems in evaluation of credit card borrowers", *Managerial Finance* 15/5, 19-27.

O'Leary, D.E. (1995), "AI in accounting, finance and management", *International Journal of Intelligent Systems in Accounting, Finance and Management* 4, 149-153.

Oral, M. and Kettani, O. (1989), "Modelling the process of multiattribute choice", *Journal of the Operational Research Society* 40/3, 281-291.

Oral, M., Kettani, O., Cosset, J.C. and Daouas, M. (1992), "An estimation model for country risk rating", *International Journal of Forecasting* 8, 583-593.

Pardalos, P.M., Michalopoulos, M. and Zopounidis, C. (1997), "On the use of multicriteria methods for the evaluation of insurance companies in Greece", in: C. Zopounidis (ed.), *New Operational Approaches for Financial Modelling*, Physica-Verlag, Berlin Heidelberg, 271-283.

Pardalos, P.M., Sandström, M. and Zopounidis, C. (1994), "On the use of optimization models for portfolio selection: A review and some computational results", *Computational Economics* 7/4, 227-244.

Pardalos, P.M., Siskos, Y. and Zopounidis, C. (1995), *Advances in Multicriteria Analysis*, Dordrecht: Kluwer Academic Publishers.

Pareto, V. (1896), *Cours d'Economie Politique*, Lausanne.

Pau, I. and Giannoti, G. (1986), *Technical Analysis of Future Markets*, Prentice Hall, New York.

Pawlak, Z. (1982), "Rough sets", *International Journal of Information and Computer Sciences* 11, 341–356.

Pinson, S. (1989), "Credit risk assessment and meta-judgement", *Theory and Decision* 27, 117-133.

Pinson, S. (1992), "A multi-expert architecture for credit risk assessment: The CREDEX system", in: D.E. O'Leary and P.R. Watkins (eds.), *Expert Systems in Finance*, Elsevier Science Publishers, 37-64.

Pomerol, J.C. (1993), "Multicriteria DSSs: State of the art and problems", *Central European Journal for Operations Research and Economics* 2/3, 197-211.

Quinlan, J.R. (1983), "Learning efficient classification procedures and their application to chess end games", in: R.S. Michalski, J.G. Carbonell and T.M. Mitchell (eds.), *Machine Learning: An Artificial Intelligence Approach*, Tioga Publishing Company, Palo Alto, CA.

Quinlan, J.R. (1986), "Induction of decision trees", *Machine Learning* 1, 81–106.

Radermacher, F.J. (1994), "Decision support systems: Scope and potential", *Decision Support Systems* 12, 257-265.

Ribarovic, Z. and Mladineo, N. (1987), "Application of multicriterional analysis to the ranking and evaluation of the investment programmes in the ready mixed concrete industry", *Engineering Costs and Production Economics* 12, 367-374.

Riquelme, H., and Rickards, T. (1992), "Hybrid conjoint analysis: An estimation probe in new venture decisions", *Journal of Business Venturing* 7, 505-518.

Ross, S. (1976), "The arbitrage theory of capital asset pricing", *Journal of Economic Theory* 13, 343-362.

Roy, B. (1968), "Classement et choix en présence de points de vue multiples: La méthode ELECTRE", *R.I.R.O* 8, 57-75.

Roy, B. (1977), "Partial preference analysis and decision aid: The fuzzy outranking relation concept", in: D. Bell, R. Keeney and H. Raiffa (eds.), *Conflicting Objectives in Decisions*.

Roy, B. (1985), *Méthodologie Multicritère d'Aide à la Décision*, Economica, Paris.

Roy, B. (1988), "Des critères multiples en recherche opérationnelle: Pourquoi?", in: G.K. Rand (ed.), *Operational Research '87*, Elsevier Science Publishers, North Holland, Amsterdam, 829-842.

Roy, B. (1991), "The outranking approach and the foundations of ELECTRE methods", *Theory and Decision* 31, 49-73.

Roy, B. (1996), *Multicriteria Methodology for Decision Aiding*, Kluwer Academic Publishers, Dordrecht.

Roy, B. and Bouyssou, D. (1993), *Aide Multicritère à la Décision: Méthodes et Cas*, Economica, Paris.

Saaty, T.L. (1980), *The Analytic Hierarchy Process*, McGraw-Hill, New York.

Saaty, T.L., Rogers, P.C. and Pell, R. (1980), "Portfolio selection through hierarchies", *The Journal of Portfolio Management*, Spring 16-21.

Sangster, A. (1995), "The bank of Scotland's COMPASS – The future of bank lending?", *Expert Systems with Applications* 9/4, 457-468.

Selly, M.A. and Forman, E. (1986), *Expert Choice*, Decision Support Software, Inc., Mc Lean, VA.

Sena, J.A. and Smith, L.M. (1987), "A sample expert system for financial statement analysis", *Journal of Accounting and EDP* 3, 15-22.

Shane, B., Fry, M. and Toro, R. (1987), "The design of an investment portfolio selection decision support system using two expert systems and a consulting system", *Journal of Management Information Systems* 3/4, 79-92.

Shao, Y.P., Wilson, A. and Oppenheim, C. (1997), "Knowledge-based systems in retail banking: A survey of current practice", *International Journal of Intelligent Systems in Finance, Accounting and Management* 6, 73-81.

Sharpe, W. (1964), "Capital asset prices: A theory of market equilibrium under conditions of risk", *Journal of Finance* 19, 425-442.

Shaw, M. and Gentry, J.A. (1988), "Using an expert system with inductive learning to evaluate business loans", *Financial Management* 17, 45-56.

Shin, K-S. and Han, I. (1999), "Case-based reasoning supported by genetic algorithms for corporate bond rating", *Expert Systems with Applications* 16, 85-95.

Siegel, S. (1956), *Nonparametric Statistics for the Behavioral Sciences*, McGraw-Hill, New York.

Simon, H.A. (1957), *Models of Man*, John Wiley and Sons, New York.

Singh, M.G. and Cook, R. (1986), "PRICE-STRAT: A Decision Support System for Determining Building Society and Bank Interest Rate Mixes", *International Journal of Bank Marketing* 4, 52-66.

Siskos, J. and Despotis, D.K. (1989), "A DSS oriented method for multiobjective linear programming problems", *Decision Support Systems* 5, 47-55.

Siskos, Y. and Yannacopoulos, D. (1985), "UTASTAR: An ordinal regression method for building additive value functions", *Investigação Operacional* 5/1, 39-53.

Siskos, J., and Zopounidis, C. (1987), "The evaluation criteria of the venture capital investment activity: An interactive assessment", *European Journal of Operational Research* 31, 304-313.

Siskos, Y. and Zopounidis, C. (eds.) (1993), "Multicriteria decision support systems" (Special issue), *Journal of Information Science and Technology* 2/2, 107-199.

Siskos, Y., Spiridakos, A. and Yannacopoulos, D. (1993), "MINORA: A multicriteria decision aiding system for discrete alternatives", *Journal of Information Science and Technology* 2, 136-149.

Siskos, Y., Spiridakos, A. and Yannacopoulos, D. (1999), "Using artificial intelligence and visual techniques into preference disaggregation analysis: The MIIDAS system", *European Journal of Operational Research* 113, 236-246.

Siskos, Y., Zopounidis, C. and Pouliezos, A. (1994), "An integrated DSS for financing firms by an industrial development bank in Greece", *Decision Support Systems* 12, 151-168.

Slade, S. (1991), "Case-based reasoning: A research paradigm", *AI Magazine* 12/1, 42-55.

Slowinski, R. (1993), "Rough set learning of preferential attitude in multi-criteria decision making", in: J. Komorowski and Z. W. Ras (eds.), *Methodologies for Intelligent Systems*, Lecture Notes in Artificial Intelligence vol. 689, Springer-Verlag, Berlin, 642–651.

Slowinski, R. and Zopounidis, C. (1995), "Application of the rough set approach to evaluation of bankruptcy risk", *International Journal of Intelligent Systems in Accounting, Finance, and Management* 4, 27-41.

Slowinski, R. and Stefanowski, J. (1994), "Rough classification with valued closeness relation", in: E. Diday et al. (eds.), *New Approaches in Classification and Data Analysis*, Springer-Verlag, Berlin, 482–488.

Slowinski, R., Zopounidis, C. and Dimitras, A.I. (1997), "Prediction of company acquisition in Greece by means of the rough set approach", *European Journal of Operational Research* 100, 1-15.

Sprague, R.H. Jr. and Carlson, E.D. (1982), *Building Effective Decision Support Systems*, Prentice-Hall, Englwood Cliffs.

Sprague, R.H. Jr. and Watson, H.J. (1976), "A decision support system for banks", *Omega* 4/6, 657-671.

Sprague, R.H. Jr. (1972), "Systems support for a financial planning model", *Management Accounting* 53, 29-34.

Spronk, J. (1981), *Interactive Multiple Goal Programming Application to Financial Planning*, Martinus Nijhoff Publishing, Boston.

Srinivasan, V. and Kim, Y.H. (1987), "Credit granting: A comparative analysis of classification procedures", *The Journal of Finance* XLII/3, 665-683.

Srinivasan, V. and Ruparel, B. (1990), "CGX: An expert support system for credit granting", *European Journal of Operational Research* 45, 293-308 (1990).

Steinbart, P. (1987), "The construction of a rule-based system as a method for studying materiality judgements", *Accounting Review* 62, 97-116.

Steuer, R.E., *Multiple Criteria Optimization: Theory, Computation and Application*, New York: John Wiley and Sons, 1986.

Steuer, R.E. (1992), *Manual for the ADBASE Multiple Objective Linear Programming Package*, Department of Management Science and Information Technology, University of Georgia, Athens, GA.

Sun M., Stam A. and Steuer R.E. (1996), "Solving multiple objective programming problems using feed-forward artificial neural networks", *Management Science* 42/6, 835-849.

Suret, J.M., Cormier, E. and Roy, J. (1991), "Un système-expert de choix d'actions", *FINÉCO* 1/1, 39-60.

Tabachnick, B.G. and Fidell, L.S. (1989), *Using Multivariate Statistics*, Harper Collins Publishers, New-York.

Tam, K.Y., Kiang, M.Y. and Chi, R.T.H. (1991), "Inducing stock screening rules for portfolio construction", *Journal of the Operational Research Society* 42/9, 747-757.

Tang, J.C.S., and Espinal, C.G. (1989), "A model to assess country risk", *Omega* 17/4, 363-367.

Teghem, J., Dufrane, D., Thauvoye, M. and Kunsch, P. (1986), "STRANGE: An interactive method for multi-objective linear programming under uncertainty", *European Journal of Operational Research* 26, 65-82.

Trippi, R.R. and Turban, R. (1996), *Neural Networks in Finance and Investing*, Irwin, Chicago.

Turban, E. (1993), *Decision Support and Expert Systems: Management Support Systems* (3rd ed.), Macmillan, New York.

Turban, E. and Watkins, P.R. (1986), "Integrating expert systems and decision support systems", *MIS Quarterly*, June, 121-136.

Valentine, J.L. (1988), "Applying expert systems to investment", *Financial Analysts Journal*, November-December, 48-53.

Vincke, Ph. (1992), *Multicriteria Decision Aid*, John Wiley and Sons, New York.

Vinso, J.D. (1982), "Financial planning for the multinational corporation with multiple goals", *Journal of International Business Studies*, Winter, 43-58.

Von Altrock, C. (1996), *Fuzzy Logic and Neurofuzzy Applications in Business and Finance*, Prentice Hall, New Jersey.

Von Neumann, J. and Morgenstern, O. (1944), *Theory of Games and Economic Behavior*, Princeton, New Jersey.

Vranes, S., Stanojevic, M., Stevanovic, V. and Lucin, M. (1996), "INVEX: Investment Advisory Expert System", *Expert Systems* 13/2, 105-119.

Wallenius, J. and Zionts, S. (1976), "Some tests of an interactive programming method for multicriteria optimization and an attempt at implementation", in: H. Thiriez and S. Zionts (eds.), *Multiple Criteria Decision making*, Lecture Notes in Economics and Mathematical Systems, Springer-Verlag, Berlin, 319-331.

Williamson, O.E. (1964), *The Economics of Discretionary Behavior: Managerial Objectives in a Theory of the Firm*, Prentice-Hall, Englewood Cliffs, N.J.

Yu, W. (1992), "ELECTRE TRI: Aspects methodologiques et manuel d'utilisation", *Document du Lamsade No 74*, Universite de Paris-Dauphine, 1992.

Zadeh, L.A. (1965), "Fuzzy sets", *Information and Control* 8, 338-353.

Zahedi, F. (1986), "The analytic hierarchy process - A survey of the method and its applications", *Interfaces* 16, 96-108.

Zeleny, M. (1977), "Multidimensional measure of risk: The Prospect Ranking Vector", in: S. Zionts (ed.), *Multiple Criteria Problem Solving*, Springer Verlag, Heidelberg, 529-548.

Zeleny, M. (1982), *Multiple Criteria Decision Making*, McGraw-Hill, New York.

Zimmermann, H.J. (1978), "Fuzzy programming and linear programming with several objective functions", *Fuzzy Sets and Systems* 1, 45-55.

Zollinger, M. (1982), "L'analyse multicritère et le risque de crédit aux entreprises", *Revue Française de Gestion*, Janvier-Février, 56-66.

Zopounidis, C. (1987), "A multicriteria decision-making methodology for the evaluation of the risk of failure and an application", *Foundations of Control Engineering* 12/1, 45-67.

Zopounidis, C. (1990), *La Gestion du Capital-Risque*, Economica, Paris.

Zopounidis, C. (1993a), "A multicriteria methodology for the evaluation and ranking of investment projects", *Bulletin of the Greek Banks Association* 10/39-40, 22-28, (in Greek).

Zopounidis, C. (1993b), "On the use of the MINORA multicriteria decision aiding system to portfolio selection and management", *Journal of Information Science and Technology* 2/2, 150-156.

Zopounidis, C. (1994), "Venture capital modelling: Evaluation criteria for the appraisal of investments", *The Financier: ACMT* 1/2, 54-64.

Zopounidis, C. (1995), *Evaluation du Risque de Défaillance de l'Entreprise: Méthodes et Cas d'Application*, Economica, Paris.

Zopounidis, C. (1998a), *Operational Tools in the Management of Financial Risks*, Kluwer Academic Publishers, Dordrecht.

Zopounidis, C. (1998b), *Analysis and Management of Financial Risks: Multicriteria Approaches*, Kleidarithmos Publishing, Athens (in Greek).

Zopounidis, C. (1999a), "Multicriteria decision aid in financial management", *European Journal of Operational Research* 119, 404-415.

Zopounidis, C. (1999b), "Les approches multicritères en finance", *Revue Banque et Marchés* 38, 57-62.

Zopounidis, C., and Doumpos, M. (1997), "Preference disaggregation methodology in segmentation problems: The case of financial distress", in: C. Zopounidis (ed.), *New Operational Approaches for Financial Modelling*, Physica-Verlag, Berlin-Heidelberg, 417-439.

Zopounidis, C., and M. Doumpos (1998a), "Developing a multicriteria decision support system for financial classification problems: The FINCLAS system", *Optimization Methods and Software* 8, 277-304.

Zopounidis, C. and Doumpos, M. (1998b), "A Multicriteria Sorting Methodology for Financial Classification Problems", in: C. Zopounidis et I. Papadimitriou (eds.), *Abstracts and Papers of the 47th Meeting of the European Working Group «Multicriteria Aid for Decisions», Vol. II*, Editions of the Technical University of Crete, Chania, 41-68.

Zopounidis C., Matsatsinis N.F. and Doumpos M. (1996a), "Developing a multicriteria knowledge-based decision support system for the assessment of corporate performance and viability: The FINEVA system", *Fuzzy Economic Review* 1/2, 35-53.

Zopounidis, C., Despotis, D.K., and Stavropoulou, E. (1995a), "Multiattribute evaluation of Greek banking performance", *Applied Stochastic Models and Data Analysis* 11/1, 97-107.

Zopounidis, C., Doumpos, M. and Matsatsinis, N.F. (1996b), "Application of the FINEVA multicriteria knowledge-based decision support system to the assessment of corporate failure risk", *Foundations of Computing and Decision Sciences* 21/4, 233-251.

Zopounidis, C., Doumpos, M. and Matsatsinis, N.F. (1997), "On the use of knowledge-based decision support systems in financial management: A survey", *Decision Support Systems* 20, 259-277.

Zopounidis, C., Godefroid, M. and Hurson, C. (1995), "Designing a multicriteria decision support system for portfolio selection and management", in: J. Janssen, C.H. Skiadas, C. Zopounidis (eds.), *Advances in Stochastic Modelling and Data Analysis*, Kluwer Academic Publishers, Dordrecht, 261-292.

Zopounidis, C., Pouliezos, A. and Yannacopoulos, D. (1992), "Designing a DSS for the assessment of company performance and viability", *Computer Science in Economics and Management* 5, 41-56.

SUBJECT INDEX

Arbitrage pricing theory, 16, 62, 66
Artificial intelligence, 18, 36, 83, 91, 100, 133, 136, 143, 173, 194
Asset/liability management, 7, 9
Backward chaining, 95, 97
Bankruptcy prediction, 2, 5, 137, 146
Bond rating, 31, 99, 136, 146, 165
Capital Asset Pricing Model, 10
Case-based reasoning, 133, 144, 165
Cash management, 155
Certainty factors, 98, 110
Classification, 21, 27, 49, 59, 68, 74, 125, 137, 160, 176, 187
Country risk, 2, 5, 9, 17, 31, 188
Credit granting, 31, 48, 99, 131, 148, 159, 178, 182, 184
Credit risk, 3, 9, 48, 52, 59, 160, 163, 182
Data mining, 125, 129, 133
Database, 39, 42, 49, 63, 112, 121, 129, 149, 152, 159, 168, 180, 186
Database management, 39, 50, 65, 124, 129, 169
Decision support systems, 2, 19, 36, 38, 121, 123
Discriminant analysis, 11, 33, 133, 164, 166
Econometrics, 11, 16, 35, 73
Efficient set, 22, 62, 132
Expert systems, 36, 83
Financial analysis, 47, 53, 99, 101, 148, 160, 186
Financial derivatives, 3
Financial engineering, 3, 10, 23, 31, 46, 71, 99, 118, 128, 141, 148, 177, 193
Financial innovation, 3, 7
Financial planning, 2, 5, 9, 23, 31, 47, 148
Financial risk management, 3, 5, 31
Financial statements, 51, 66, 160
Financial theory, 2, 9, 14
FINCLAS system, 48, 59, 68
FINEVA system, 101, 111, 117, 178, 185, 188
Forward chaining, 95
Frames, 88, 91, 101, 151
Fuzzy set theory, 98, 137, 142, 176, 188
Global optimization, 7
Goal programming, 16, 20, 22, 30, 69, 169, 171, 175
Heuristics, 84, 87, 106, 109, 118, 182
Ill-structured problems, 37
Immunization models, 9
Inductive learning, 94, 140, 159
Inference engine, 86, 94
Information technology, 5, 83, 194
Integer programming, 7, 79, 154
Internal rate of return, 2, 14, 190
Investment appraisal, 190
INVESTOR system, 47, 61, 63, 70, 71
Knowledge acquisition, 86, 93, 101, 106, 119, 149

Knowledge engineer, 86, 92
Knowledge representation, 88, 91, 93, 151, 178
Linear programming, 31, 59, 74, 77, 155, 186
Marginal utilities, 29, 60, 75, 77, 187
Markowitz, 2, 4, 16, 62, 149
Mean-variance model, 16
Membership function, 142, 190
Mergers and acquisitions, 2, 8, 32, 141, 163
Meta-rules, 89, 106, 109
Model base management, 39, 44, 50, 123, 129, 169
Model development, 42, 129, 163, 169, 172
Model formulation, 44
Model validation, 44, 46, 128
Multiattribute utility theory, 15, 21, 171, 175
Multicriteria decision aid, 2, 14, 18, 127
Multiobjective programming, 22, 175, 177
Net present value, 2, 14, 182, 190
Network optimization, 7, 11
Neural networks, 133, 136, 143, 163, 175
Non-linear programming, 11
Operations research, 2, 7, 9, 18, 33, 45, 195
Optimization, 2, 10, 16, 21, 29, 33, 62, 70, 128, 146, 166
Option pricing, 4
Ordinal regression, 59, 74, 186
Organizations, 193
Outranking relations, 19, 21, 25, 30, 141, 171, 176
Portfolio construction, 63, 71, 128, 148, 152
Portfolio selection and management, 2, 5, 9, 62, 126, 148, 152, 168
Preference disaggregation, 20, 27, 49, 59, 74, 117, 171
Principal components analysis, 68, 186
Problem structuring, 129, 158, 170, 194
Production rules, 88, 93, 101, 109, 118, 151, 157, 160
Rough set theory, 94, 137, 163, 176
Semantic networks, 88, 93
Sensitivity analysis, 78, 125, 128, 156, 170, 190
Simulation, 2, 14, 83, 190
Statistical analysis, 11, 33, 68, 132
Stochastic programming, 7
Technical analysis, 152
Tradeoffs, 22, 28, 49
Trading, 3, 8, 127, 136, 149, 152
Uncertainty, 25, 98, 118, 137, 156, 175
User interface, 39, 44, 49, 65, 86, 99, 123, 157, 168, 174
UTADIS method, 20, 59, 68, 74, 186
UTADIS I method, 59, 79, 81
UTADIS II method, 59, 81
UTADIS III method, 59, 81
UTASTAR method, 117, 186, 188
Utility functions, 24, 29, 76, 175
Venture capital, 2, 5, 9, 31, 188
Visual interactive modeling, 126, 174

Applied Optimization

1. D.-Z. Du and D.F. Hsu (eds.): *Combinatorial Network Theory*. 1996
ISBN 0-7923-3777-8
2. M.J. Panik: *Linear Programming: Mathematics, Theory and Algorithms*. 1996
ISBN 0-7923-3782-4
3. R.B. Kearfott and V. Kreinovich (eds.): *Applications of Interval Computations*. 1996 ISBN 0-7923-3847-2
4. N. Hritonenko and Y. Yatsenko: *Modeling and Optimimization of the Lifetime of Technology*. 1996 ISBN 0-7923-4014-0
5. T. Terlaky (ed.): *Interior Point Methods of Mathematical Programming*. 1996
ISBN 0-7923-4201-1
6. B. Jansen: *Interior Point Techniques in Optimization*. Complementarity, Sensitivity and Algorithms. 1997 ISBN 0-7923-4430-8
7. A. Migdalas, P.M. Pardalos and S. Storøy (eds.): *Parallel Computing in Optimization*. 1997 ISBN 0-7923-4583-5
8. F.A. Lootsma: *Fuzzy Logic for Planning and Decision Making*. 1997
ISBN 0-7923-4681-5
9. J.A. dos Santos Gromicho: *Quasiconvex Optimization and Location Theory*. 1998
ISBN 0-7923-4694-7
10. V. Kreinovich, A. Lakeyev, J. Rohn and P. Kahl: *Computational Complexity and Feasibility of Data Processing and Interval Computations*. 1998
ISBN 0-7923-4865-6
11. J. Gil-Aluja: *The Interactive Management of Human Resources in Uncertainty*. 1998
ISBN 0-7923-4886-9
12. C. Zopounidis and A.I. Dimitras: *Multicriteria Decision Aid Methods for the Prediction of Business Failure*. 1998 ISBN 0-7923-4900-8
13. F. Giannessi, S. Komlósi and T. Rapcsák (eds.): *New Trends in Mathematical Programming*. Homage to Steven Vajda. 1998 ISBN 0-7923-5036-7
14. Ya-xiang Yuan (ed.): *Advances in Nonlinear Programming*. Proceedings of the '96 International Conference on Nonlinear Programming. 1998 ISBN 0-7923-5053-7
15. W.W. Hager and P.M. Pardalos: *Optimal Control*. Theory, Algorithms, and Applications. 1998 ISBN 0-7923-5067-7
16. Gang Yu (ed.): *Industrial Applications of Combinatorial Optimization*. 1998
ISBN 0-7923-5073-1
17. D. Braha and O. Maimon (eds.): *A Mathematical Theory of Design: Foundations, Algorithms and Applications*. 1998 ISBN 0-7923-5079-0

Applied Optimization

18. O. Maimon, E. Khmelnitsky and K. Kogan: *Optimal Flow Control in Manufacturing.* Production Planning and Scheduling. 1998 ISBN 0-7923-5106-1
19. C. Zopounidis and P.M. Pardalos (eds.): *Managing in Uncertainty: Theory and Practice.* 1998 ISBN 0-7923-5110-X
20. A.S. Belenky: *Operations Research in Transportation Systems:* Ideas and Schemes of Optimization Methods for Strategic Planning and Operations Management. 1998 ISBN 0-7923-5157-6
21. J. Gil-Aluja: *Investment in Uncertainty.* 1999 ISBN 0-7923-5296-3
22. M. Fukushima and L. Qi (eds.): *Reformulation: Nonsmooth, Piecewise Smooth, Semismooth and Smooting Methods.* 1999 ISBN 0-7923-5320-X
23. M. Patriksson: *Nonlinear Programming and Variational Inequality Problems.* A Unified Approach. 1999 ISBN 0-7923-5455-9
24. R. De Leone, A. Murli, P.M. Pardalos and G. Toraldo (eds.): *High Performance Algorithms and Software in Nonlinear Optimization.* 1999 ISBN 0-7923-5483-4
25. A. Schöbel: *Locating Lines and Hyperplanes.* Theory and Algorithms. 1999 ISBN 0-7923-5559-8
26. R.B. Statnikov: *Multicriteria Design.* Optimization and Identification. 1999 ISBN 0-7923-5560-1
27. V. Tsurkov and A. Mironov: *Minimax under Transportation Constrains.* 1999 ISBN 0-7923-5609-8
28. V.I. Ivanov: *Model Development and Optimization.* 1999 ISBN 0-7923-5610-1
29. F.A. Lootsma: *Multi-Criteria Decision Analysis via Ratio and Difference Judgement.* 1999 ISBN 0-7923-5669-1
30. A. Eberhard, R. Hill, D. Ralph and B.M. Glover (eds.): *Progress in Optimization.* Contributions from Australasia. 1999 ISBN 0-7923-5733-7
31. T. Hürlimann: *Mathematical Modeling and Optimization.* An Essay for the Design of Computer-Based Modeling Tools. 1999 ISBN 0-7923-5927-5
32. J. Gil-Aluja: *Elements for a Theory of Decision in Uncertainty.* 1999 ISBN 0-7923-5987-9
33. H. Frenk, K. Roos, T. Terlaky and S. Zhang (eds.): *High Performance Optimization.* 1999 ISBN 0-7923-6013-3
34. N. Hritonenko and Y. Yatsenko: *Mathematical Modeling in Economics, Ecology and the Environment.* 1999 ISBN 0-7923-6015-X
35. J. Virant: *Design Considerations of Time in Fuzzy Systems.* 2000 ISBN 0-7923-6100-8

Applied Optimization

36. G. Di Pillo and F. Giannessi (eds.): *Nonlinear Optimization and Related Topics.* 2000
ISBN 0-7923-6109-1
37. V. Tsurkov: *Hierarchical Optimization and Mathematical Physics.* 2000
ISBN 0-7923-6175-X
38. C. Zopounidis and M. Doumpos: *Intelligent Decision Aiding Systems Based on Multiple Criteria for Financial Engineering.* 2000 ISBN 0-7923-6273-X
39. X. Yang, A.I. Mees, M. Fisher and L.Jennings (eds.): *Progress in Optimization.* Contributions from Australasia. 2000 ISBN 0-7923-6286-1

KLUWER ACADEMIC PUBLISHERS – DORDRECHT / BOSTON / LONDON

GPSR Compliance

The European Union's (EU) General Product Safety Regulation (GPSR) is a set of rules that requires consumer products to be safe and our obligations to ensure this.

If you have any concerns about our products, you can contact us on ProductSafety@springernature.com

In case Publisher is established outside the EU, the EU authorized representative is:

Springer Nature Customer Service Center GmbH
Europaplatz 3
69115 Heidelberg, Germany

Batch number: 10837190

Printed by Printforce, the Netherlands